PENGUI

BEFORE

Charles Tyng was born in Newburypor
cabin boy to prosperous merchant and se
took him across the Atlantic, the Pac
China, Europe, and Indonesia, among o
land in 1879.

Susan Fels, who edited the text, is his great-great-granddaughter. She is an editor and indexer in Washington, D.C.

Praise for *Before the Wind*

"Charles Tyng writes with the confident forcefulness that saved him countless times at sea, yet with the open-eyed wonder of a child. [This] lyrical memoir is a testimonial to an ambitious but likable man with a penchant for the unusual. Tyng not only went around the world, but went into it wholeheartedly. A novelist's eye for detail and a storyteller's flair make this yarn a page turner."
— *The New York Times Book Review*

"Between the summonings of port life—from opium dens to wharf-side eateries—architectural descriptions, and landscape delineations, there are North Sea gales to reckon with, pirates to outrace, boils to lance, unwanted tattoos to carve off, spells in prison to survive, and mutinies, some to partake in, others to quash. [Charles] Tyng's saga grips with its lively immediacy and transports with its mildly antique but always expressive language."
— *Kirkus Reviews*

"And oh, the things he saw: British ships blockading American shores in the War of 1812. Lord Byron; Princess Victoria before she ascended the throne. This is a book of commerce as much as it is a sea tale. Tyng recounts commercial transactions as enthusiastically as, and usually in greater detail than adventures at sea."
— *Chicago Sun Times*

"This is social history at its best, told in an authentic New England voice dryly recounting the story of a life from reluctant schoolboy to ship's captain and owner. Tyng's ancedotes come thick and fast, serious and humorous. The memoir ends with Tyng struck down by cholera, but he survived and lived to a ripe seventy-eight. *Before the Wind* left this reader wishing for more."
— Alan Gurney, author of *Below the Convergence: Voyages Toward Antarctica, 1699–1839*

"Without a doubt, this belongs on every sailor's bookshelf. It's an honest, uncluttered account of a sailor's life and sheds light on areas of seafaring I never knew existed. His writing comes from the same rich stock as books like *Two Years Before the Mast* or the works of Patrick O'Brian."
— Daniel Hays, author of *My Old Man and the Sea*

"The only serious complaint I have about this book is that its author did not live to tell the whole tale."
— Jonathon Yardley, *The Washington Post*

BEFORE THE WIND

The Memoir of
an American Sea Captain,
1808–1833

CHARLES TYNG

EDITED BY *Susan Fels*
PREFACE BY *William T. LaMoy*
AFTERWORD BY *Thomas Philbrick*

PENGUIN BOOKS

PENGUIN BOOKS
Published by the Penguin Group
Penguin Putnam Inc., 375 Hudson Street,
New York, New York 10014, U.S.A.
Penguin Books Ltd, 27 Wrights Lane, London W8 5TZ, England
Penguin Books Australia Ltd, Ringwood, Victoria, Australia
Penguin Books Canada Ltd, 10 Alcorn Avenue,
Toronto, Ontario, Canada M4V 3B2
Penguin Books (N.Z.) Ltd, 182–190 Wairau Road,
Auckland 10, New Zealand

Penguin Books Ltd, Registered Offices:
Harmondsworth, Middlesex, England

First published in the United States of America by Viking Penguin,
a member of Penguin Putnam Inc. 1999
Published in Penguin Books 2000

1   3   5   7   9   10   8   6   4   2

THE LIBRARY OF CONGRESS HAS CATALOGED
THE HARDCOVER EDITION AS FOLLOWS:
Tyng, Charles, 1801–1879.
Before the wind: the memoir of an American sea captain,
1801–1833/Charles Tyng.
p. cm.
ISBN 0-670-88632-7 (hc.)
ISBN 0 14 02.9191 1 (pbk.)
I. Tyng, Charles, 1801–1878.   2. Ship captains—United States—Biography.
3. Merchant mariners—United States—Biography.
I. Title.
VK140.T93A3   1999
387.5´4044—dc21   [B] 98–53477

Printed in the United States of America
Set in Bembo
Designed by Mia Risberg

CONTENTS

❧

PREFACE VII

ACKNOWLEDGMENTS XI

INTRODUCTION XIII

1 A Boston Boyhood 3

2 First Voyage 16

3 Return to China 45

4 A Leaky Trip to Havana 53

5 Pirates and Promotions 64

6 Sharks, Monkeys, and Lord Byron 78

7 Mutinies and the Mermaid 86

8 The Schooner *Zephyr* 118

9 More Pirates and a Sudden Squall 127

10 A Belated Honeymoon 163

11 A Man Overboard! 169

12 The Brig *Creole* 183

13 The Wreck of the *Munroe* 194

14 A Painful Loss 206

15 Rough Passages 214

16 Dining Out in London and Paris 229

17 Out of the Frying Pan and into the Fire 240

AFTERWORD 251

EXPLANATORY NOTES 257

INDEX 265

PREFACE

❧

THE PHILLIPS LIBRARY of the Peabody Essex Museum was approached by Susan Fels and her uncle, Charles Tyng, in May 1997 to inquire as to whether the library had any interest in acquiring for its collection a memoir written by their ancestor Charles Tyng. His narrative is remarkable because it is so obviously an ingenuous tale of a Boston and Newburyport, Massachusetts, youth who had to contend with early adversity. Due to the untimely death of his mother when he was seven and the remarriage of his father, Charles Tyng was largely reared and educated in an environment controlled by independent schoolmasters, one in which he did not especially thrive. His father, accepting Charles's inability to succeed in his schooling, offered him the difficult option of a life at sea. From this point forward, the story that emerges is an engaging one of the personal growth of an individual in the midst of a fascinating period in American history.

At the outset of the nineteenth century, the United States had just assumed its rightful place in the world of nations. It had worn down Great Britain in its battle for independence and was just beginning to contend with other countries in a global marketplace that was governed by sea power. It was into this exotic milieu that Charles Tyng was catapulted. Having accepted his fate as a seafaring man, he evolves before us in this memoir into a skillful mariner and an astute merchant.

Charles Tyng was first mate aboard the Cadet *in 1823*
when he and Captain Magee jointly purchased a mummified mermaid.
Page 157 of the memoir, reproduced here from the original manuscript,
describes the circumstances (see book pages 94 and 95).

This is not a simple and painless process, however. He must attain strength not in keeping with his physical stature and a composure that could control mutinous crews. The charm of the manuscript is that we observe this gradual transition in a manner that is completely natural and devoid of self-promotion. He genuinely appears to be recalling his story as frankly and honestly as he can.

The memoir is most focused on the daily run of shipboard activities. In fact, one is provided with an astonishing amount of detail on life at sea. The topics touched upon include the diet on board vessels, navigational procedures and techniques, interactions with the crew, and the need to engage in a continuous round of successful commerce all over the world. The commentary documents the usually mundane nature of this way of life, but the routine could be punctuated with moments of sheer terror, as the following excerpt demonstrates:

In the course of half an hour, the steward rushed into my room with a large carving knife in his hand, his eyes glaring most wildly. He made towards me. I sprung up, reached my hand for my pistol. He seemed confused, evidently expecting to find me asleep. He went for the cabin door, but instantly turned and came to the door of my room. I pointed my pistol at him, he threw his knife down, and run up on the deck. At once there was the cry "A man overboard." I went up on deck and found that the steward had jumped overboard, and looked over the side and saw him about a fathom under water with his face downwards, his arms and legs stretched out, and without motion, sinking fast, so that it would have been useless to try to save him. I related to Capt. Magee what had just occurred in my room, and one of the boys then told me that he had threatened several times, that he would knife me, but he did not believe him, and therefore did not tell me. Capt. Magee said I had a very narrow escape. I found afterwards a pot half full of rum, which he had been drinking from, until he became frenzied, and produced that awful glare of his eyes, which I shall never forget.

While the general portrait that is conveyed is that of a seaman engaged in the course of his daily occupations, we are offered glimpses of celebrities, most notably Lord Byron. This glamorous encounter does not succeed in overwhelming the levelheaded Charles Tyng:

As Mr. Cabot took lodgings on shore as soon as the ship arrived I saw but little of him. He was a great admirer of Byron's poems, and as Lord

Byron was in Leghorn at the time, Mr. Cabot made his acquaintance, and one day they came on board of the ship together. I was struck with his appearance, and rather disappointed, as on the passage I had read some of his works and formed a high opinion of him. He appeared to me as an ordinary Englishman. He was under size, and walked lame. His face was pleasing, with a high forehead and good shaped head. He wore a high shirt collar, turned over on the side and quite open in front, which was different from the fashion at that time, as gentlemen wore generally wide stiff black stocks.

The memoir of Charles Tyng presents a wonderfully full and captivating picture of the life of an American shipmaster coming of age in the exhilarating period of the first third of the nineteenth century. In many respects, he embodies the characteristics that we would perhaps prefer to be associated with the American spirit: his is impartial, open-minded, entrepreneurial, and rugged when the occasion warrants it. His own recounting of this part of his life will be welcomed as a splendid contribution to the literature of the sea as well as an authentic rendering of the period when America began shaping and defining itself.

Along with the satisfaction of seeing this memoir obtain the audience that it deserves with its publication by Viking Penguin, it is also a great pleasure to be able to announce that the Tyng family intends to donate the manuscript of this memoir to the Phillips Library of the Peabody Essex Museum, where it will be preserved in our climate-controlled and fireproof vaults and stored with our extensive collections in perpetuity. Such original documentation of our cultural patrimony is invaluable, and it certainly merits its proud place in a rare-book-and-manuscript repository.

—WILLIAM T. LAMOY
James Duncan Phillips Librarian
Peabody Essex Museum
Salem, Massachusetts

ACKNOWLEDGMENTS

ON BEHALF OF CHARLES TYNG, who lived and wrote his story with such verve, I offer sincerest thanks to the other people who made this book possible. Charles's namesakes, his grandson Charles and great-grandson Charles, each in turn inherited and preserved the manuscript. The latter Charles, my mother's brother, gave his delighted consent to publication, and provided pictures of the Captain and his vessels. Lage E. Carlson expertly cleaned, de-acidified, mended, and encapsulated the document's most fragile pages. Sarah Fels suggested Jessica Dorfman Jones as a literary agent. Jessica ably represented the book to senior editor Wendy Wolf at Viking. Wendy bought the book, chose the title, judiciously trimmed the text, and coordinated the project. At her invitation, William T. LaMoy, the James Duncan Phillips Librarian at the Peabody Essex Museum in Salem, Massachusetts, agreed to write the Preface, and Thomas Philbrick, retired professor of English at the University of Pittsburgh, the Afterword. In addition to his fine analysis and appreciation of the memoir, Mr. Philbrick kindly offered some corrections to the text and additions to the book's explanatory notes. Roland Ottewell performed a praiseworthy job of copyediting. Senior production editor Kate Griggs, and editorial assistant Reeve Chace, of Viking, also deserve recognition for their fine work.

Others who helped with their interest, encouragement, and practical suggestions include Phyllis G. Sidorsky, now retired from library work but active as an artist, gardener, and critic of children's literature; book editor Barbara Brownell at the National Geographic Society; Jane E. Ward, Curator of Manuscripts at the Phillips Library of the Peabody Essex Museum; and Peter R. Haack of the Historical Society of Old Newbury. Mr. Haack was particularly kind to Uncle Chuck and me during our impromptu visit to Newburyport in May 1997. Ruth Quattlebaum, archivist at the Phillips Academy, Andover, added helpful information on Charles Tyng's later life.

My brother, William T. McEwan Jr., and my neighbor, architectural historian Jane C. Loeffler, generously shared their experience in research and publication. Other friends allowed their ears to be bent about the project, and responded with gratifying enthusiasm. My husband, Nicholas W. Fels, and our beloved daughter, Sarah, contributed, as always, their affection, their excellent judgment, and their acute senses of humor. Responsibility for any inadvertent errors in the book is, of course, mine.

—SUSAN TYNG MCEWAN FELS

INTRODUCTION

❧❦❧

A Family Note

CHARLES TYNG (1801–1879), a sea captain and merchant of Boston and Newburyport, Massachusetts, was the fifth of eight children born to Dudley Atkins (1762–1829), a lawyer who took the last name of Tyng to inherit a female relative's modest legacy, and his first wife, Sarah (1766–1808), daughter of the Boston merchant Stephen Higginson (1743–1828). The name "Tyng" is pronounced "ting" (with a short i) and is of English origin.

Despite his family's wide network of friends and relations, Charles did not have an especially privileged upbringing. His mother died when he was seven. He was farmed out to his paternal grandmother in Newburyport, who then died within a year or so; his father had remarried, but his stepmother (his mother's sister Elizabeth) took charge of only her two youngest stepchildren, with help from their two teenaged sisters. Charles and three of his brothers (two older, one younger) were sent to separate boarding schools outside of Boston. As a schoolboy in Cohasset during the War of 1812, Charles joined townsfolk in repelling British marines raiding the harbor, and watched American and British warships patrolling offshore. He was an eyewitness to the epic naval battle between the British frigate *Shannon* and the U.S. ship *Chesapeake*, described from the British point of view in Patrick O'Brian's novel *The Fortune of War*. Charles's account, though somewhat inaccurate, gives us the personal dramas and miscalculations that occurred on the American side of the conflict.

Unlike his four brothers, who all attended college (three followed their father to Harvard), Charles proved to be a lackluster and even rebellious student, whose outspoken tendencies often got him into trouble. What to do with this barely adolescent black sheep? The very small—under five feet—but hardy thirteen-year-old was sent to sea as a "sailor boy" on a merchant vessel belonging to two of his Perkins uncles. His first voyage, a year and a half long, took him to China and back, around the world. On his return, the youngster told his father he never wished to go to sea again. His father replied that Charles had made a choice of career and must stick with it. Fortunately, his second voyage was less grueling than his first, and he formed a new ambition: to captain a ship as soon as he possibly could.

Some sixty years later, after a long and prosperous career as a captain, ship owner, and merchant, Tyng decided to record the details of his eventful early life on land and sea, completing the account as far as his 1833 bout with cholera. The handwritten memoir from 1878, a handsome French watercolor painting of Tyng's first two ships meeting in the Mediterranean (dated 1830), and some photographs have survived in the Tyng family—most recently, in the hands of my uncle Charles Tyng, the captain's great-grandson and namesake.

I first learned about this manuscript in June of 1996, when Uncle Chuck and I got together at his home in Santa Fe, New Mexico, to collaborate on preserving his family photos and papers. After we had gone through the photos, Chuck, saving the best for last, gave me his great-grandfather's memoir to read—about 419 handwritten pages. I was immediately struck by the quality of the writing: direct, colorful, dramatic, humorous, informative, and, in places, touchingly personal, recounting heartaches, gnawing ambition, moments of terror and ex-hilaration. Here was an astonishingly lively and believable self-portrait of an affectionate, spirited, and impulsive boy growing into an enter-prising, ambitious, determined, warmhearted young man.

No less remarkably, the memoir offered cinematically vivid stories of Charles's adventures at sea, his maritime trading experiences, and his highly diverse travel observations—the rich historical and social context of his life on shipboard and on shore, in Boston, Canton, Indonesia, Havana, London, Paris, Italy, the Sandwich Islands, and other worldwide ports of call. The sheer number and intensity of near-death experiences—in storms at sea, shipwrecks, mutinies among his crews, pirate attacks, and a cholera epidemic—were truly phenomenal.

Tyng's lack of formal education seems to have hindered neither his writing ability nor his pursuit of aesthetic interests, to judge from his strong reactions to scenery, architecture, painting, literature, and cui-sine. His chance meeting with Lord Byron came after he had already read the poet's works, which no doubt appealed to the impetuous, ro-mantic side of Charles's nature. He also showed an affectionate interest in young children, taking pleasure in describing those he encountered in his travels.

About actual romance, Tyng had rather little to say, although in sev-eral instances he revealed his susceptibility to feminine charm. He mentioned boyhood "sweet hearts" and an early, unrequited crush on a Boston girl, Sarah Hickling, whose initials he wore in a tattoo. Although he chose not to describe his courtship of Anna Arnold (1804–1831), his first wife, we know from a surviving diary (or "sentimental jour-nal") of Charles's voyage in the *Zephyr* that he had developed a strong emotional attachment during his preceding six months at home. They married in November 1826, following Charles's successful voyage in the *Eight Sons*. His subsequent remarks about their life together made it sound highly companionable and affectionate. The adaptable Anna, despite her ill health, shared Charles's enthusiasm for seafaring and travel abroad. After Anna's death, which he mourned acutely, Charles wistfully noted a brief acquaintance in 1832 with the three vivacious FitzGerald sisters, whom he met on board a Channel steamer.

Charles's second marriage took place in Chaseville, Florida (near

Jacksonville), in November of 1833, just a few months after the cholera attack that marks the end of the memoir. We know from other family records that Charles's second bride was also named Anna—Anna Amelia (or, in some sources, Amelia Anna) McAlpine (1816–1885). She was the seventeen-year-old daughter of John H. McAlpine—a millwright and mechanical engineer born in Beaufort, South Carolina, who moved to New York City and Albany—and his wife, Elizabeth Jarvis, from a Connecticut family active in the Episcopal Church. Anna's older brother, William Jarvis McAlpine (1812–1890), became a renowned civil engineer, responsible for numerous major city water supply projects, railroads, buildings, bridges, and highways.

Possibly Charles and Anna became acquainted through their families' Episcopalian connections, although it is hard to guess exactly where they met, or why the wedding was in Florida. Anna's mother's cousin was the learned Dr. Samuel Farmar Jarvis, rector from 1820 to 1826 of St. Paul's Church in Boston, where he was well acquainted with Charles's father. Judging Anna by her relatives and children (for lack of other evidence), we can reasonably suppose she brought an attractive combination of brains and energy to the marriage, along with her youthful appeal.

Anna Amelia and Charles Tyng spent thirty years of their married life living in Havana, Cuba, where Charles continued his mercantile ventures, hiring others to captain the ships that he owned. The family eventually retired to Newburyport, to the house formerly belonging to Charles's grandmother, the one he had visited as a small boy. In older age, Charles and Anna visited Providence, Rhode Island, where their daughter was living. Charles died there at the age of seventy-eight. His obituary in the June 24, 1879, *Newburyport Herald* remembered him as "a man of great enterprise, daring, and spirit . . . [who] by these qualities several times acquired enormous fortunes, but again met with reverses. . . . Capt. Tyng was a man of great benevolence, genial disposition, and with the faculty of making many friends."

Three of Anna and Charles's five children lived to maturity, spending enough of their younger years in Havana to speak fluent Spanish. The oldest son, Charles (1836–1906), worked there as an insurance underwriter's agent and a correspondent for the New York Associated Press, authoring a guidebook to the Caribbean called *The Stranger in the Tropics* (1868). From 1874 to 1876 he served as a private secretary to Caleb Cushing, a distinguished lawyer and family friend then serving as U.S. minister to Spain, but seems never to have settled on a career, diplomatic or otherwise. Anita Elena (1838–1914) became one of the very few women M.D.s in the United States at that time, studying in Boston and Philadelphia and practicing gynecological medicine (including surgery) in Providence, Rhode Island, before returning to head the Women's Hospital in Philadelphia. She retired in later life to Florida, where she lived with her unmarried older brother.

George (1842–1906), the younger son, studied engineering in Germany, a career choice no doubt encouraged by his Uncle William McAlpine. He began his career in New York, then sailed via Central America to California, where he married Elena Anita Carrillo Thompson of Santa Barbara in 1869. (Elena's father, Alpheus Thompson, a Maine sea captain, and her mother, Francisca Carrillo, daughter of a Hispanic landowner, make cameo appearances in chapters 10 and 11 of R. H. Dana Jr.'s *Two Years Before the Mast*.) Of George and Elena's three sons, the youngest, Francis, born in Mexico City, became my grandfather.

George spent some years in Yuma, Arizona, serving there as U.S. marshal, sheriff, and editor of the *Yuma Sentinel*. He later became involved in a Mexican railroad construction project across the Isthmus of Tehuantepec, and worked as a manager for a British landowning company in the Texas panhandle. He died in a snow slide at American Fork, Utah, where he was engaged in silver mining. Each in his or her own way, Charles Tyng's children seemed to have inherited their father's restless and enterprising spirit.

Although we might wish that Charles Tyng had completed the written account of his life, it seems likely that the years he describes in his memoir were his most adventurous and dramatic. And so we are grateful that the manuscript survived to give us a privileged look into this headstrong New Englander's turbulent world.

In editing the manuscript, we aimed to enhance its readability by standardizing Tyng's spelling and punctuation. We also broke it into paragraphs and chapters, adding chapter headings and a modest number of explanatory notes. Tyng's word choices and writing style, direct and effective as they are, have been left intact.

We did not leave out the evidence of Tyng's racial biases, deplorable and offensive though they are, because we did not want to represent him as being more progressive than he actually was. Readers are entitled to make their own judgments on Tyng's character and to know him and his era as they were, not as we might wish they had been. However, we did cut some portions of the memoir to improve the flow of the narrative, balance its different sections, and achieve publishable length. The complete text of the memoir is preserved in the manuscript, which will be at the Phillips Library of the Peabody Essex Museum, a wonderful collection devoted to New England's seafaring history.

—SUSAN FELS

BEFORE THE WIND

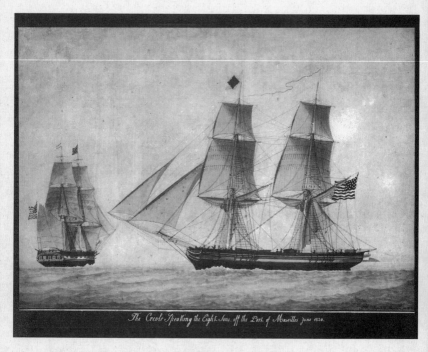

The Creole Speaking the Eight Sons. off the Port. of Marseilles June 1830.

The Creole & Eight Sons belonged to Charles Tyng—who began a sailor boy at 14 years old—in the yr 1815—At the time the two vessels met at sea near Marseilis [Marseille] as this picture represents, he commanded the *Creole* & Capt Parsons, his former mate, commanded the *Eight Sons*, which was bound to Havana. The *Creole*, with a cargo of Sugar, was from Havana bound to Marseiles. This picture represents *correctly* their meeting, and should be kept by C Tyngs children, &c—as a memento of their fathers perseverance, who from a sailor, without a dollar, by his own industry & perseverance, became a Captain and owner of these and other vessels—before he was 30 years old. This *act* of meeting his own vessel at sea, was particularly pleasant to him, as he had been out 70 days, and was quite short of provisions, he was supplied with refreshments by Capt Parsons—for which he ever felt thankful.

Newburyport *1831*—
CHAS TYNG
[*note on the back of the original painting*]

I

A Boston Boyhood

M Y MOTHER HAVING PASSED AWAY when I was 7 years old, I was left in a measure to shift for myself amongst my relations, sometimes staying in one place, and then at another, and finally found a home at my Grandmother Atkins's in Newbury, and there went to school at the academy in Belleville. Mr. McFales, a Scotch gentleman, was the principal. He was an excellent teacher and a good man, very kind to his scholars, and at this distant day I recollect him with pleasure.

My grandmother's family consisted of a maiden daughter (my Aunt Rebecka) and a grand daughter (my cousin Peggy Searle). My grandmother was somewhere about 80, a most excellent and kind hearted woman, & I loved her very much, as she always took my part when any little difference occurred between me and my dear Aunt Becka, which was *not* seldom as I was what they called "a bad boy" and this good woman frequently saw the necessity of a little punishment to keep my refractory spirit under proper restraint.

I remained there nearly a year, when my good father sent me to

Bridgewater Academy, and placed me to board with the Rev. Doctor Sanger. I was between 8 and 9 at that time. I was there about a year, and my impressions of the time I passed there are not pleasant. Doctor Sanger was a man between 60 and 70, a very large man, of a stern and disengaging look. He was a rigid Congregationalist, and had been settled in that parish for thirty years. There were several other boys from Boston placed there, amongst them Frank Lowell, & Henry Hubbard, both of whom were sons of leading families and became leading men in Boston.

In those days there were no public schools, and gentlemen sent their sons to school in the country towns, to board with the ministers, who most generally kept school in their houses for a dozen or more boys from the city. My father was left with five boys, beside three girls, to provide for. Four of us boys were big enough to be disposed of in the above way. My father, after a widowhood of a year or more, married again, and we boys were allowed to come home twice a year, once in the fall, to get our winter clothes, and once in the spring to get our spring clothes. We were never allowed to be at home at the same time, so that years passed without our seeing one another.

I once was so discontented in Bridgewater that I determined to run away, and [began] watching my opportunity, when the stage passed through town, which it did daily, and stopped at the town for the passengers to dine. The driver hitched his horses and went into the tavern, and there was no one in sight. I got into the stage, lifted up the back seat, & crawled in and let down the cover, and soon the driver came out, and mounted his seat and drove away. As I heard no one get into the stage, I pressed up the cover, and found no one sitting in the seat. I took a lookout, and no one [was] in the stage. I laid still in the box, until I thought the driver had got to a distance that he would not put me out to walk back again, when I lifted up the seat and got out, and sat down as unconcerned as if I was a passenger, and had paid my passage money. The driver did not see me until we got to the first stopping place. He knew who I was, as I often went for the Dr.'s paper when the stage came in from Boston. He expressed his surprise in a good humored way, and I had a very pleasant journey.

It was getting late in the afternoon when we arrived in Boston, and as I had some misgivings about going home, thinking my father would be angry, I stopped about the stable looking at the horses & the men at work until it became dark, when I went to the house, [and] came in the back way, into the kitchen. My father then lived in Milk St., where are now large blocks of granite stores. There was a strange woman for the cook, & who had never seen me. She asked me what I wanted. I said, "Give me a piece of bread and butter." She asked me what was my name. I told her none of her business. She was thinking of putting me out, when the man Warrick Jones came in (he had lived with the family for several years), and at once, said "Why, Charlie, where did you come from?"

As soon as the woman found I was Mr. Tyng's son, she gave me a piece of bread & butter. Warrick went up stairs (the kitchen was in the basement) and told the folks I was down stairs. My new mother (whom I had not seen since her marriage) told Warrick to take me up to such a room and put me to bed. It was Saturday night and I lay thinking of my exploit, and that as tomorrow was Sunday, I should have one day at home, and went to sleep. At daylight I was awoke by Warrick, who told me I must get up and come down to breakfast, which I did. Warrick waited for me, and took me down to the kitchen, where the strange woman gave me something to eat. When [I was] done, Warrick took me out to the front door, where stood a horse & chaise. Soon my father came & told me to get in, and off he drove. I do not remember that he spoke a word to me during the ride of about twenty miles. I saw no one of the family, and had not much of a visit at home.

We arrived at Dr. Sanger's house about noon. I sat and listened to the conversation between my father and the Dr., which was not much in my favour. Among other things my father told the Dr. he had rather I should be employed at some work, even picking up stones, than to be playing with the other boys. My father bid me good bye, and away he drove back to Boston, I remember to this day how dreadfully I felt, no friend, no sympathy. I did not wish to live.

I passed through many unpleasant scenes during the year I was at

Bridgewater, which did anything but assuage the high temper I had from childhood. Finally, my father became convinced that I was so discontented & unhappy that it was necessary to take me away from Bridgewater, so I was allowed to come home, where I stayed two weeks to have some new clothes made. I was then put under the charge of the Rev. Dr. Jacob Flint, the minister at Cohasset. I soon found that the change was from the frying pan to the fire. Doctor Flint was a large man with a forbidding countenance. He was morose & cross in his family, which consisted of his wife, three sons, and an infant daughter, whose names were Barker, Jacob, William, & Elizabeth. Mrs. Flint was very kind to me, would let me rock the baby in the cradle, and sometimes would let me hold the baby in my lap, which was my delight. I loved that little child.

As I had my sweet heart in Newbury and in Bridgewater, I felt it necessary for my happiness to have one in Cohasset, so the first Sunday I went to church I looked all round to find one. At last I discovered a pretty little girl, about 6 or 7 years old, with a straw hat surrounded with a wreath of artificial roses, which took my fancy, and although I was at Cohasset nearly a year, I never spoke to her, & I believe I never knew her name. It was all the same to me, I had chosen her for my sweet heart, and I used to see her every Sunday, which was the only pleasure I had in going to church—as I dreaded Sunday, the Dr. was so very strict, made us boys sit in the house, reading our Bibles, or learning hymns.

The school room was on the side of the house toward the bay. As the house stood on high ground, not far from the water, we had an excellent view of the bay, and the ocean. My desk was at the window, and I watched the vessels as they sailed up and down the coast, and was more interested in keeping the account, on the underside of my desk cover, of the sloops, schooners, &c. that passed, than I was with my studies. The war with England had commenced, and the British men of war would be often seen in the offing, and I watched their movements with the greatest interest. They sometimes would come in near the shore and send their boats in to destroy the vessels in the harbours along the coast.

The state supplied all the towns that were exposed to that danger with cannon for their defense, which were kept in small houses built for that purpose called gun houses, wherein were kept all the necessary equipments and powder, ready for use in case of alarum, as it was called, which was a quick pounding on the meeting house bell, when every male inhabitant run to quarters, as it was called, which was on the green round the meeting house, the militia men with their muskets, and cartridge boxes well filled, and the rest to drag the big cannon down to the cove, as the harbour was called.

Never shall I forget one forenoon whilst in school, we heard the alarum. In a moment all was excitement. The cry, "The Britishers are coming," was in every mouth, and we boys left school in a hurry, not waiting to be dismissed, and ran to the green to get hold of the drag rope to help haul the cannon down to the cove. I was frantic with excitement. We soon run the cannon down to the water where we found the English man of war boat was in the harbour and had already set fire to two schooners, which we saw burning when we arrived, and the boat in sight. How we blazed away at her. She soon turned her head seawards. I could not see that any of our shot hit her.

The channel from the harbour was through a narrow passage way. The militia, and every man who had a shot gun, had at once run down to the banks of this channel to get a shot at them as they went out, and they peppered them well. The boat was armed with swivel guns, and had a company of marines with carbines, who returned the fire, whilst the sailors rowed for their lives. It was supposed that many of them were wounded, and some killed. I believe none of our men were hurt. The Britishers never again attempted to come into Cohasset harbour, but the vessels were burnt in Scituate, and some other harbours in the bay.

THE BRITISH SEVENTY-FOUR GUN SHIP called the *Bulwark* was to be seen most every day, sailing about in the offing. She was blockading Boston harbour, watching for some of the American war vessels, particularly the ship *Chesapeake*, which was laying at the Navy Yard at

Charleston. The English frigate *Shannon*, which had been cruising in the bay for some time, exercising her men, sent a challenge in to the *Chesapeake* to come out & fight. The gallant Lawrence, who had just taken command, was too proud to refuse the challenge and against everyone's advice, as the ship was not in fighting trim—the crew were mostly new and not acquainted with their officers, had never been drilled or had any exercise—and was no match for the *Shannon*, although of about equal number of guns. In vain, all his friends advised him to wait a few days, until his ship could be got in perfect order for the fight. He sailed the following morning, stopped in Nantasket roads to land the women which were on board, & proceeded down the bay in search of the *Shannon*, when he knew the men were still labouring under the effects of rum, and in a half mutinous state.

We had heard that the *Shannon* had sent in a challenge, and I had watched her sailing back and forward for several days, & knew her well by sight. On the day of the battle I saw her sail by pretty close in between 11 and 12 o'clock up towards Boston. I was intensely interested, and watched sharp, until I saw her sailing out again with all colours flying, and an hour afterwards I saw the old *Chesapeake* come sailing out under full sail and all colours flying at about 2 o'clock. She followed after the *Shannon*, both keeping in the middle of the bay, not near enough for us to see very plain. We boys went down on the high rocks, which were covered with the town people watching the action of the two ships. Many had spy glasses [and] would tell us what they saw. By & by the two ships came near together, and we heard the cannon roaring, and soon the ships were enshrouded in the smoke, and I saw no more of them, but the roar of the cannon continued for a long time, as it appeared to me.

Days passed, and we heard nothing about the battle, and finally the news came that the *Shannon* had captured the *Chesapeake*. The particulars were soon heard, which were that the first broadside from the *Shannon* swept the decks of the *Chesapeake*, killing Lawrence, the first and second lieutenants. Lawrence's last words were "Don't give up the ship," which are on his monument in the Trinity church yard where he was buried. The third lieutenant then took command, & fought the ship as well as he could, with the mutinous crew, until they had battered the *Shannon* almost to pieces, when Captain Dacres by good fortune was able to run his ship down upon the *Chesapeake,* so that they could throw their boarders on board, when [in] a hand to hand fight with cutlasses, they gained, and struck the *Chesapeake*'s flag. Both then repaired damages as well as they could, and sailed for Halifax.

I WAS AT SCHOOL IN COHASSET somewhere about a year. I was far from being contented, and felt no interest in my studies. Dr. Flint was a tyrannical man, and very severe, particularly with his own children. Hardly a day passed without his whipping them. Us Boston boys did not get it so often, although I often felt the effects of the rod. He probably was deterred from whipping those who boarded with him, as his disposition would have induced him, had he not thought our parents would take us away. It was fortunate for me that my dear father had not given him the same instructions he gave to Dr. Sanger, or I should have had it with a vengeance.

I became very discontented, and constantly complained in my letters to my father of my unhappiness, which he did not seem to take much notice of. I at last became so worked up at the ill treatment I got that I ran away to Hingham, and got on board of a Hingham packet which run to Boston. A vessel was my delight, and this was the first one I ever stepped on board. When I got in Boston, I tried to get the captain to take me as a cabin boy, but he would not and I had to go home. The family then lived in the corner house of a block of 4 brick houses built by my grandfather Higginson, in Mount Vernon and Belknap Streets, since changed to Joy St. I went to the house in the afternoon, [and] was coolly received by my [step]mother.

My father was not at home when I got there but soon afterwards came in. He merely said "How do you do," [and] asked no questions about Dr. Flint or Cohasset. No one [was] at home besides my father & mother, except my sister Mary, who was about 6 years old, and my little brother James, who was about 3. I could have wished he had given me a whipping, or at least a good scolding for coming away from Cohasset without leave, for this entire silence on the subject was more galling than a whipping would have been, for then I should have felt as if I was forgiven.

My father decided to let me stay at home for a while, and he put me at school under the Chauncy Street meeting house, kept by Master Howe, a celebrated teacher of those days. But before I went to Mr. Howe's, I was put to a smaller school for a short time. I forget the master's name, but I well remember among the scholars a little fellow by the name of Goldsborough, whose father had procured a midshipman's warrant for him. He used to come to school in his uniform, with his little dirk hanging by his side. How much I envied him, and wished my father would procure me a warrant in the Navy. I had made my [mind] up then, if I could not go in the Navy I would go to sea.

Mr. Howe was a good master, a good teacher and a strict disciplinarian. He had a large school, some 60 to 70 boys. We all sat in rows, to desks fronting the monitor, who was one of the largest scholars. He had a desk upon a small platform raised about two feet above the floor, so that he could see every boy in the school. His duty was to watch the boys, and any one breaking the rules, he would make a mark against their names, and when one got three marks, he was reported to Mr. Howe, who in some way punished them, sometimes by a reprimand, or not allowing them to go out at intermission, or keeping them an hour after the school was dismissed. He very seldom administered corporal punishment, except in extreme cases.

There were many of my schoolmates whom I liked, some still living, and are men of consideration. There was Ralph Emerson, a boy of my age, who became a minister, as his father was before him. He now lives in Concord and is called "a sage." There was Robert C. Winthrop, the son of Lieut. Governor Winthrop, one of the old aristocracy. He graduated from Harvard College, and I believe he never attempted any profession. He still lives, one of the most respected of men in Boston. There was Russell Sturgis, a very handsome boy, whom all liked. After graduating from Harvard I believe he studied law but never practiced. He preferred mercantile pursuits and in after years established a mercantile house in Canton, China, and was successful, and when Joshua Bates died he was invited by the Barings of London to take Bates's place in the great banking house of Baring Bros. & Co. He is still a partner. Then there were many more who became men of note—Horace Gray, S. Parkman Blake, Benj. Rich, and others, which were older than me, and with whom I was not intimate, as I was with those of my age.

My impressions of that school are pleasant. Of those boyhood days, I have a vivid remembrance, and of the many wild and scampish tricks the boys who lived in our neighborhood were up to, as I was never kept under any restrictions during the time I lived at home. I used to mix & play with those boys, and often be a leader in their wild exploits. I formed a hoop company, as driving hoop was a common amusement at that time. We were between 15 and 20 boys.

The company was quite an affair. We paraded every Thursday and Saturday afternoon, and exercised on the Common, sometime in single file, sometime double, and sometimes, all in a line. It was grand fun. We used to press all hoops the other boys drove that did not have the right number of notches cut on them, and sometimes we got ourselves in difficulty. Once we had pressed a Black boy's hoop, which raised the indignation of the Blacks, and they came in force to attack us, and if it had not been for man who lived with us, we should have been badly whipped. He was a large stout built Scotchman, and seeing from our gate the fight going on, and that the Negroes were larger, he came to our assistance and soon dispersed them.

It was war time, and soldiers were almost every day drilling, and the drum was constantly heard. I was much interested in the army which was forming for old General Hull to take Canada, when finally it started and passed through Boston, with all their equipments, a great number of large, long covered wagons, with their tents, camp kettles, &c., each drawn by 4 mules, and the large number of cannon, also drawn by mules, and the great number of men. It took most of one day for them to march through the town. They marched up to Canada, and were defeated, owing to some fault of General Hull, it was said. The country was disgusted, and the poor man was court martialed, and cashiered from the army, and hung in effigy on Boston Common, and other parts of the country.

About the same time, I forget whether it was before or after, we were all astounded by the arrival in our harbour of the old frigate *Constitution*, Commodore Hull, who had fought the British frigate *Guerrière*, and sunk her. They were both of the same size, and metal. What a time of rejoicing, flags flying everywhere, the town beautifully illuminated. Fire works on the Common, no school for a week, and how we boys did enjoy the merry time. The town gave a great ball and public reception to the Commodore, and his officers, in the Boston Exchange coffee house, which was an immense building five or six stories high, with an immense circular hall in the centre of the building, from the second story up to the dome which was covered with glass. Galleries were round each story, with doors entering to each room. It was a magnificent affair, and every one felt a deep interest in its success.

I REMAINED IN BOSTON some 8 or 10 months, when my Father decided it would be better for me to go to a school out of the city, and sent me and my brother Stephen to Phillips Academy in Andover, and as he thought it would not be prudent for both of us to board in the same family, Stephen was placed at a farmer's, where there were other Boston boys, and I was put to board with the Rev. John Adams, who was the principal of the Academy. There were several Boston boys boarding there but I do not recollect their names, excepting Josiah Quincy. He was a very good fellow. He graduated from Harvard College. I believe he studied for no profession, but was always an active man, connected with many undertakings, one in which he became much embarrassed and lost his property, this was the Vermont rail road. He was at one time mayor of Boston, and is now living.

I have no pleasant recollections of Andover. Mr. Adams was excessively severe, both in his family and in the Academy. He was a strict Presbyterian—of the Puritan stamp. Sunday commenced at sundown on Saturday, and ended Sunday at sundown. Between those hours, all was silent, no one was allowed to laugh, or make any noise. Us boys had to pass our time in the house, reading the Bible, and learning hymns. How we learned to hate Sunday.

Mr. Zebulon Shaw was the assistant at the Academy, and had the younger boys in his class. I was one. We had a separate room from the larger scholars. I had no wish to study or learn anything, and as for Latin, I abominated it, and never would get my lesson, for which I used to be whipped, and finally after a term and a half Mr. Adams wrote to my father that I never would make a scholar, and advised him to take me away (that is, as I was told), and I came home to live.

During the time I was in Andover my father moved to Cambridge, as my brother Dudley had entered college, and Stephen was to enter the next year. I presume he thought it better that they should live at home than board at the college, besides being more retired & quiet for him, as Boston on account of the war had become very noisy. I found the family quartered in the former residence of Judge Dana, a large mansion house standing on high ground about a quarter of a mile this side of the college. It was surrounded by the farm, no house being near excepting the farm house, which was inhabited by Mr. Make-peace and his family. Mr. M. hired the farm, and carried on the milk business, keeping about 60 cows.

My father then told me if I would go to school, and study, I could go to sea as soon as the war was over. Uncle Perkins, whom he had consulted, had advised him by no means to put me in the navy as I had desired, as the war would soon be over and our navy would not amount to much, but to put me in the merchant service where I could advance & become a captain & a merchant, and perhaps become a wealthy man like him. As my father thought a boy that did not go through the Cambridge college was hardly worth raising, I suppose he did not care whether I went in the navy or the merchant service, as long as something was done with me.

I WAS THEN SENT to the school formerly kept by Dr. Allen, in Brighton, but at that time was kept by a Revd.—I forget his name. It was a boarding school, with boys mostly from Boston, who came Monday morning and went home Saturdays. I do not remember anything particular happening, until the winter of 1815 in the month of February, when one forenoon a man on horseback rode by on a gallop crying out "Peace has been declared."

All was excitement through the country, cannon firing and flags flying, and every show of rejoicing. At about the same time we got news of Gen. Jackson's great battle near New Orleans, and his victory with 3500 raw troops over the English invading army of 15,000. Great indeed were the rejoicings—Boston was illuminated, splendid fireworks in the Common, and a procession of all the trades passed through the streets.

Quite an enlivening time commenced in all branches. Vessels that had been tied up at the docks, under cover for years, were brought out, and work commenced to refit them for sea. Amongst the number was the ship *Cordelia*, which belonged to Messrs. Bray & Boit, who sold her to Messrs. James and Thomas Perkins, who were brothers to my uncle Samuel Perkins. They had her overhauled and fitted for sea. She had been laying up for over four years, and was much out of repair. She was about the largest ship then belonging in Boston, although she was only 349 tons. John King was appointed Capt., a man past middle life, and a most excellent man. The Perkinses had her fitted out for an India voyage, and my uncle John Higginson was to go supercargo. He had commanded a vessel, some ten or fifteen years before. He was an eccentric man of about 50 years of age, although looking much older, having grey hair, and large grey whiskers, not a very prepossessing countenance, and most certainly, his countenance did not belie his character. It was decided that I should go as one of the sailor boys in that ship. How delighted I felt that at last my long wished for idea was about to be realized.

My father, not knowing what I required for an outfit for the voyage, requested my Uncle John to provide for me what was necessary. He, being either too proud or too busy, requested Mr. Tom Lee, his cousin, and a much younger man, to attend to getting my clothes &c. Mr. Lee in after life became wealthy, and presented the city of Boston with a very handsome monument to the discoverer of ether for the unconsciousness of pain, in surgical operations &c. It now stands in the Public Garden at the bottom of the Common.

Mr. Lee did as my Uncle John told him, and procured from a slop shop a couple suits of sailor's clothes, some checked shirts &c., but no pea jacket or over coat, as it would not be needed. These, with my jacket and trousers which I then wore, the trousers buttoning on to the jacket, with a shirt ruffled and spreading over my shoulders, with one pair of new shoes, some pocket handkerchiefs, and a sailor's cap were packed away nicely, in a sea chest which Mr. Lee had got for me, by my mother. She also rolled up a piece of stair carpet as hard as she could to make it firm, and sewed some strong cotton round it for a pillow which was also packed in my sea chest. This chest I took with me in all of my first voyages, whilst I was a sailor, and it is now in the garret of the old house as a memorial of my sailor's life.

This pillow often amused my ship mates, they said it was capital to crack nuts on, and was good to press my ears to my head &c. I also had a sailor's mattress, jack knife, and tin pot. I mention my outfit for an eighteen month voyage, as it is so strongly impressed on my mind that I shall never forget it, and I had reason to remember it, as will be seen further on. I was however delighted to get my sailor clothes, being the first I ever had with suspenders. I had always wore jacket and trousers, the latter buttoning round the jacket. I soon put them on with my sailor's cap, a blue woolen one with a white stripe round the lower part, worn generally by sailors in those days, and as my check shirts were not ready, I put on my ruffle shirt which spread over my shoulders. I felt very proud and paraded the streets, when I heard some boys crying "A fresh water sailor, a fresh water sailor." I felt very angry, but I soon realized my want of a check shirt, as my boy's shirt appeared ridiculous over my sailor's jacket to the boys, and I made for home about the quickest.

2

First Voyage

Now i come to my voyage in the *Cordelia*, which even to this day has a sickening effect on my mind, & I would willingly leave it out, but as I began to tell the history of my adventurous life, I presume I must go on and tell the whole, however unpleasant it may be to renew the thoughts of that first voyage. My father procured my protection as an American citizen, signed by Governor Strong, giving my age as thirteen years and some months, my height as four feet & ten inches, and various scars on my person &c. This was to protect me as a citizen of the United States, from being pressed on board of any English man of war that might board us at sea, as an English subject.

The ship *Cordelia* having been hauled off in the stream to take on board the specie, for the purchase of a cargo of tea in Canton, China, amounting to four hundred thousand Spanish dollars, in one hundred iron kegs, the crew were ordered on board. This was on the 13th of May 1815. I among the rest went on board. I felt as if I was doing something dreadful, and as near as I remember, that feeling never left me until I got back from that voyage.

The ship's company were Capt. John King, a good man, Charles Magee (a brute), first mate. The second mate was a good sailor, about 30 years old and a so, so, sort of man, rather hard on the boys, of which there were two besides me, Henry Dow and William Hickling, both older, and much larger than me. Then there was a carpenter who was the meanest man on board. He lived in the steerage, and I was placed with him. There were eight old sailors, and six green hands. There was also a coloured cook, and steward, and my uncle Mr. John Higginson, supercargo, making in all twenty five persons on board, all, as it were, strangers to me, and I the smallest one on board.

I was put on board in the fore noon of the day before she sailed, and the first order I received was from Magee, the first mate, "Boy, coil up that rigging." I was completely puzzled, as I thought the shrouds was the rigging, and I looked up to them, wondering how I could coil them up, and as I was hesitating what to do, Magee (who was a large man) came up to me and took me by the ear and lifted me up from the deck, and roared out like a bull, "I tell a boy once to do a thing, beware of the second time," and dashed me down on the deck. A sailor then showed me how to coil the ropes, which were lying about the decks, on the belaying pins at the side of the vessel. If Mr. Magee had told me to coil up the ropes, I should have understood him what to do. I had not been on board one hour when this took place, and if I could have got on shore, I never would have gone to sea, but have studied like a good one, and have gone to college, or anywhere else my father wanted me to, but it was too late. My fate was sealed.

I listened with horror to the profane language of the sailors, who were under the influence of rum, and saw their disgusting looks and actions, and the idea that I was to be a companion with such creatures perfectly shocked me. I had no appetite to eat the dirty messes, and passed the night as best I could, crying most of the time, overcome with such an indescribable feeling of loneliness, and friendlessness, that almost drove me crazy. The morning came at last, and all hands were called to wash down the decks. I was given a broom, and with the other two boys, scrubbed the decks, and swept the water down the scupper holes. Sometime in the forenoon the pilot came on board, and the sailors manned the windlass and hove up the anchor, and the ship sailed down the bay. I soon became very seasick from the motion of the ship. Oh, how dreadful I felt.

In the evening the watches were set, half of the men in the starboard, and half in the larboard watch. I was in the first mate's watch. The watches are of four hours, excepting the dog watches, which are from four in the afternoon until six, and from six until eight, two hours each. The bell is struck every half hour, commencing at eight in the evening, which is called the first watch, until 12 o'clock, which is eight bells, and from 12 until 4 is called the middle watch, and from 4 till 8 is called the morning watch, but all hands are called at seven bells, or half past 7, when they have half an hour to eat their breakfast, and are set to work at 8 o'clock.

The seamen, as they are called, take turns steering the ship. Each one has two hours, night and day. The first mate's watch always is the first watch sailing from port, and our watch commenced at 8 o'clock. I was very sea sick, and Magee amused himself by tormenting me, would not let me set down, but insisted upon my walking the deck, as the ship was rolling. It was almost impossible, in vain I begged him to let me sit down. He put a stick in my hands, and told me to walk guard as a marine. I would stagger about and fall down, and finally I was so overcome that I could not get up, when he took the end of a rope and commenced beating me, and threw a bucket of water over me, as he said to learn me to keep awake, in my watch on deck. And when he found I could not get up, he got some tar and grease mixed together and rubbed it on my face and neck. How I wished I could die.

I could not wash the stuff that he put on me off with salt water, and we were put on an allowance of fresh water the first day out, of two or three quarts a day. That was for our coffee, tea, and soup, if we had any, as well as to drink. Each one was given a small keg to keep it in. The water was dealt out every evening, each one carrying his keg to the cask between decks where it was dealt out by the second mate, so the tar & grease had to remain until it wore off. The old sailors said it was a shame to treat a little boy that way, was all the sympathy I got.

The other boys were not treated so bad. Time wore on, and when we had been out a month, I got more used to it, and got along pretty well.

I was called *the* boy, I suppose because I was the smallest, and the youngest, and was called to all the dirty jobs. The sailors were kind to me, but the carpenter was a cross, malignant scoundrel, of under size. I had to wait on him, bring the food from the cook, & clean up his dirt. I soon began to hate him. My Uncle John looked down the steerage hatch one day and said "Carpenter, why don't you flog that boy?" This was the first time I had heard his voice since we sailed. So after that, the carpenter thought he had full right to pound me, but before the voyage was up I became strong enough to pound him, and did I not give it to him, was a caution.

Time rolled on, and we got down to the equator and crossed the line, as the sailors called it, and such a time I never forget. The Captain gave the crew extra allowance of grog on that day. Jack Campbell, one of the oldest and best seamen on board, rigged himself up as Neptune, with long beard and hair made from rope yarns, with a sort of crown on his head, with a speaking trumpet in one hand and a trident in the other. He came in on deck from over the bow of the ship dripping wet as the Father of the Sea, to christen his new children, which were all those who had never crossed the line before. Each one was blind-folded by tying a handkerchief over his eyes, and had to kneel down on deck, when Neptune administered the oath, which was a long rig-marole medley of sayings—among them was, "never to eat brown bread, when you could get white, never to kiss the maid when you could kiss the mistress," which was repeated after Neptune, when he gave the individual the speaking trumpet telling him to hail Neptune & thank him for permitting him to join his family, when a pot full of dirty water was dashed in their faces. Some of them took it very kindly, & others did not, when they would get a daub of tar in their faces. Neptune treated me very kindly, patted my head & told me to be a good boy, and I should be one of Mother Carey's chickens.

Jack was a good friend to me, always took my part, when any mis-understanding occurred between me and any of the crew. I used to give Jack my grog, when any was given to me. Grog, or New England rum, was dealt to the crew daily, each having one gill, measured to him by the steward. I, being in the steerage, did not receive it regularly, only when the steward, who was my friend, chose to give it to me, which he stealthily did sometimes. I did not like it, and never drank it, but gave it to the old sailors, who used to teach me to splice ropes and make the various kinds of knots used on shipboard.

I became quite a favourite with the old sailors during the voyage. They would tell me long stories during the midnight watches of their many experiences. They were very superstitious, believed in haunted ships, in ghosts, &c. Some of them had seen a coffin with an open Bible in it float by the ship, a sign of shipwreck which always happened in such cases. Some had seen black bears walking in the yards, a sure sign that a heavy gale was going to blow, and that the ship would lose some of her spars, and many such preposterous vagaries filled their minds.

The mates took good care to keep us all at work. We boys were employed in making five yarn sennit, from rope yarns, which was braiding five rope yarns together, which was much used about the rigging of the ship. We made thousands of fathoms during the voyage and at other times we picked oakum. The boys generally did all the light work aloft, such as loosing and furling the light sails. I was a great climber before I went to sea, no tree or pole that I would not undertake to climb. This had made me strong in the arms. Soon after I recovered from my seasickness, I began to climb up the rigging, and soon could go higher on the masts than the other boys.

After we had been out two months or so, one very pleasant Sunday afternoon, I made a bet with William Hickling that I could go up to the truck of the main mast, which is the tip top of the mast. The sky sail pole, as it was called, had no shroud, so that it was a bare pole of 8 to 10 feet long, with the truck on the end, and as the ship was rolling, the end of the pole was making something of a sweep in the skies. It was rather a dangerous exploit, but I did it and gained the bet, which was a dollar, and which William paid me.

An hour afterward, Magee, having heard of it, called me aft, and took the dollar from me, and gave me a severe whipping with the end of a rope. That is what I got for trying to be smart. But it did not dampen my ardour for climbing, as by constant practice, I became an expert before the voyage was over. I could go up a rope hand over hand, higher than any one on board. I could hold on with one hand longer, and in fact I had more confidence in my hands and arms, than in my feet when going about the ship, for I always felt safe as long as I had hold of a rope. This practice was of great benefit to me. It gave great strength to the muscles of the arms, and many a time saved me pitching into the sea.

TIME PASSED ON and we sailed south into cold latitudes, as we were to go round Cape Horn to arrive at Coquimbo, where the ship was to stop to take on board a cargo of copper for Canton. It was in the month of August, the middle of winter, and very cold, [that] we came in sight of land, after being at sea over three months. I think we did not see a sail, from the time we left Boston, so that the sight of the coast of Patagonia was quite a treat to us as we sailed quite near the coast, and went through the Straits of Le Maire, a narrow passage between an island and the main land, which was high and rocky—the island being quite low, having a wide beach of very white sand, and some straggling shrubs and desolate looking trees in the interior.

What was most curious to me was the swarms of penguins, marching along the shores, and swimming around the ship. On the beach they looked like men, as they are perfectly upright when they are on the land, their short legs being as it were, in the place of a tail. There were several kinds, some three feet and over in height, with red and yellow feathers about the neck and head, with black bodies & white breasts. They looked like regiments of soldiers.

We passed through this Strait in the afternoon and the next day the land of Tierra del Fuego was in sight, and a gale commenced from the north, which lasted for nearly three weeks, some of the time blowing most violently. All the upper masts & yards had been sent down on deck, and the ship lying to under a staysail and bare poles, nothing above the top masts, and drifting all the time to the south, until we got somewhere about 60° South. It was cold, hail & snow, and ice forming on deck. I suffered dreadfully, having no outside coat, or pea jacket, no boots & my shoes worn out, no woolen socks, as my mother was told I should not want anything of the kind going to the East Indies. All the rest had pea jackets, woolen socks, tarpaulin hats &c. I was the poorest clad of any one on board, and all for that brute of an uncle, who would not give me anything when he was told by the second mate how much I was suffering from the want of warm clothes & shoes.

I had sometime previous been changed from the first mate's watch to the second mate's. He was kind to me, gave me a pair of his woolen socks, and a guernsey frock. As he was a large man & I a small boy they did not fit very well. The guernsey frock answered for an outside coat, & helped to keep me a little warm. William Hickling, who was in the other watch, would lend me his peajacket & tarpaulin hat, when he went below, which I was thankful for.

One night in the midst of the storm, about two o'clock, in the middle watch, and my watch below, Magee gave orders to call up that boy, and I had to go on deck, the ship tossing about among the heavy seas which were running. Magee ordered me up to the mizzen top, to take off a rope yarn blowing from there, which he called an "Irish pennant." I never felt so completely worked up before in my life as I was at this piece of cruelty. I went up the shrouds and pulled off the rope yarn, and coming down, I came to the conclusion to jump over-board and drown myself, not wishing to live suffering this man's bru-tality any longer. I got halfway down, and turned round, and was on the point of jumping, when a thought, which seemed a voice, said "No, no, go in on deck," and I mechanically stepped in on deck. I was allowed to go below again, and although all wet and cold, I fell into a sweet sleep and dreamed of my own mother. I do not remember my dream, only I recollect it had a very soothing effect on my discouraged spirit.

To give some idea of this man's brutality, I will mention one [inci-dent] which the rest of the crew thought worse than all. They had been accustomed to see him whip me, which he always did in the for-ward of the ship so as the Capt. would not hear me cry, and they had often told me to cry louder & make a noise so as to be heard aft. So one day when he was whipping me for nothing but for his amusement, I began to scream, and he pushed me into the hog pen and shut down the cover, where there were two or three large hogs, and told me they were my brothers, &c. I got up in one corner and had as much as I could do to fight them off from biting me. I was kept there but a short time, as I suppose he saw that he was doing wrong. Magee bullied over me and the other two boys, and once began upon others of the crew, when they mutinied—and it like to have been a very serious affair. So much for Magee, and no more, only to say he kept up his abuse of me the whole voyage.

We at last arrived in the harbour of Coquimbo, having had a passage of 160 days, over five months. The latter part of the time we were on short allowance of water, salt beef, and mouldy bread. Beans, sugar, coffee, tea, and flour, as well as molasses & vinegar, had been all out long before. This was a most outrageous fault of the owners of the ship, in not putting on board sufficient supplies of water and food for the ship's crew, which was in ballast, and there was plenty of room for many more water casks. So there would have been no need of putting the crew on an allowance of water, a thing unheard of the present day, except in very extraordinary cases. There is nothing which causes more aggravating suffering than the want of water, especially at sea in warm latitudes, and living on salt beef & bread. We were all glad enough to get into port again.

Coquimbo is a port in Chile some hundreds of miles to the north of Valparaiso. The entrance to the harbour is through a narrow passage, large black rocks on each side, which were covered with thousands of seal that tumbled off into the water as the ship approached. There had been no vessel in the harbour for a very long time, on account of the wars which raged for a length of time, between England and America, that drove the whalers and other merchant vessels from the Pacific Ocean. At this time, the revolution of the Chileans was in full force, fighting for their liberties, and to get themselves clear of the tyrannical government of Spain.

Soon after the ship came to anchor, several canoes came alongside to trade chickens, ducks, and many other things. Those of us who had money, of which I was one (as my father had given me five silver dollars the day I went on board the ship, in Boston harbour), traded with the Indian looking fellows for what they had. I bought a dozen chickens. The cook made us a good soup of half of them, and the steward put the other half in the chicken coop, and fed them with the others which the captain bought.

Our object in stopping at Coquimbo was to procure a cargo of copper to carry to China. There are large copper mines there, and in former times great quantities were shipped to Spain, and there was plenty there then, but we did not stop for a cargo, for the following reason. The day after our arrival the Captain and supercargo were invited to dine with the Governor, and other high officers on shore. As the Capt. did not understand Spanish and the supercargo could not speak the language, but could understand the most of what was said, which he did not let the company mistrust, an interpreter was employed, and all due honours were paid to the guests.

The Capt. invited them to visit the ship the next day, and about midday they all came on board. We fired a salute, and made all the show we could. They were very particular in examining the ship, her guns, &c., and there seemed to be a good deal of suspicious talk and whispering amongst them and when in the cabin, drinking wine, some observations were made which the supercargo understood to be planning to seize the ship, rob the money, and making a Chilean war ship of her. At all events to be on the safe side, and prevent blood shed, our Captain thought best to get out of the harbour as soon as possible, so when it became dark we got the ship underway and sailed out. Most fortunately, we had filled up our water casks the day before, as well as procured some potatoes and other provisions. At daylight the high land of Chile was seen in the distance, and our friends the Chileans left to wonder what had become of us.

We sailed away across the Pacific Ocean towards the Sandwich Islands, where it was intended to take on board a cargo of sandalwood, if we could obtain it, as it grows in the Islands to perfection. The only thing that is impressed on my mind particularly occurred when about half passage. It seems that my Uncle John had been in the habit of amusing himself in feeding and watching the chickens in the coops, mine amongst the rest, he however not suspecting that *I* had any interest in them, and it so happened that he took a great fancy to two of mine, which were of a peculiar colour, and very pretty. An old Italian sailor by the name of Luis, who had always been very kind to me— taught me many things about the ship such as stropping the blocks, making splices, &c., became sick, and I felt much sympathy for him, and I had asked the steward for two chickens at different times, to make some soup for him. It so happened that he had taken the two so much admired by my uncle, who one morning missed them, and when told they were the boy's, and he had taken them, his rage knew no bounds.

He sent for me, and for the first time spoke to me since we left Boston, and in the most violent manner demanded, what had I done with the two chickens I had stolen from the coop. I told him I had not stolen them, that they were mine, that I had bought them in Co- quimbo, and that I had given them to Luis who was sick to make some soup. The way he cursed me, and the profane language he used in his threats to annihilate me, was to say the least most dreadful.

One bright morning to my astonishment we first saw the land up in the clouds. It was the high peak of a mountain on the island of Owhyhee, and it must have been a great way off, as we sailed with a good breeze until towards night before we reached the land. It was so late that the Captain thought it not prudent to try to find a harbour until the next morning, so the ship was hove to with her head off the land until the next morning, when we sailed in towards the land, which had a beautiful appearance. The high mountain in the distance with the sun shining on it was of different colours, some green, brown, and purple. The sight was fine.

This is the island where Capt. Cook was killed, and eaten, and I was told the Indian who killed him was still living. Soon after the ship was brought to anchor, the Captain & supercargo went on shore, and many of the Indians swam off alongside of the ship, and some of them came on board, but as no one could understand them, they did not stay long, but looked round the ship & then jumped overboard. They seemed to be as much at home in the water as the fish, swam round and dove like porpoises. The Capt. sent the boat back to the ship loaded with yams, bread fruit, and other eatables, which gave us a good treat for supper, as we had had no vegetables for months, and the scurvy began to show among the ship's company.

The next morning I was surprised to be called aft by my Uncle John, and told I might go on shore in the boat when he went, and to wash, and to put on my best clothes &c. This order was a little amusing, as I had worn out my clothes, excepting the jacket & trousers, and boy's shirt which I used to wear to school, and my mother thoughtfully had put in my chest. My shoes had been gone for a long time, and the bottom of my feet had become quite hard by running up and down the rigging, so that I had not felt the want of them since we had got into warm latitudes. Luis had made me a pair of light shoes out of canvas, a short time before we arrived, which answered a good purpose, and I dressed myself as well as I could in my jacket and trousers buttoning on to the jacket, with my boy's shirt spread over my shoulders, much to the amusement of the sailors. I do not remember what I did for a hat, only I know I had none.

I went on shore with my uncle, who seemed to have changed wonderfully & spoke kindly to me. Perhaps his conscience was a little unsettled at the manner he treated me during the voyage. We were soon surrounded by the natives, large and small. All of them seemed to be staring at me. I suppose so small a white man was a curiosity to them. We went into the palace, the king's house, which was about ten feet high made with poles stuck into the ground, interwoven with a species of coarse grass or reeds. There seemed to be several of these huts connected together, which were fenced round with strong poles fastened into the ground. Quite a space was enclosed in this way, which was guarded by the king's troops. The furniture was very simple, appeared to be the cabin furniture of some ship, which might have been wrecked on the island, nothing very kingly in appearance, but there sat King Tamehameha, in all his glory.

He had a *kanaka,* which is the name given to the male Indians, who spoke English and acted as an interpreter. He had been on a whale ship on her voyage to the Bering Straits and had learned English. The king took quite a fancy to me, took me in to another part to see his wives, or that his queens might see me. They were laying down on a mat, and looked to me more like three great brown hogs, than like queens, as they were naked, and their skins oiled. They were hideous looking beings, and they pawed over me, to my great disgust, taking a great fancy to my ruffled shirt. My uncle, who came into the room, told me to kiss them, which I declined to do, but he threatened me with a flogging if I did not, so rather than take a flogging I kissed three queens.

The king had some dinner prepared for us, which was baked dog, yams, and some other messes. The dog was very good, more like a young pig than anything else. The manner of cooking is curious. They make a hollow in the earth, and line it with hot stones, put in the dog, and cover it with more stones, then cover it with sea weed, something on the principle of a Rhode Island clambake. I made a capital dinner, not having tasted fresh meat for some time. They also gave me some bananas to eat, a fruit I had never seen before, it was the most delicious thing I had ever tasted, also some bread fruit, which was good, but not to be compared with the banana.

Previous to the war we had many whaling ships in the Pacific Ocean which stopped at the Sandwich Islands to get supplies of provisions and water, but for three years or more there had been none. Our ship being the first after the war was quite a treat to the Islanders. I never knew the cause that prevented our not being able to procure a cargo of sandalwood, but we could not, and therefore made sail for Canton.

I THINK WE WERE about a month on the way, and when we approached the shores of China, we saw many of the Chinese vessels, or "junks," as they are called, most strange looking craft, nothing like our vessels, either in hull or rigging. The hull looks like a bunch of boards put together in a most clumsy manner, apparently open at the bow and the stern, not painted, excepting two large eyes, one on each side of the bows. The rudder is a large square thing, entirely different shape from ours. Their anchors are of wood with a big stone lashed on the crown. The stern is much higher than the forward part, it rises from the centre, something like a pair of steps, altogether a strange looking thing, at first sight, but one soon gets used to them after a while. They have one large mast a little forward of the entire centre of the vessel with a large lateen sail, curiously made of bamboo, and rushes. It seems a big unwieldy affair to a sailor. They also have another small mast on the stern, with a small sail, of similar shape as the large one, no bowsprit and no other sails than these two. All their vessels large and small, as well as their boats, have eyes painted in the bows. I asked a Chinaman why they painted eyes on their vessels. He replied "How can see no got eye?"

We sailed up the Yellow Sea, on which Canton is situated, or I should say in which the river empties on which Canton is situated, and finally saw the land, which was not very high, and as we drew near, a pilot boat came alongside and put a pilot on board, to me quite a curiosity, with his shaved head, excepting his long queue hanging down behind, and his curious dress. It was quite a funny sight to me. His shoes and cap took my fancy. He was as great a sight to me as I was to the Sandwich Island Indians.

We soon entered in amongst the islands, sailing close to them. All looked curious. We entered the mouth of the river, between two for-tifications, one on each side, singularly formed, being built on the side of the hills, which sloped gradually to the edge of the river. They were in shape of a half circle, the circle part being up the hill, and the straight part along the river, where the cannon were placed, all sur-rounded by a white wall, so that the whole interior of the forts could be seen as we sailed by. Any kind of an armed vessel could destroy such fortifications in short order by shot and shells.

From the mouth of the river, which is called Chinpee, to Wham-poa, where all foreign vessels must anchor, is about 35 miles. The scenery along the river, which is thickly settled, is exceedingly inter-esting, and to one like me, who never saw anything of the kind before, it was wonderful. We passed a pagoda of large size, seven stories high. It was about a mile from the banks of the river. It is exactly of the same form as pictures & models of pagodas which I had seen before— all excepting the bells at the various angles on the different stories. The houses were curious, similar in appearance as those seen on china plates, and other ware. The country seemed crowded with inhabitants, young and old, all moving about like ants round an ant hill.

We finally arrived at Whampoa, and came to an anchor. Very soon a large "harpoo" boat came alongside and made fast to the side of the after part of the ship, also a comprador's boat. The comprador is a very important personage, every vessel has to have one, who are hired to attend to the ship during their stay. They attend to everything. They speak a broken English mixed up with Portuguese, some Dutch, and French, the same as most of the Chinamen who come about the ship. It is rather difficult to understand them at first, but one soon gets used to hearing them.

The harpoo boat is more of a custom house affair, it is curiously built, has in the middle a room covered with a circular bamboo top. This is for the mandarin, or custom house officer. He has a little table in the centre, with his writing materials, as he signs all the papers connected with the discharge or loading of cargoes.. These papers are called "chops." This part of the boat is entirely devoted to him. The after part of the boat is one story higher, also covered with a bamboo cover. There are two or three China men, or women, who have charge, and live quite comfortably. I very soon formed an acquaintance with them, and they were always very kind to me. They would make a nice omelette, which I liked, and I learned to count in the Chinese language, which I have not forgotten to this day.

It was fortunate that I had a little money [so] that I could enjoy this luxury. Eggs and everything of the sort were cheap & a dollar would go a great way. The exchange [rate] was 8 mace for a dollar. A mace, equal to 12½ cents of our currency, was a string of 80 cash, as they are called. A cash is a round metal coin with a square hole, so a dollar in "cash" went a long way, and I could treat my friends among the crew with an omelette once in a while, which was one of my greatest pleasures. All this visiting was done on the sly, in the evening when Magee was below, as he would, I don't know what, if he knew I was enjoying an innocent pleasure.

Then there was the washwoman's boat, would come alongside of the forward part of the ship. Her price for washing the sailor's clothes was one dollar each, no matter how many, or how long the ship was there. There was also a barber. His name was Tom Kin. He came on board every Sunday to shave the crew. He charged half a dollar for the whole time, no matter how long, one month or six. He got his pay when the ship went away, that is, if the sailors were a mind to pay him. I, who had not seen the least sign of a beard, used to ask him how much he would ask me. He always answered "Half a dollar, all same pricee."

The river was covered with boats, always sculled by women, who lived on board with their children, and they of all sizes until they were big enough to work on shore or to catch fish. Until they could crawl about, they were carried on their mother's back in a sort of band, which did not interfere with her work. When they got so that they could crawl, they had fastened to their back a life preserver, which was made from a peculiar wood more like the pith of a reed than wood, and was lighter than cork. They frequently fell overboard. The mother, or anyone, would reach out and pick them up. Men were seldom seen in these boats, without they were very old and could not work. These boats seemed to be all alike, and very near of a size, about 12 feet long and 5 feet wide, each covered about half way over with a bamboo cover, under which they lived, and raised their families. They were sculled by an oar of a different shape from ours, being in two pieces spliced together, and resting on an iron pivot in the stern of the boat, and it was astonishing with what ease they would propel their boats along.

We laid at anchor at Whampoa between two & three months, so that I got pretty well acquainted with the habits of the people and the appearances of things on the water. The following day after our arrival, the specie was taken up to the city in the long boat of the ship, towed up by the pinnace with six oars. Our ship had three boats. The long boat was a large boat carried on deck in the middle of the ship, lashed to large iron ring bolts, which were fastened to the beams under the deck. The pinnace was a little smaller and was stowed inside of the long boat, and the jolly boat was carried at the stern.

The hundred kegs, each containing four thousand dollars, were stowed in the long boat, also the jolly boat with six oars, and covered over with a tarpaulin, and the pinnace with six seamen and second mate rowed up to Canton, through the thousands of boats which covered the river, towing a boat with four hundred thousand silver dollars, without the thought of being robbed. I presume the comprador boat and perhaps some other guard boat accompanied the expedition.

It soon became my turn to row up to Canton. Being quite green at this work, I was given the bow oar in the jolly boat. There were four rowers beside me. I made witch work with my oar at first, but by the kind words of Capt. King who was in the stern seats, I soon learned to put my oar in the water, to feather edge it, and keep time with the others, and as I felt ambitious to learn, I kept at it without faltering until we reached the landing, although I was very tired, and my hands sore, by rowing 7 miles the first time I ever used an oar.

For two or three miles from the landing the river was covered with boats, in which families lived, all the time, scarcely ever going ashore. How they existed is the greatest wonder. A passage through this floating town was always kept open as a public road, by a sort of police guard, who did not mind using their bamboo clubs to keep order. It was only a little wider than required for the boats to row through, so that we were close to, on both sides of this high way through this floating town, and could look into their houses, as it were, and see all that was going on. They would good naturedly greet us with the word *pangui, pangui,* which I understood to mean stranger, which I learned afterwards was "foreign friend." The banks of the river were quite low. There is very little tide in the river, not more than a foot difference between high and low water, which is generally the case in the tropics. It is the same in Havana, which is in the same latitude as Canton, 23½° north.

There is only one place for foreigners to land, which is a large space, fenced in on two sides, with the factories, or hongs, on the other sides, fronting the river. This space, or common as it is called, is about forty rods square. The hongs are high buildings, built more in the European style of brick covered with stucco. They are about

50 feet wide in front, and run back several hundred feet, divided by openings from the top every 40 or 50 feet, which gives a little yard, and lets light and air in to the building. These openings are about 12 feet wide, with galleries on each side so as to connect the whole together. There is a large passage way from the front to the rear of the hong. The front part, second story, is generally the counting rooms, the third story contains sleeping rooms. The second division is devoted mostly to family purposes, the others [in] back more as ware houses. On the square in front, each hong has a high flag pole, on which the flag of the nation that has the hong is hoisted every day. The American, Dutch, French, and English flags were flying. All commercial business is done in the hongs. Only certain Chinese merchants are allowed to trade with the foreigners—and this company are the hong merchants. Houqua was at the head of the hong, at the time we were there. Mr. John Cushing, a nephew of the Perkinses (our owner) was at the head of the American hong when we were there, and of course did the business of our ship.

I did not leave the boat, whilst we were there this time, as I was very tired, and glad to sit still. The boat's crew walked about the square. We remained there about an hour, when we were ordered to return, and I rowed 7 miles back to the ship, making 14 miles the first time I ever rowed a boat. I was tired enough to sleep sound that night. My hands, which were pretty hard from pulling on the ropes, and climbing the rigging, were pretty well blistered.

We had now to hoist out the ballast, which were large paving stones. We discharged a large part of the ballast, keeping only enough in the hold to keep the ship upright until the cargo was ready to be brought on board, which took some time to be prepared as every chest, half chest, and quarter chest of tea had to be examined to see that it corresponded with the sample, as the Chinamen are great cheats, and frequently if they are not watched sharp will put in stones to make it weigh, or even fill the boxes with the hulls of rice, instead of tea, as well as to put in poorer qualities of tea, of which there is plenty, as they are in the habit of drying the leaves of black teas, after they have been once used, and selling them again to supply the poorer class, as well as to pass them off to foreign purchasers. Also it takes much time to prepare the boxes, which are to be lined with lead and paper, and covered with oiled paper and each one marked with the ship's name as well as the name of the hong merchant who supplies the cargo.

The crew in the meantime were employed in overhauling the rigging and putting everything in order, and there was plenty of work for all hands. I was employed, as well as the other boys, in tarring the rigging, and help[ing] the older sailors in serving the ropes, which is to wind spun [rope] yarn round them with a serving mallet, and we [had] to pop the ball of yarn spun round the rope as the mallet went round. Those who knew how to sew on the sails were employed to mend them. Making and mending sails is quite an art in good seamanship. The men of war always carry a sail maker, who is considered an officer on board. Merchant ships depend upon the crew. The ship had to be caulked outside from the copper up, as well as the deck (this was more the carpenter's work, but some of the crew did the most of it), then to scrape the outside and inside of the ship, and then to paint her throughout, so that there was more than a plenty of work for all of us from morning till night all the time we were at Whampoa.

The boats were frequently sent up to Canton, and I was most always one of the boat's crew, so that I had plenty opportunities to see what was to be seen, and at last I became a good oarsman, and so used to rowing, that I did not mind rowing thirteen or fourteen miles a day. I also had a chance whilst the boat lay at the landing to walk round and see the people, and get some idea of what was going on. From the common were two streets, or lanes, running back about half of a mile, on which foreigners were allowed to walk. No one was allowed to enter the gates of the city, and there never was a foreigner inside of the city, until years afterwards when in the war with the English, the city was taken. At the end of these two walks, there were Chinamen stationed, armed with bamboo clubs to stop further progress, and drive us back. These streets or lanes were called China Street and Hog Lane. The first was about 12 feet wide, with stores on each side. Hog Lane was about 10 feet wide, also shops, not so fine as on China St.

There were more eating places, and small traders there. The principal resort of sailors was at Jemmy Young Tom's. He spoke pretty good English and we used to go to his place, and get what we wanted to eat and drink. He was a middle aged Chinaman, and was always very good to me.

The shops in China Street were large, and almost everything the country produces was to be found for sale there. The stores were apparently all open on the street, so that one could see in, what was for sale. There was always one standing at the door beckoning us to come in and buy. The first thing in the trade was a "kumshaw," that is a gift, a silk handkerchief, or something of the kind, and if you accepted the gift and did not buy anything, and went on to another store, you would not receive a kumshaw, as notice would be given that you already had one.

I had some money left from the five dollars my father gave me, and bought many little things. And one day when I was up there, my Uncle John met me, and to my surprise, said "Boy, do you want some money?" I thanked him and said "Yes, sir"—and he gave me twenty silver dollars, and my jacket not holding them I took what would not go in the jacket in my hand, and what to do with them, I could not think, but to deposit them somewhere was quite necessary, so I took them round to Jemmy Young Tom's, as he was the only person I had become acquainted with, and asked him to take care of them for me, which he did most faithfully—giving them to me every time I went up to town, as many as I wanted at a time, and not cheating me out of one cent.

In the stores in China St. there were all kinds of silks, china sets, carved ivory and tortoise shell work, and a great variety of ornamental boxes, & a variety of nic nacs made from rice, and bamboo. In fact, there was everything that one had never seen before. It was like a museum, and I used to go into the shops and store rooms, and instead of giving them offense, they seemed more pleased than I was myself, and would take things down to show me, and sometimes would give me something of not much value.

The Americans usually went to Jemmy's, as he had a small American flag stuck up over his door. They all kept "sampshu" for sale, which is a very disagreeable smelling drink made from rice, something the same as whiskey is, distilled from corn and rye. I do not think I ever tasted of it, the smell was enough. The sailors would take a glass now and then, but I never saw one of them intoxicated, neither did I ever see a Chinese the least so. They prefer the use of opium.

It was strange to me, to see them smoking opium. The pipe is made from a joint of bamboo, about the size of a pipe, open in one end, the division being left in the other. A little way from the division is inserted the bowl of the pipe, which is of metal, about the size of half of a large cherry stone. The opium when prepared for smoking looks like thick tar. This is in a china box. An opium needle, which looks like a large packing needle, sharp and curved at the end, & a small lamp is necessary. Now all being ready, the Chinaman stretches himself out on a bench, lights the lamp, puts the open end of the bamboo into his mouth, and with the needle takes a little opium from the box on the point and holds it over the bowl of the pipe, in the blaze of the lamp, and draws in the smoke, which he seems to swallow, as none comes out of his mouth. They take only three or four whiffs, then shut up their eyes, and pass off into dream land. They are also great smokers of a peculiar looking tobacco, very fine, and made from some weed entirely different from our tobacco, and their pipes are different from ours, being a long small reed for a stem, with a small metal bowl the size of a child's thimble. It is said the tobacco is wet with a solution of opium.

The dry ducks piled up in the provision shops was a curiosity to me. They are picked of their feathers, split open down the back, placed under a heavy press, which flattens them out, and then kept in the sun until all the moisture is dried out, when they look more like a smoked salmon than any thing else. This kind of provision seems to be more abundant than any other kind in the stores for sale.

Their markets are curious and well worth seeing. Each man has a sort of table, with a perpendicular framework in front of him made with two uprights, with several bars of wood running horizontal from one upright to the other, on which are iron hooks, to hang the meats he has for sale, composed of almost every kind of creeping thing. You will there find rats, mice, frogs, &c. to your heart's content, as well as all kinds of poultry, and various kinds of meats, in small pieces, which are hung about the frame work. The Chinaman stands at the table opposite the frame, and looks as important as a hong merchant.

They have beside the mace, and cash, which I have already mentioned, "chiky" silver as currency, which goes by weight, and every trader will always have a little pair of scales by which he ascertains the amount. This chiky silver is from broken dollars, as the singular custom prevails for every trader who receives a silver dollar to put his stamp on it, by striking with a hammer, an iron punch with his stamp on it, so that after a dollar has passed about for some time it gets broken up in small pieces, and passes by weight.

There is a curious law in China, which was put in force during our stay. That is, if a Chinese is killed, or loses his life while working on board of a foreign vessel, one of the foreigners must be given in return. When the English got power there they abolished that law, as well many other of their curious laws. The case I refer to was on board of another vessel, to a Chinaman who was at work taking on board the cargo. I do not recollect how it was done. I think he fell in the hold. The authorities demanded one of the crew should be given up, which the Captain refused to do, and the work of sending his cargo was stopped. The Captain would not allow a man to be taken out of his ship. The Chinese insisted upon it, and the mandarins came down in their big boat, also the American consul, and held a sort of court on board, and after some time it was decided that the man who was working nearest to the Chinaman, when the accident happened, should go up to the city under the solemn promise that he should not be harmed, but only to explain to the higher mandarins how it happened. Under this agreement the Captain let the man go. That night, as we learned afterwards, he was squeezed to death, by tying a rope round his body, and two men with bamboo sticks twisting the strap round him until he was a dead man.

Our cargo being ready, it was sent down in lighters called "chap" boats. The first part of the cargo was boxes of china tea sets, dinner sets &c. These were placed in the bottom of the ship, being much heavier that the rest of the cargo. They answered for ballast. Then came tea of various kinds, in whole boxes, half boxes, and in ten

- Mail
- Napoleon

caddy boxes. These different sizes were to make good stowage. Also small packages of cassia or cinnamon in mats, to put in every crevice, so that the ship's hold was completely filled.

We soon passed out the river, and sailed down the China Sea, through the Gaspar Straits, having passed the island of Borneo. We came into the Java Sea, and stopped at Angier Point, which is on the western part of the island of Java, opposite the island of Sumatra. We stopped there to fill up our water casks, as most ships do from China, and to leave our mail for the next ship to take, as we took the mail left there by the ship which stopped there before us. We then sailed through the Straits of Sunda, which separate the islands of Java & Sumatra, into the Indian Ocean.

WE HAD NOW CLEAR SAILING of about two thousand five hundred miles to the Cape of Good Hope, which took us a little over a month, we having the trade wind in our favour. When abreast of the Cape, we sighted the table land, which is a high mountain perfectly flat on the top, which gives the name. At times very heavy blows of wind come off from the land, as the ship doubles the Cape, of which sailors are warned by heavy clouds settling over the table land, and call it, the devil's table cloth, which he is now spreading, &c.

Passing the Cape, we were in the Atlantic Ocean again. I remember a happy feeling I had at the time, thinking we were again in the same ocean which washed the shores of our home. I was at the helm steering the ship, which I had learnt during the voyage, in smooth weather. I did not take a regular trick, but was placed there for hours in calm, or light winds. We now shaped our course to the north, as we intended to have stopped at the island of St. Helena, to fill up our water. We saw the island and sailed pretty close to it, when an English man of war came off to us, and forbid our going any nearer to the island, as no vessel was allowed to have any communication with the shore, that Napoleon Bonaparte was a prisoner there under guard of the English government. This was the first news we had received about the battle of Waterloo. When we left Boston, Napoleon was a prisoner on the island of Elba. The English were afraid he would again make his escape, and therefore kept armed vessels cruising round the island, ordering every vessel away. Passing through the South Atlantic Ocean, and having the south east trade wind, which was nearly aft, we had a pretty quick run up to the "line"—equator. There we were becalmed for some days, and having heavy rains, we again filled up the water casks. These rains were a great luxury to us, as we could drink and bathe to our hearts' content.

We were out of all kinds of vegetables. That is, there were none for the crew. They had plenty for the cabin. Salt beef which had been more than one year on board, and which never was good, had become not fit to eat. The sailors called it "old horse." Flour and rice, and beans were nearly out, and our allowance was short. The bill of fare for the crew, which was fixed when we left Boston, was, Sunday beef and pudding, Mondays beef and bread, Tuesdays pork & beans, Wednesdays beef and potatoes, Thursdays beef and pudding, Fridays pork and beans, Saturdays salt fish & potatoes. This bill of fare was not given us, not half of the time. Potatoes, flour, and beans were scarce articles with us. And now we had got into the Atlantic Ocean, with nothing but ship bread, and salt beef, both having been on board more than a year. The bread had got weevils into it and was unfit to eat. The sailors bore it patiently, and made no complaint to the Captain.

After we crossed the line, we fell in with the northeast trade winds and variable winds, and as we advanced north, had some heavy gales so that reefing again became the order of the day. We were bound into Cowes on the Isle of Wight in the English Channel, for orders, where to deliver our cargo. We at last got sight of the land, which proved to be Land's End, the southwest part of England. A pilot boat came alongside and put a pilot on board, which piloted the ship into Cowes roads, and we came to anchor, having had a passage of about five months from China.

We laid at anchor in the roads for several days, and I enjoyed the sight of the vessels passing and repassing, as it was new to me to watch the evolution of vessels similar to ours. Soon after we came to anchor, bom boats and traders came off to the vessel, to see what they could sell & what they could buy. We were all short of money. I had the glass jar of pressed oranges which the wash woman in Canton gave me as a kumshaw, when I paid her the dollar for washing my clothes during our stay there. This I sold for a little more than a dollar, and I bought tobacco, which I gave to the sailors, as they had been out for some-time, and they were very thankful to me for it, and it gave me more pleasure than anything else, as they were indeed my friends.

I went in the boat ashore once, and walked up a little ways from the boat to a small woods, to see how things looked on land, and feeling that I was in a civilized country, I thought I should enjoy the sight af-ter being at sea so long—when to my surprise and disgust I noticed a sign stuck up with "Dogs and sailors are forbidden to trespass here," and that is about all the impression I had of Cowes at that time.

Our orders being received to deliver our cargo in Hamburg, we weighed anchor and sailed through the Straits of Dover between France and England, both shores being in sight, and passed into the North Sea. It being a pleasant season of the year (the summer of 1816), we had a delightful sail to the island of Helgoland, which lies off be-tween the mouths of the Elbe and the Weser. This is a high bluff looking island with the English flag flying. We entered the Elbe, and sailed up the river as far as Stadt where we anchored, as this was in the Hanoverian dominions, and all vessels have to pay a duty to the Hanoverian government.

A large government boat having the Hanover flag flying, which is a red flag with a white horse in the centre and in the upper inner corner the English union, came alongside. Several officers in bright uniforms, in which a goodly show of gilt braid was displayed to show their dig-nity, came on board, after making the enquiry, the name of the ship, where from, and what was the cargo &c. The doctor, who was one of the officers, had the crew called aft and examined us all, and finding all right, gave us a bill of health. The other officers were to examine the list of our cargo, and to get such information as to enable them to re-port to their superiors, if they had any, the amount of Stadt duties to be levied by the Hanover government, for the privilege of passing through their premises. In after years the American government re-sisted paying this tax upon their vessels going up the Elbe, and it was rescinded.

Hamburg is one of the Hanseatic cities, Bremen and Lübeck being the other two. They were independent, have their own governments and their own flags. The Hamburg flag is red, with a castle in white in the centre. Hamburg was a walled city, but the walls were leveled by Bonaparte in his wars with other European powers. They now form the ramparts, and are laid out in gravel walks and flower gardens, very beautiful.

For about twenty years, there had been scarcely any foreign trade with Hamburg on account of the French wars, and all their ships had been destroyed, or rotted in the harbour. There were a few vessels in the river when we arrived, English and American. We were the first from the East Indies, I believe, with a cargo of tea. The European markets were entirely bare of this article and our cargo brought a great price. It was consigned to the house of John Berrenburg Gosler & Co. In after years when I was in Hamburg I became acquainted with Mr. Gosler, who told me that he remitted from the net sales over eight hundred thousand dollars to the London bankers for account of Messrs. James & Thomas Perkins, the owners of the ship. This was more than one hundred per cent, a splendid profit.

We were soon boarded by almost all description of traders, all trying to sell something to the ship's company. There were tailors, shoemakers, and others taking measure for clothes, shoes &c., all willing to give credit to the crew, as they supposed coming from India they would have plenty of money, and by the appearance of their clothing they would require something of the kind. The wardrobes of the crew had run short for some time. As for mine, it was reduced to one pair of duck trousers, and a guernsey frock, no jacket, shoes, or socks. I still had my jacket and trousers, which I wore before we left Boston, but I had grown so the past year that they were too small for me, and I kept them to cover the bottom of my sea chest, which would be entirely empty without them. I took advantage of their kind offers to give me credit until I was paid some money, and had a jacket, trousers, and waistcoat made, also two shirts, socks, and shoes, and with a pocket handkerchief which I had not seen since I left home, I really felt made, and felt as dandified as possible.

It was over a year since the ship left Boston, and the crew had received not a cent of their wages during the time. They applied to the Captain for some money, and he told them as soon as the cargo was discharged, they should be paid. He no doubt thought it more prudent to retain their money as long as he required their work, as they might supply them selves with more drink than was necessary for their good. At last the cargo was discharged, all came out right, and the crew were paid their wages in part, and they had liberty to go on shore. I never saw a happier or a more jolly set of beings than they were.

I was not permitted to go on shore, that is, when I asked for permission of the chief mate, he always said no, but I did contrive to go sometimes, and as I found where my uncle lived, I went to his boarding place, and asked him for some money to buy me some clothes. He was very busy then and told me to ask Mr. Magee for permission to come on shore the next day, which I did, but was refused. Some days afterward he came on board of the ship, and asked me why I did not come on shore as he had directed me. I told him that the mate would not let me. How he blowed up Magee was a caution. He told him that he had abused me enough and it must be stopped. They had hard words together, and I was glad of it. I forgave my uncle for all the coldness I had experienced from him during the voyage, and really felt I had a friend in the world. I went on shore the next day and got the cost of my tailor's bill & took it to my uncle. He gave me the money to pay it, beside something more for spending money. I really felt happy for once.

The ship was again ballasted, and after being in Hamburg about six weeks, a pilot came on board and piloted her down to Cuxhaven, where we lay at anchor some days waiting for Captain King, who had remained up to the city to finish the ship's business. The Capt., having finished his business, came on board, the anchors were hove up, and we started on our voyage back to Boston.

We sailed out of the river, down the North Sea, having very fine weather until we reached the Straits of Dover, when we encountered a heavy gale blowing directly up the Straits. We beat there for some days, and finding that we were losing ground, the Captain decided to go round to the north of England and Scotland into the Atlantic, so we bore away to the north, making the head gale a fair wind, and passed round the north of the Shetland and Orkney Islands, thus going as far north as 61°. We then steered west, and had a long and boisterous passage. When about half way across the Atlantic, it was suddenly found out that we had become short of provision. The beef and bread was about giving out, and we poor sailors were put on a short allowance of both beef and bread. The beans, flour, & potatoes had been gone some time.

This was an unaccountable piece of neglect in the officers of the ship in not procuring provisions for the voyage before leaving Hamburg. And as the beef and the bread that was weighed out to us was put on board in Boston, and both had become wormy and was unfit to eat, the crew became mutinous, taking their kids aft to show the Capt. the allowance and the quality of the food. They met with no satisfaction, excepting the regrets of the Captain and that he would speak to the first vessel we met, and try to get a supply. Magee undertook to bully them & ordered them forward, when some words passed between an English sailor, called Mike, and Magee. [Magee] struck him with an iron belaying pin, and broke his arm, and put him in irons. The crew then came forward, of course in a very discontented state, but as they could not help themselves, bore their troubles as well as they could, until we fell in with a brig from Halifax, from whom we procured a barrel of beef, and some bread, when our troubles were partially removed.

The *Cordelia* was a slow sailer, and as her bottom was pretty well covered with barnacles, we had a long passage, I do not remember how many days, but at last we made the land off Cape Cod, and sailed up the bay until we got near Boston light house, when a pilot came on board, and piloted her up to the city, where we came to an anchor. The ship had been eighteen months absent on this voyage, having sailed the middle of May 1815, and now arrived back again the middle of November 1816. She had passed every degree of longitude, and been as far south as 60° and as far north as 60°, passing Cape Horn in the south and the Shetland Islands at the north, thus circumnavigated the globe of 360° of longitude, and 120° of latitude, a remarkable voyage, as far as navigation was concerned, for a merchant ship. To say that we were glad the voyage was ended, would have been but a poor expression of our feelings.

The next forenoon we hauled the ship to India Wharf, and made her well fast, and the crew went on shore. The first person I met on the wharf was Colonel Perkins, who accosted me, "Why have they not thrown you overboard?" I smiled, and *perhaps* thought it affectionate. I soon found my way to Cambridge, and was received with a kind welcome from all the family, particularly from my dear sister Mary.

The next day the crew were to be paid their wages, which was due them, and all of them assembled at the counting room of the owners on the end of India Wharf, and after all the rest had been settled with, I stepped up to the desk, at which sat Mr. James Perkins, the senior partner, who had been settling with the crew, and asked him for my wages. He replied that there was no wages due me. I said, "I have received no wages during the voyage." He again said in a very cross way, "There is nothing due you." My heart almost sunk within me as I had witnessed all the men, and the other two boys receive their money, and to be told that I should have none. I found out that when my name was put on the crew list there was no wages put down. All the rest received two months' pay at the time of shipping, and the monthly wages placed against their names, as is always done, but as I had no one to look out for me when I shipped it was not done.

I went out to Capt. King's house at once, he lived in Medford, and waited till he came home, when I asked him if I had not earned wages as well as the other boys. He replied "Most certainly you have," and was surprised to hear that Mr. Perkins had made any objections to pay me the same as the other boys, and said he would see to it the next day when he went in town. That quite pacified me, and the next day I was at hand watching for the Captain to go into the store. After some hours I saw him and I followed him in to the counting room, and heard him tell Mr. Perkins that I was the smartest of the three boys, and did as much work, and that although my father had omitted to have any wages put on the crew list, I ought to receive the same as the other boys. Mr. P—— then without saying a word, paid me five dollars a month. William Hickling and Henry Dow, the other two boys, had six dollars. The sum due me was $90. He deducted 20 cents per month as hospital money, paying me $86.40. I have thought since I knew what a splendid profit they made, that it was rather small business for them.

I never saw Captain King, or Mr. James Perkins from that hour. They both died whilst I was on my next voyage. I had formed a strong friendship with William Hickling during the voyage, and became intimate with his family when we arrived in Boston. The family consisted of his mother, a most excellent woman (sister of Alden Bradford, then secretary of state), [and] a brother by the name of Charles, who was then a clerk in a broker's office, afterwards went into the stationery business, became well off, [and] married Eliza Eades, daughter of Capt. Eades of Charleston [Massachusetts], of mermaid fame. Charles and I were intimate friends for many years, he lived to an old age.

There were two [Hickling] sisters, Sarah and Mary. Sarah was a beautiful girl and I fell in love with her, but whilst I was on a voyage to India, she became engaged to a young man by the name of Switser. He died in New Orleans, shortly before I returned from India. I found her in mourning for him. I then found my love had somewhat dampened.

William [Hickling] made several short voyages, and became to be second mate. I think he was lost at sea on that voyage. Harry Dow died young. I never met him but once after we arrived, neither have I met any of the crew, excepting Caleb Williams, whom I have met several times. He never went to sea again, but joined his father who had a cotton mill at Pawtucket, R.I. Mr. Magee, who was a connection of the Perkins family, took command of the *Cordelia* her next voyage. My Aunt Perkins, having found out the manner he treated me on the voyage, gave him a piece of her mind, which no doubt had a great effect on him.

I was sick enough of the seas, and wanted to stay at home and study, but my father said I had chosen my profession and must stick to it, and that I must study navigation until I had a chance to go another voyage. I therefore went to Mr. John Hendricks who kept a navigation school in Boston.

3

Return to China

I N FEBRUARY 1817, the ship *Suffolk*, Captain Uran, was ready to sail for Canton, and I shipped as one of her crew. This ship was about the size of the *Cordelia*, but was more modern built, and a finer vessel. She was owned by Mr. Edmund Dwight, who married my cousin Mary Elliot, and some other persons living in Salem. Richard Uran was Captain. My uncle Henry Higginson was the super cargo, Mr. Baxter the chief mate, and most of the crew were from Cape Cod.

This ship was much better found, in provisions and water, than the *Cordelia*, and as I was a more experienced sailor, I fared and got along much better than I did on board of the *Cordelia*. I got along very well with the officers and crew, and my impression of that voyage is rather pleasant than otherwise. We had a good passage of about four and a half months, 135 days to Canton.

The crew were shipped in Boston as a very steady set of men, and it was agreed between the Capt. and men at the time of the shipping that they were to have the privilege of taking the altitude of the sun at meridian each day in fine weather, as several of them had their quad-

rants, and they wished to keep their journals and practise their navigation. They also stipulated about the provisions, that they should have
flour puddings twice a week, beans and pork twice a week, and vegetables every day, also a gill of vinegar daily, good salt beef, or fresh,
four times a week, and as much bread as they wished for. There was to
be no allowance of water or provisions, good coffee in the morning,
and good tea for supper, molasses and sugar, rice & other necessaries.
This arrangement was fairly carried out during the voyage.

The crew did no work on Sundays, except what was necessary for
the safe navigation of the ship, but used to employ their spare time
reading, or singing psalm tunes. Most of them had their music books,
and I used to try to sing with them, but could not make out very well,
although I was taught at Andover Academy by the singing master
Mr. Blanchard, but somehow I had not the talent to learn. I was always
fond of music—and listened with pleasure to the sailors' songs on
board the *Cordelia*, and now not only listened but tried to join in the
psalm singing with the sailors on board of the *Suffolk*.

Capt. Uran had great confidence in the crew, and placed the two
barrels of New England rum in the between decks, lashed to the main
mast, on the heads. There was also there the barrels of vinegar, molasses &c. Most of the crew had provided themselves with a bunch of
quills for their pens during the voyage to write their journals &c. Steel
pens were not known in those days.

There was one amongst the crew by the name of Braddock Black.
He was rather a black sheep amongst the crew, although a real jolly fellow. He had been in one of our men of war during the war with England, and had been a prisoner in the famous Dartmoor prison in
England. He introduced the plan to suck the rum out of the barrels
between decks with a quill, and although they were allowed a half of a
gill everyday, they all soon joined in sucking the rum with their quills,
through a gimlet hole in the head of the barrel. Soon one quill was
not long enough, then two were put together, and when they failed to
reach the rum, the third, and fourth, and so on were joined together
until the barrels were sucked most out. The crew showed no signs of
intoxication and were not suspected by the officers of the ship.

The rum getting short, they found some wine casks, and a cask of cherry rum which was sent out for Mr. Cushing. These were stowed away in the hold of the ship, but they soon found a way to introduce their quills into the casks—when about two thirds of the passage, one day the second mate was down in the hold when one of the crew was sucking at Mr. Cushing's cherry rum, and was discovered by the mate.

This broke the spell, as the mate informed the Capt., and an examination took place, when several of the wine casks were [found to be] partly out, as well as the cherry rum cask. Mr. Baxter said "Let us look at the rum barrels." The two barrels in the between decks had not been used from, as there was a barrel in the steward's pantry which had supplied the crew so far on the passage. What was Mr. B.'s surprise to find both barrels nearly empty. The crew were called aft, and Captain Uran held a kind of court on the quarterdeck. It so happened that I was among the innocent ones, as I had no quills, and I could not bear the taste of New England rum, I never had sucked.

The captain was very angry, and made many threats, what he would do, called us d——d scoundrels, and said "I sent down to Cape Cod to get a steady set of men, but if I had raked hell with a fine tooth comb I could not have got a bigger set of rascals." In a short time, the Captain's anger passed off, and there seemed to be no difference in the treatment of the crew, excepting their daily grog was stopped, and the rum kept to splice the main brace, as it is called, that is to give the crew an extra glass of grog when all hands are called in the night to reef topsails &c. in rainy, and stormy weather. The custom of those days, giving grog to sailors, has been for some time abolished, and now the owners never think of putting rum on board of their ships as stores. It is also abolished on board of our armed vessels, where the custom was followed for some time after it had been given up in the merchant service.

The passage to Macao was about one hundred and forty days. We there took a pilot for Canton River, and the second day we came to anchor at Whampoa.

There was a little more style in the visit of the mandarins (the custom house officers) than there was on my last voyage. Their visit was introduced by a kumshaw of a dozen jars of "sampshu," a liquor made from rice, horrid smelling stuff, and a lot of pressed ducks, and some other eatables, which was given to the comprador, as they were no use to us. He probably sold them back to the givers for a trifling sum, to be used as a kumshaw to the next vessel arriving, they charging full price to their government.

This visit over, all was right for the Capt. and supercargo to go up to the city. The Capt.'s gig, as we called the jolly boat, was lowered, and Mr. Baxter picked out the crew, four in number. I was honoured by being named as after oarsman. This I considered quite a feather in my cap. As Mr. Baxter was a Cape Cod man, he naturally would have given someone of his townsman the place, as the after oarsman is considered the director, or manager of the boat. I felt quite proud of the situation, and did my best to give satisfaction.

We rowed up to the city. To me the scenery and the crowded state of the river was quite natural, but to the others, not one of whom had ever been there before, all was strange, and the Captain would occasionally ask me some question, for information. I had rowed up and down something like twenty times, and of course was pretty well acquainted. We remained at the landing several hours, the Captain giving us some money to get our dinner, as he would be detained to attend to his business.

I took the boat's crew round to my old friend Jemmy Young Tom. He recollected me at once, and expressed his delight to meet me again, and gave us all as much as we could eat. I think I never enjoyed a meal better than I did that. We all stuffed ourselves, with fried fish, stewed meat, and baked duck, and I don't know what else, and Jemmy was not disposed to charge us anything, but I told him the Captain had given us money to pay, and he must take his pay, which he finally did. This was a treat indeed, as we had been out at sea almost five months living on ship's provision, and one can imagine how much we enjoyed a good dinner on fresh provisions.

We rowed back to the ship in the afternoon, bringing the Capt. on board. I was not in the least tired, but the others who were not accustomed to row, were pretty well tired out. The same wash woman, and the old barber, Tom Kin, were employed. They both remembered me, and I felt as if I had got amongst old friends.

We remained at anchor at Whampoa about six weeks, passing the time very similar to that described on board the *Cordelia*. The cargo being all on board, the sails were bent, and everything got ready to go to sea, we weighed anchor, and sailed down the river. We had a pleasant passage through the China Sea, nothing particular occurring until we came to anchor off Angier Point, where we remained one day filling up the water casks. There were several canoes came alongside, with monkeys, birds, sea shells, &c. to sell to the crew, as is the custom. After filling our water & procuring a quantity of vegetables & fruit we weighed anchor and sailed out through the Straits of Sunda, into the Indian Ocean, on our course to the Cape of Good Hope. We had a good and smooth time of about forty days, when we made the land of the Cape, nothing particular occurring as I remember.

During this passage, Black, who had procured some cakes of India ink when in Canton, commenced to prick it into the arms of the crew who wished it. I had often noticed it on the hands and arms of sailors, but never had seen the operation. Black seemed to be a master of the art, having learned it when a prisoner in the Dartmoor prison. His instrument was three common sewing needles fastened round a pointed stick, the points being a little separated from one another, and a small saucer with a little of the ink mixed with water. He would dip the needles in to the saucer and commence pricking just raising the skin, not bringing blood, on the letters or figures previously marked out with the ink.

I had letters, anchors, hearts, on my hands and arms, and a fancy double heart with C.T. in one, and S.H. in the other, red roses between, each heart pierced with cupid's dart, the red showing the drops of blood dropping from the wound. This was on the left arm. On the right was pricked a cross, with the Saviour nailed to it, and red showing the wounds in the hands, feet, and side, an anchor and a large letter T. On the back of my left hand was an anchor and on my middle finger was a heart representing a ring.

Most of the crew had various representations pricked on their persons, mostly on their hands and arms. These impressions remain for life. There is but one way to get clear of them and that is by cutting them out. Some years after, I became very much ashamed of them, and got my brother Dudley to try to remove them by caustics. He tried several things on the finger, but nothing would remove them. The anchor on the back of my left hand was very annoying to me as it appeared to me everybody was looking at it and I was determined to get rid of it. Finding my brother, who was a physician, could not remove them, I marked the anchor with aqua fortis, which deadened the skin, and with my knife cut it out. It was rather a dangerous operation, over the veins and chords on the back of the hand, but the anchor was gone, leaving rather a bad scar.

During the passage we caught many porpoises, dolphins, and barracudas. The porpoise come in large numbers, and play about the bows of the vessel when she is going five or six miles an hour. There is some art in catching them, and requires practice. The mate, if he understands it, generally undertakes to strike them with the harpoon, which is on the end of a pole about ten feet long, the end in the socket of the harpoon, not fastened. A small rope is rove through a block on the bow sprit, then passed through a becket on the pole and made well fast to the harpoon. The other end is on deck, with several men ready to haul in. The mate throws the harpoon into the porpoise as he comes out of water, the pole comes out of the socket, when the men haul, and the porpoise is hauled up to the block, when a bowline is put round above his tail, and he is hauled in on deck. I became quite an expert in harpooning when I was mate.

The porpoise is called the sea pig, as the internal arrangements, the heart, liver &c. are just like the pig. The meat is darker, otherwise it is like pork. The ribs are similar to a pig's, and it is very good eating. A good size porpoise will weigh 150 lbs. Dolphin and other fish are caught by a hook, or struck with the grains, an instrument composed of a dozen more or less of small barbed irons, harpoon shape, which spread out from a socket into which a pole of about ten feet is fastened, and with a small line to it, which is held in the hand, and when the fish comes near the vessel, this is thrown into it, and most generally secures the fish. We caught a good many on this passage, and fairly feasted.

The skin of the dolphin is a favourite tie for the queue, which was then in fashion with those who had hair long enough. I had aspired to a queue for a long time, but could never let my hair grow long enough. I had now longer hair than ever before, and I got Black, who was the factotum in all such things, to do up my hair into a queue. He combed it back together, and put on the dolphin skin, as I thought too tight, as it hauled the skin up on my forehead, and I had difficulty in closing my eyes to go to sleep. Queues were going out of fashion. None but old sailors wore them, and they made fun of me so young to wear a queue, and I soon got tired of it and gave it up.

We passed round the Cape of Good Hope, giving it a pretty good berth, as the weather was stormy. We could just see the high land in the distance, and shaped our course north to the equator. During that part of the passage I was much troubled with boils, that were very painful. I applied to the Captain for some salts, which were in the medicine chest. Every vessel going a foreign voyage was obliged to carry a medicine chest. The Captain seemed not disposed to take the trouble to give me any, when my uncle who had overheard me asking for some Epsom salts, called me, and asked me what was the matter with me. I told him I had several boils on my person, and I was told that Epsom salts was good in such a case. He told me to show them to him. I pulled off my jacket & shirt, and he expressed astonishment to see my body covered with them, most of them discharging and look- ing as well as feeling very bad. I had no rags to bind over them. He immediately took me down in the cabin, and tore up one of his linen shirts and bound them up as well as he could, had some words with the Captain, said he never saw such a sight. The Captain gave me the salts, and scolded me for not letting him know before.

About the first of February we made the land somewhere between Nantucket & the Cape and were full of expectation to be in Boston the next day, but we were doomed to disappointment, for a heavy gale from the northwest broke upon us with great fury and drove us off the coast, and for over three weeks we struggled against it, suffering in- tensely from the cold. Sometimes the rigging would be encased with ice, and at one time the ice had collected on the fore part of the ship to such an extent, that we were obliged to bear away for the Gulf Stream to melt it off. I, as well as the rest of the crew, were not prepared for such severe cold weather. I had no mittens and but one pair of woolen socks. We were all more or less frost bitten. At last the gale subsided, and the wind came out fair and we soon made for Boston, where we arrived about the 25th of February 1818, to our great joy.

I remained at home until spring, attended school to study navigation, and riding horses, as the man who had formerly lived with us kept a livery stable in Bowdoin Square at this time, and I used to patronize him, paying cash at first, but when that came short, would leave the bill for my father to pay. I felt now that I had made up my mind to follow my profession, which was to be a captain of a vessel as soon as I could, and I was soon ready to go to sea again, but I thought I would like a short voyage, and looked around for one. In the month of May an opportunity offered in the brig *General Stark*, Capt. Farris, for Hamburg. I never had been in a brig, and thought I should like the change from a ship, so I shipped on board of her for a voyage to Hamburg, and back to Boston.

It being in the summer time the passages both ways were quite pleasant, nothing particular occurring, excepting that when we had passed through the English Channel, and just entering the Atlantic Ocean, we discovered one morning a smoke on the horizon, which we supposed to be some vessel on fire. It was quite calm, or we should have run down for it, to render any assistance that we could. We soon perceived that it altered its bearing and was moving fast towards the English Channel. The Capt. and all on board were puzzled, as there was not a breath of wind to move the craft and she was near enough to see the masts with the spy glass, and the smoke pouring out of her, but no blaze. She kept on her course until out of sight, to our perfect astonishment. When we arrived in Boston and reported this strange occurrence, we were informed that it was a steam ship called the *Savannah* which had sailed for Russia, being the first vessel that ever crossed the Atlantic Ocean with steam. She was ship rigged and used steam only when it was calm or the wind ahead. It was a wonder for us, for no one on board suspected that it was a steam vessel.

4

A Leaky Trip to Havana

AN OPPORTUNITY OFFERING in the brig *Augusta*, Captain Pelham, to go to Havana, I concluded to ship on board of her, as I wished to go to the West Indies. Having been two voyages to the East Indies, and one to Europe, I thought I would like to see how Havana looked. My father had moved from Cambridge to Boston, when my brothers graduated from college, and lived in Gouch St., a very respectable street at the time, but has of late been inhabited by a low vagabond set.

About the first of December, the brig being ready for sea I signed the articles, and got my things ready to go on board, when my [step]mother, who had never expressed much interest in my affairs, surprised me by asking if there was anything else I wanted to make me comfortable. I told her more in joke than anything else that I believed I had everything but a waist coat. Now this was an article of dress which sailors never wear on board of a vessel. She said she would go up stairs and see if she could not find one of my brothers' old ones. After hunting round for some time she returned, saying she could not find any of my brothers', but [there] was one of my father's. I told

53

her that it was much too large, and it was of no consequence, but she insisted that she could soon alter it. My father was a very large man of six feet high, and his waistcoat would go round three common sized men.

As my mother was so kindly disposed, and being the first time she had expressed a sympathy for me, I could not deny her the pleasure of trying to fit me out with this waistcoat. So she put it on, and marked out the arm holes to be cut out, and rolled the back up in several folds so that it would button tight round me, saying it would keep me warm. I of course thanked her for her kindness, thinking it the greatest joke of the season. It was a curious garment, old fashioned, the pockets covered with a lapel, and came down to my ankles, so that when I wanted to put my hand in the pockets I had to squat down. It was of no use to me, excepting as a pea jacket without sleeves, and I used to sleep in it to keep me warm nights.

The *Augusta* was an old vessel, some where about twenty years, and her model was of olden times, called a half decker, that is with the quarter deck or after part eight feet higher that the rest of the deck. She was deeply laden with lumber, mostly pine boards, the hold being full, and a large deck load, running from the bulkhead of the quarter deck forward to near the fore mast, leaving a space abaft the mainmast, for the pumps, which were close to the bulkhead. She was a strange looking craft to go to sea, in the wintertime. The Captain [was] a middle aged man, but a brutish sort of a fellow, who would use more profane language in one day than a good swearer would in a week.

So one very cold day the first part of December, the crew on board, and all being ready, we made sail and proceeded to sea. The vessel's hull was so deep in the water that the sea was continually washing over the decks, and we soon found out that she was the most uncomfortable craft that could float, and certainly she was the slowest sailer. After being out a few days, we had a heavy gale, and she sprung a leak, which kept us at work at the pumps night and day. During this time we spoke a vessel bound to Boston, which reported having fallen in with us leaking badly.

The leak continued the whole passage, but did not increase except when the sea run heavy. Two of us had to be at the pump pretty much the whole time to keep her free, and one at the helm. The pumps were down in the deep space, or hold, made by the high bulkhead of the quarter deck on the after part. To man the pumps we had to get down in this hold, the water washing under us, and the sea frequently breaking over, so that sometimes it would be half full of water, and we like drowned rats pumping for our lives. We would take turns, as one man could pump. I have many a time when it was the other's turn to pump set down in the water and had a good sleep. I was so exhausted that I would fall right asleep as soon as I sat down. We changed every eight or ten minutes, and in this way we had to work to keep her free, until we arrived in Havana, which was after a very long passage of forty eight days. A vessel having sailed from Havana for Boston the day before we arrived reported that the *Augusta* had not arrived, and as she was spoken a few days out leaking badly, she was supposed to be lost.

We had got down near the island of Abaco, when sailing along with a fine wind, and being my turn at the helm between the hours of six and eight o'clock P.M., a large ship run down towards us and fired a gun for us to heave to, which we did, and she sent a boat alongside and an officer in uniform came on board, who said it was the Colombian privateer *Bolivia*, fitted out in Baltimore, which was cruising for Spanish vessels, as at that time the Colombians in South America were fighting for their independence. He said that they had captured a number of Spanish vessels, and he wished us to take some of the prisoners, as their ship was crowded. Our Captain said that our vessel had no accommodations, and that he did not see how he could take any. The officer, who evidently was an American, said we must take some, and that the Capt. might say how many. It was finally agreed that we should take three.

The boat went back to the ship and brought three persons, who were either English or Americans. They had much more baggage than prisoners would have, and a different kind, large square trunks, and things that no Spanish crew or any other crew ever had. They also sent from the ship a box of tea, boxes of raisins, beef, potatoes, rice, and sugar, enough for a voyage. All this was very strange to me. I soon found out that something was wrong, by questioning them. They all seemed to tell different stories. Their trunks contained no clothes, but almost everything else, such as are found in a dry good store. Each one had a wide belt with doubloons stitched in, which they wore round their waists, and all of them had silver spoons, and other silver ware in three large trunks. They told us that they gambled with the crew, and won all these things &c.

When we arrived in Havana, they went on shore, and left their baggage on board. I met one of them on shore after some time, who told me that they had drawn the high prize in the Havana lottery, and that they would come after their baggage soon. Some of our crew broke open their trunks and robbed the silver spoons &c. It was not very long after, that we got Savannah newspapers, which gave the following account:

Capt. Almira, having obtained from the Colombian government "a letter of marque," fitted out in Baltimore the ship *Cortez* as a Colombian privateer. She cleared as an American merchantman with the usual number of men, and dropped down the bay to a point previously arranged and took on board men, guns & ammunition, and proceeded to sea. A few days out, the crew rose upon the officers & put them in irons. They chose the boatswain as commander, and other officers from the crew, which consisted of sixty men. They then started as a pirate, and robbed every vessel they came across, putting one of the captured officers on board each vessel as prisoners, until they got clear of all of them. They then went into the harbour of St. Marys, one of the Canary Islands, landed in the night, and robbed the town. After making many robberies, they began, by choosing lots, to separate, some going on board of every vessel they met, represented as prisoners from Spanish prizes, until reduced to a small number, who run the ship in near the coast of Georgia, and taking their boats, destroyed the ship, and landed near Tybee light, giving out that they were ship-wrecked sailors. They were suspected of something wrong, as they all had so much gold, and could not buy a glass of grog without offering a Spanish doubloon for the pay. They were taken up by the police, and one of them confessed and told the whole story, naming the vessels on which the crew went, and among the rest, the three which were put on board of our vessel. Many of them were caught, tried for piracy, and hanged.

We first made the land on the island of Abaco, [and] passed the Hole in the Wall, a celebrated point at the entrance to the passage across the Bahama Banks. It is a mass of coral rock, against which the Atlantic Ocean has beat for ages, and the Hole in the Wall is a circular passage made by the waves through these rocks. There is a lighthouse on that point now. There was none then. We sailed on through this channel between Abaco and Nassau until we came to the Bahama Banks, which we crossed to the Florida Gulf, about sixty miles to the Orange Keys, which are on the western edge. The Bahama Bank is very shoal, averaging about twelve feet, so that it is not safe for any vessel drawing more, to pass over them. It has a curious appearance, looking as white as snow, on account of the bottom being a white marl like chalk. It is said that there is no living creature in these waters.

We crossed the Gulf Stream and got in sight of the island of Cuba. The first land we saw was the Pan of Matanza, a high mountain, shape of a loaf of bread, about fifty miles from the Morro Castle, which is on the eastern side of the entrance to the harbour of Havana. The following day we sighted the Morro, & passed between it and the Punta castle on the west, quite a narrow entrance, not more than twenty rods in width. The harbour commences almost at the entrance and spreads out into a large bay, with deep water, large enough to hold the navies of the world. A pilot boarded us and took us to our anchorage. We were then boarded by the health and custom house boats, called *falunes,* which soon dispatched us, and the Captain and passengers went on shore.

The crew were a curious mixture of several different nations, and as superstitious a set as well could come together. They believed the vessel was haunted, they thought they heard strange noises, sometimes a child crying, at others groans from someone in distress. They insisted that the chests were moved about the forecastle by some evil spirit, and there was no end to their silly stories about ghosts and haunted vessels.

We soon commenced discharging the cargo, which was a very tedious job. The boards were shoved into the water and large rafts were
made. The mark of measurement of each board [was] called out, and
taken down by the mate, and the clerk of the purchaser of the cargo.
It would be a long day's work to make one of these rafts, and in the
middle of the day working in the hot sun, it was hard work. When the
raft was finished we had to tow it with our boat to the lumber yard of
the purchaser which was more than half a mile from the vessel.

The crew had become dreadfully disgusted with the vessel and soon
commenced to desert. Three of them had run away before the cargo
was discharged, which of course made it harder for those which were
left, and the mate was more disagreeable than ever. The crew insisted
upon it that the vessel was haunted, and although she had arrived
safely in Havana, she never would arrive again in the United States,
which she never did.

We had taken on board empty molasses hogsheads, which had been
stowed in the bottom of the vessel, ready to be filled with molasses, as
it was intended to load her with molasses back to Boston. One night a
Dutch sailor by the name of George who was determined to convince
me of the truth, that the vessel was haunted, called me up on deck
to hear the groans in the hold. The main hatch was off, and sure
enough there was sounds similar to one in great distress, and at the
same time there was the kitten purring round George, which was a
wild little thing and would never come to any one. This was proof to
him that the kitten saw the ghost, although we could not.

The noise in the hold continued, which began to alarm me. I
thought I would go aft and call the mate, but when I got as far as the
main hatch, I listened more carefully, and satisfied myself that it was
the cook who was sleeping in the hold on top of the casks. He snored
tremendously, and it rung through the empty casks, producing a most
unearthly sound. I went back to George, but could not convince him,
that it was the cook. The next night he run away.

Mr. Curson, who married my cousin Peggy Searle, was then a partner in the house of Muralles Knight & Co. I went there but found that
Mr. Curson was in the States, but his wife was there. I sent my name

up to her. She was sick in her room. She had me brought up at once, and our meeting was extremely pleasant. She was sitting in an easy chair with a flannel robe wrapped round her, and after sitting some time, she removed the robe, or wrapper, and asked me to see her little boy, which was born after Mr. Curson had left. This was George Curson who is now living, being sixty years old.

I related how unpleasantly I was situated, and she said she would tell Mr. Knight, which she did, and he spoke to a captain who was consigned to him, who said I might go on board of his vessel. She laid at anchor more than a half of mile from where our vessel lay, and the only way for me to get on board was to swim, which was rather a dangerous undertaking, as there were occasionally large sharks in the harbour, but I was determined to leave the vessel, so I tied up a few things and fastened them to my back, and at midnight I jumped overboard, and struck out for the brig I was to go on board. I forget her name. I got on board all right, the mate had been told to receive me.

I had been on board but two days when I saw Captain Pelham row by in his boat, and got sight of me. I knew he would have a soldier after me, and in the evening I went on shore, to Mr. Knight, and told him the Captain had found me. Mr. Knight told me to stay at the house and he would find me an opportunity to go home. In a day or two, he had a small vessel that was going to Charleston, and I could go passenger in her. The morning she was to sail I went on board, expecting the schooner to sail every moment, when the first thing I knew Captain Pelham came alongside with a soldier, and took me a prisoner, and I was put into the Spanish prison, a place too horrid to think of.

The prison, which was under the captain general's palace, was the only place to put every kind of criminal, as well as those who were crazy. There were old and young, Black and white. In the centre there was a yard about two rods square, with walls of the palace about fifty feet high on each side. There were no windows in these walls, which were built on stone arches, about ten feet high, and all under the palace, excepting about twelve feet all round, was for the prisoners. This space outside was occupied in various offices, opening out on the streets. There was a thick stone wall separating them from the prison.

Under these dark arches, loathsome places, the prisoners were kept, no air excepting the small centre yard, and only a few of them could get there at a time.

There were several stout Negro prisoners who were called *alcaldes*, who carried big clubs, with a lash of green hide in the end, and it was heart sickening to see how these great naked Black fellows would lash any one who did not do just as they ordered them, and frequently the lash would come before the word. Mr. Knight soon became acquainted with my situation, and applied to the American consul, who had not the least power, as the Spanish government did not acknowledge consuls in any of their colonies, and he could do nothing towards getting me out.

I was kept in that awful hole three days and nights, when I was taken out in the cage. This is a small room made with iron bars, with an iron door which enters the prison and another door made of iron bars, which opened into the guard room, where there were always a guard of soldiers with loaded muskets, ready to fire through the iron gratings, when ordered by the officer of the guard. I was kept there until the captain brought the order to let me out. I was sent on board of the vessel, for the mate to work me up for running away, which he did his utmost to do, by keeping me at work on all the dirty jobs he could think of, among others blacking the yards with coal tar.

One forenoon as I was blacking the fore yard, a bom boat came alongside with fruit to sell, and the mate was leaning over the side buying some oranges, exactly under me and my bucket of coal tar. There was in the fore top close by, an Irish sailor by the name of Sam, who by motion of his hands gave me a hint to let some coal tar fall upon the mate. I gave the bucket a tip, and at the same time slipped from the yard, and caught by one hand on the foot rope by which I hung, Sam singing out "Hold on, I will come and help you." I was calling for help, & pretending I must fall to the deck. About a pint of coal tar went on the mate's neck, giving his long queue a good soaking, and a part went upon the Negro and his oranges. There was a tremendous splutter, the Negro cussing me in Spanish, and the mate cussing me in English, whilst Sam was trying to help me from falling by putting a rope round my waist, telling the mate it would be sure death if I fell to the deck, he swearing and saying he believed I did it on purpose. Sam knew very well I could hang by one hand, and recover myself by the other, but he wanted to carry out the joke. It was as much as I could do to keep from laughing.

I was determined not to go to sea in that vessel, and I gave as much trouble as I could. The owners of the *Augusta* had another vessel in port called the *Volant*, Capt. Brown. She was a schooner which was loaded with molasses, and ready for sea. Most of the crew had run away, and Capt. Brown found difficulty in finding others. Captain Pelham told me if I would ship on board the *Volant* which was bound to Boston I might go. I took him at his word, and went on board. She was a strange vessel, deeply loaded with molasses, had a large brick fire place in the steerage, one also in the cabin.

The crew consisted of four, two in a watch. Capt. Brown was a good natured man, which was his best qualification, as he was as ignorant as one could be to have command of any vessel. The mate was a Frenchman, spoke imperfect English. There were two sailors, beside the cook. I made the third, and Capt. Brown picked up the fourth, making seven in all, about as motley a set as ever got together. Everything ready, we weighed anchor and proceeded to sea. I never had been in a schooner before. It was new and amusing to me to see the management. The crew and the cook slept down in the small hold called the steerage, two berths were for the four sailors, so that when one watch turned out, the other turned in, and the watch in the morning from four to eight were nearly smothered by the smoke which filled the steerage when the cook made the fire.

There was no time piece on board, neither Capt. or mate had a watch, and it was amusing sometimes to see how they managed about finding the time for the watch on deck to begin or to end. I was in the Captain's watch, and he was sure to fall asleep by the time he had been on deck for a half hour. When I was at the helm, and finding him fast asleep, I would call him and say, "Capt. Brown, I think it must be about twelve o'clock," when I knew it was not more than nine. He would rouse up rubbing his eyes, saying "Yes, I guess it is," and down he would go and call the mate, and the other watch, and we would go below to sleep. When the mate got tired he would think it was four o'clock, and call the Captain, so instead of three watches, from eight in the evening to eight in the morning, we would have half a dozen, and as it was in the winter time the nights were very long as we went north.

We had a very long passage, as the Captain was not much of a navigator, knew but little of longitude, and trusted wholly to his quadrant for the latitude. We sailed north west, until we got in to the latitude of Boston and then steered west. We were fortunate in having good winds and fine weather for the month of March, which is generally considered one of the worst months on our coast, or we certainly would have been shipwrecked, as the Captain did not know the exact position of the vessel any day after we left Havana.

We at last arrived in Boston harbour, and I was glad enough to get clear of her. I had but a poor wardrobe. My best suit consisted of a pair of duck trousers, not very clean, a red woolen shirt, and my father's waistcoat which my mother had so kindly fixed for me, and a straw hat rather worse for wear. I trudged up for home, which was in Gouch St., where the family lived when I went away. Going through Bowdoin Square I met my old father. I spoke to him, but as he did not hear me, I passed on, till I got to the house, and rung the bell, and after waiting sometime, no one coming, and being very cold, I commenced pulling the bell handle until the door opened. When a strange young man I had never seen before asked me what I wanted, I pushed by him, and went through the entry into the kitchen. The parlour was in the second story, and my father's library and study was in the basement, fronting the street, and the kitchen directly behind it.

My mother came to the head of the parlour stairs and asked the boy who had come. He said a sailor had gone into the kitchen. She told him to call Mr. Tyng. In the meantime I was in the kitchen, and Mrs. Saunders, who had lived some years in the family, asked what I wanted. I told her to get me something to eat. She at first had not the least idea who I was, and was upon the point of turning me out, when all at once she recognized it was me, and there never was a woman more glad to see one than she was to see me.

Soon after my mother came down and walked into the kitchen in the most dignified manner and looking at me a moment, without speaking to me, said "Mrs. Saunders, put on a kettle of water." Now the good woman had every reason to think I wanted a good scrubbing, as I was very dirty, not being able to wash the tar off with salt water. Her surprise at seeing me, and in such a condition no doubt prevented her from expressing her motherly feelings. My dear little sister Mary came in running up to me, and throwing her arms round my neck, saying, "Oh, my dear brother Charles, how glad I am you have come. I thought you was drowned." My sister Susan also came in to the kitchen and expressed her surprise by saying "What an object to behold." Mrs. Saunders soon had a tub of warm water, and with soap, I was soon cleaned, and my mother had hunted up an old suit of Stephen's clothes, and with a white shirt, I looked like another being.

It seems, that they had not heard of the arrival of the *Augusta* in Havana, and as they saw by the papers that she was spoken on the passage out leaking badly they had given me up as lost. The *Augusta* was loaded with molasses, and sailed from Havana for Boston, and that was the last ever heard from her, or of Capt. Pelham and his mate with a long queue, so it proved a piece of luck that I joined the *Volant*.

5

Pirates and Promotions

It was now the last of March, and I remained at home about six weeks or more, looking round for an East India voyage, as I had had enough experience of West India, and European voyages. At last an opportunity offered in the new ship *Houqua*, built by the house of Thomas Perkins & Co., the same owner that had the ship *Cordelia*. She was a larger vessel than either the *Cordelia* or *Suffolk*, and more modern in her rig. I shipped on board of her the 19th of May 1819 bound for Canton.

Captain Conant was the commander, and Joshua Nash was the first mate. The second mate's name was Henry. The crew consisted of sixteen, a carpenter, a cook and steward making in all twenty-two persons, no one amongst them that I had ever seen before. Mr. Nash was a man of about 35 years, and just returned from Calcutta in the brig *Barbara*, belonging to my Uncle Perkins. He was a smart man and a good seaman. Mr. Henry was also a young man, and a very good fellow. There were two of about my age, although they had not been at sea so long as I had and were not quite so expert sailors, as I was, but they were smart clever fellows, and we were very good friends. Their names were Henry Neef and Nat Carnes.

I had made my mind up to get out of the forecastle as soon as I could, and the only way it was to be done was to be the smartest sailor on board. I probably knew more of seamanship than any of them, and I was more agile. I had learned to make all kinds of splices, hitches, knots, turk's heads, &c. In fact there was nothing on board of the ship to be done that I was not able to do, as far as my strength would let me, and I was determined to do my duty most thoroughly, so as to gain the good will of the officers of the ship. When it was my turn at the helm in the night watch, I would not take my clothes off when it was my watch below but lay down on my chest, all ready to jump upon deck when the watch was called and go to the helm. I always tried to be the first man up the rigging. I could run up the ratlines faster than any one on board. The mates soon saw that I was always on hand when anything was to be done, and they generally gave me the nicest jobs.

The ship was well found in everything, plenty of provisions and water, so that the word "allowance" was not known on board. I was in the first mate's watch and soon gained his confidence in everything. The ship being new, the rigging was all new from the rigger's hands, and all wanted fixing up a little, and Mr. Nash was just the man who had the taste to plan out the work he proposed to have done, such as grafting all the block strops, pointing all the ropes, making handsome mats to cover the shrouds, where they were likely to be chafed. He divided the work amongst the best seamen, placing two to the fore and main mast, and giving me the mizzen mast, which I considered quite an honour, and it quickened my ambition. I had the greatest pleasure in overhauling every splice, and restropping and grafting every block strop on the mizzen mast. It was quite a work and I enjoyed it much.

The passage passed away very pleasantly. The weather was generally good excepting off the Cape of Good Hope, it being the dead of winter there when we passed. We met with several heavy gales of wind, which was always my delight, and I took good care, when it was my watch below, to be the first man up, when all hands were called to shorten sail. I had several narrow escapes, during the passage. I will mention two.

One night when off the Cape, the wind blowing a gale, and the sea running high, which caused the ship to labour badly, Mr. Nash asked me if I could not send down the fore top gallant yard, as it was straining the mast when the ship pitched and rolled heavy. I jumped up the rigging, followed by Nat Carnes, who was one of the smartest. We soon had the tie stopped out on the yard and the yard was hoisted up a cock bill, the parrel was cut, and the lifts and braces taken off, and I followed the yard down the rigging, which with the sail soaking wet was very heavy, and every time the ship rolled to the leeward, the yard had to be held to the rigging by taking a turn round the shroud with the end of the gasket to keep it from swinging off.

I got down with it very well until I got down to the top, when the end of the gasket slipped from my hand, and the yard swung off some fifty feet with me clinging to it. I held on tight, looking at the heavy seas below me, until it swung back again, which fortunately for me, came in against the rigging with me outside. Had I been inside I should have been crushed between the yard and rigging. They lowered away on deck as quick as they could, and when within a few feet of the deck the rope broke and the yard came down on the deck with full force, it was a marvel to all that the rope did not break when it swung off with my weight on it. Had it broke then, that would have been the last of me.

The other time was when we were sailing along in the Indian Ocean, the main top gallant studding sails were ordered to be set. I ran up the rigging, with the halliards, and went on the end of the yard and rove the starboard side and brought the end down in the top, then went up and rove the larboard side, and brought the end down in the top and was in the act of bending it on to the sail, when a sudden gust struck the ship and carried away the yard in the slings, so that both yard arms went forward, and had I been on either of them at the time, I would have been pitched into the sea or on deck.

———

AS I HAVE PREVIOUSLY DESCRIBED the Canton River, and the various transactions on the arrival at Whampoa, I will not repeat them, as there was no difference this time from the others. I was the only one on board who had been there before, and it was amusing how soon I was recognized by the comprador, wash woman, barber, and others. All pretended they were very glad to see me again. We remained at anchor in Whampoa for about six weeks, taking out the ballast, overhauling the sails, painting ship, and taking on board the cargo. The boat went up to the city frequently. I was the after oarsman, and always went in the boat. When up to the city landing I called on my old friend Jemmy Young Tom, who expressed surprise, and great delight in seeing me again.

Shortly before we sailed, Capt. Conant had invited the old hong merchant Houqua to a reception on board of the ship, as she was named for him. Great preparations were made, everything put in the nicest order, as Nat Cushing the consignee, the American Consul, and other nabobs were coming down from Canton. A large mandarin boat came alongside, splendidly decorated with flags, lanterns, and any quantity of gilt work, bringing the expected guests. All hands were dressed in their best to receive them. This was the first time Mr. Cushing had ever spoken to me. He made several pleasant enquiries about myself and others at home. It brought me up a notch in my own opinion, as well as in the ship's company to have Mr. Cushing acknowledge my acquaintance. I began to feel as if I was somebody.

Houqua came on board magnificently dressed in silks and satins of various rich colours. He was an old man, I should think near seventy, not bad looking, with rather a long mustache, all the rest of face and head nicely shaved, excepting the queue. He presented the ship with a beautiful set of silk flags, and a portrait of himself. He also sent on board a large variety of eatables, for the ship's company. We gave him salute of 12 guns, as the company went away. It was a great time at Whampoa. All the ships had their flags hoisted, and as the mandarin boat went away all the crews gave three cheers. Most of the Captains were invited to the reception, and all arrangements made amongst them to celebrate the occasion.

The cargo being on board, the ship was soon got ready to proceed on our homeward bound passage, and everything being ready, we weighed our anchors, and sailed for Cowes in England to receive orders where to land the cargo. Nothing particular occurred as we sailed through the China Sea, until we came to the Straits of Sunda, where we came to anchor to fill up our water. We had passed Angier Point in the night where vessels generally stop for water. But there was another watering place on the island of Crocetoe between it and Sumatra, up a narrow strait out of sight of the ship.

The pinnace was got ready with water casks on board, and six of the crew to man the boat, with Mr. Henry in charge. I was out of the way when the boat was ready and Harry Neef was called to take my place. Loaded muskets and swords were put on board, in case the natives should give them trouble. The boat being ready rowed away for the land and was soon out of sight, passing up the little channel between the islands. They had not got far before they saw a large canoe coming down towards them from the opposite direction. They did not apprehend any difficulty until the canoe sheared up alongside, and one of the Indians jumped on board and seized one of the muskets which were laying on the after seats. The after oarsman, who was a big Dutch man, seized the musket from him and threw him overboard. Mr. Henry seeing that there were a large number of Indians in the canoe ordered the boat turned round, and for the men to pull with all their might, which they did.

The canoe stopped to pick up the Indian that was thrown overboard, and our boat got the start on them. They however gave chase and just before our boat got out of the channel, the canoe had got near them, and took down a board which concealed a small brass swivel which was loaded up to the muzzle with small stones. This they fired into the boat, and then turned back. The boat came alongside, with everyone in the boat wounded, Mr. Henry much the worst, as the heaviest of the charge took him in the arm. He had on a blue nankin jacket, and part of the sleeve was driven into the arm, which made a very bad wound, and did not heal up the whole passage and after he arrived in Europe the arm was opened & a large piece of the blue nankin was taken out of the wound. The others were slightly hurt. Harry got off with the least as he was stooping down to get the muskets from the bottom of the boat.

The next day a Philadelphia ship called the *Caledonia*, which sailed from Canton about the same time that we did, came to anchor close by us, and it was agreed between the Captains to send an armed expedition to procure water and to punish the Indians for firing upon our boat. Four boats were manned, with about twenty men, each carrying muskets, & swords, and cartridges, also a dozen boarding pikes, the two long boats having the water casks. Both ships hauled nearer into the land, and in a position to see up the creek, and fired several cannons, before the boats started, to give the Indians notice that our ships were armed. The boats rowed up the creek, and filled the casks with water and not an Indian or canoe was seen.

We sailed through the Straits of Sunda into the Indian Ocean, and had a very pleasant passage to the Cape of Good Hope, which we passed without seeing land. We soon took the south-east trade winds and had a good run up to the island of St. Helena which we saw at a distance. The island being guarded by British men of war, we did not attempt to go in for water, but filled up our casks from the heavy rains we encountered when crossing the equator. We shaped our course to the northward, passed in sight of the Azores Islands, and sailed on our way up to the English Channel without anything particular occurring.

Mr. Henry was a sufferer the whole passage and I was placed in his watch to look out when the weather was so bad that he could not be on deck. I considered this confidence in [me] rather a step up on the ladder for promotion, and had strong expectations that I should get Mr. Henry's berth when we arrived at our destined port, as he would go home to America.

We at last arrived in Cowes roads off the Isle of Wight, and the following day received orders to proceed to Rotterdam. We took a North Sea pilot, [and] sailed up the North Sea to the river Scheldt, which is one of the many mouths of the river Rhine. Rotterdam is situated on another entrance, which our ship could not enter, as she drew too much water. The river pilot came on board and piloted us up the river to Dort, which is a very pretty Dutch village about ten miles from Rotterdam.

The dykes or artificial banks of the river, are almost crowded with wind mills, large heavy structures. I could count over one hundred in sight from where we anchored, each of these connected with a pump, to raise the water from the land at the side, which was much lower than the water in the river. It appeared curious to me, who had never seen anything of the kind before, when walking on the dyke to see the water in the river several feet higher than the land. They have to keep a constant watch upon the dykes to see at once any weak place, and to repair it at once, for if the dyke gave way the country would be inundated, and thousands of lives would be lost.

Large lighters were sent down from the city to receive the cargo, and labourers hired from the shore to hoist it out. The crew were discharged and paid their wages, and we all went up to the city. Most of us had silk suits, which were cheap in Canton. I had a blue silk jacket, waistcoat and trousers. We had a jolly time up in Rotterdam for a few days.

Mr. Nash had told me that Capt. Conant intended to leave the ship if she went to Canton again before she went home, and that he [Nash] probably would take command, in which case he wanted me to go second mate. That of course had a great effect on my mind, and I told the crew that I was going the voyage to Canton second mate, and persuaded some of them to stick by the ship. Nat Carnes, and Harry Neef, and two or three more decided to go with me, and after a few days of liberty, seeing the sights in Rotterdam, we returned to the ship. They all liked Mr. Nash, and had no objection to the ship, but sailor like, they liked a change, and most of them shipped in other vessels.

I parted with Mr. Henry as an old friend. I felt so sorry for his suffering. The doctor thought at first the arm would have to be amputated, but concluded to cut it open, and getting the piece of the blue nankin out, he thought it might heal up and the arm be saved, which was the case. On the passage I used to help him bathe the wound, dress it, and bind it up, and he felt grateful to me, and we feelingly bid one another goodbye. Several years after, I met him, in command of a fine ship. His arm was always weak, and the large scars showed how bad the wound must have been.

The cargo being all discharged, the ship was ordered to London to take on board a cargo for Canton. We took a pilot and sailed from the Scheldt, crossed the North Sea and soon arrived in the Thames, which was a very interesting river, though a very tedious one to get up, as the wind blew right down, and we had to work up with the tide, constantly tacking from one side to the other, and when the tide changed we had to come to an anchor. We were two or three days after we entered the river before we got up to the London docks.

Late one afternoon we came to an anchor near an island, which was called Gibbet Island, where pirates were hung in gibbets. There was at the time four lascars hanging, who had been condemned for piracy. This gibbet consisted of a large spar which was secured in the ground. About thirty feet from the ground was a square frame work made of joists. On each corner was the skeleton of one of the lascars, standing upright, secured with iron hoops. I do not know if they were alive when they were put there or not. They had been there a number of years, and there was nothing left but their bones. The frame turned round on the spar by the wind, and kept up a hideous noise all the night.

We passed the town of Greenwich, on the banks of the river, celebrated for the large marble marine hospital, which formerly was Queen Elizabeth's palace, and the great Observatory which stands on a hill, from where all longitude is reckoned, on all charts of the day. Both of these buildings were near the river. We also passed Chelsea, situated on a large inlet like a bay from the river, where all the old wooden 74 gun ships were moored, called the wooden walls of England, something like sixty or seventy of them. All had three tiers of guns, most of them without masts and roofed over. They made quite a show, being painted black with three wide streaks of white, with black port holes.

About six miles from the docks commenced the "Pool," where all the collier brigs and other coasting vessels lay moored, filling a space of four abreast nearly the whole distance to the docks. Their masts had the appearance of a forest from a distance. We at last arrived at the great London dock, which covers many acres of ground. Underneath this dock are the great wine cellars of London, considered one of the greatest curiosities. In after years when I was in London I visited these cellars with my banker. It consists of a mass of stone arches which supports the dock above, and this ground is laid out in regular alley ways, running in straight angles, leaving square places between sufficiently large to hold five casks of wine which is called a bin. Three casks are placed in the first tier, two in the second, and one in the third. Many of these casks had been for years there and were covered with a mass of fungus, that made them look like anything rather than wine casks.

It is wonderful, the order and arrangement of these cellars, every cask is numbered, as well as every bin, and each cask recorded in a book. The alley ways are marked by letters to those running north and south and by figures to those running east and west, so that if a cask that has been there for twenty years of more, is enquired for, all the clerk has to do is to look in the books, and find the number, against which is the letter and number of the alleys, and he can take a light and go direct to the casks. There were some thousand of casks there, all held in bond, as the duties are not called for until they are entered for consumption.

Our ship was hauled into this dock and had a good berth near the gates, as she was entered to receive on board a cargo. Colonel Perkins, the owner of the ship, had arrived in London as a passenger in the ship *London Packet*, and came on board as soon as the ship was docked. After being in the cabin some time talking with Capt. and Mr. Nash, he came up on deck. I was called aft, and the Colonel said to me, that he had heard that I was told that I should go as second officer. He said that he had promised the berth to one of the crew of the *London Packet*, but that I should go as third mate, that I was very young and there was time enough for me to get ahead. My heart fell within me. I made no reply, as I was so disappointed that I could not speak. A third mate's berth was a miserable place, it was neither one thing or the other, a sort of boatswain, and I partly made my mind up that I would leave the ship—but after a night's reflection, I thought it best to accept of the situation.

A new chief mate was engaged, an Englishman. I do not remember his name. He was a disagreeable fellow and not much of a seaman. The second mate, Mr. Wendall, came on board. He was a smart man and a good seaman. I rather liked him than otherwise. A new crew was shipped, all but three of the old crew, who remained with me, most of them a drunken quarrelsome set, and I had much trouble in getting along with them. They were disposed to resist my authority, looking upon me as a boy, and we had several serious fights, my old shipmates always taking my part.

It was in the spring of 1820 when we sailed from London. I was very much disgusted with my situation, and had serious thoughts of leaving the ship in the Channel in the pilot boat, as everything foreboded a very disagreeable passage. My good judgment however, decided me to continue, as I had got the first step to my advancement, and it would be very injurious to my future prospects, to take a step backward. I had got out of the forecastle into the cabin, which had been my great desire.

We had a fine run through the China Seas. In Macao, a Mr. Beal, an English gentleman, called upon us, and finding that we were from London, was much interested in the news we brought, as they had not heard for sometime anything from Europe. It was quite an interesting time in England, as the trial was going on, by George the fourth for a divorce from his queen, Caroline. Mr. Beal seemed very anxious to know if the green bag had been opened. Dr. McLoud, a young Scotchman who was a passenger, was posted up and could tell him all the proceedings until the time we left.

Mr. B. was a wealthy Englishman, had been connected with the English factory at Canton, but now retired from business. He was a man of about fifty five years, and as we understood had no family. He invited us to breakfast the next morning, and sent one of his Chinese servants to escort us to his house. The house and surroundings was a magnificent affair. At nine o'clock we accompanied the Chinaman to the house, entered a large gate in the high stone wall that surrounded extensive grounds, filled with all kinds of strange looking trees and shrubbery, the house not visible from the gate, but by a circuitous path it soon came in sight. It appeared of large dimensions, two stories high. We ascended high steps, and entered a wide hall way of some length. On both sides were shelves, filled with handsome books, having glass doors in front. The Dr. thought they were more for show than use, as they looked to him very much as if they were made of wood, lettered and gilded.

At the end of the hall way we entered a large parlour, some forty feet in length, wide in proportion, the floor covered with a most magnificent Turkish carpet, sofas, and other furniture to correspond, several large mirrors on the sides of the room. At one end of the room were large windows looking into an extensive aviary, made of wire, and filled with beautiful birds. The bird of Paradise, in all its beauty, and the mandarin drake were magnificent. The sacred dove of which there were many, is a lovely looking bird, half as big as a common pigeon, as white as snow, on the breast is a round spot, as big as a ten cent piece, of crimson feathers, which gives the appearance of blood, from a wound. I never have seen them any where else, although I have seen a great many collections of stuffed birds and looked them through in vain to find a similar specimen. This aviary was a grand affair. There was a stream of water running through it, in which the various kinds of water fowl were sporting themselves. There were also small trees growing within, and all kinds of beautiful birds flying about. I never saw anything of the kind before or since to compare with it.

We had been there but a short time before Mr. Beal came in, and breakfast was served up in great style. Four Chinese servants attended upon table. The dishes were numerous, meats, chicken, and eggs in various ways, all in covered silver dishes, tea and coffee in silver pots, sugar and cream in gold, large spoons silver, small ones gold. We had a grand breakfast.

On the arrival of the ship at Whampoa, I recognized many of my old acquaintance, and had quite a home feeling amongst them. Mr. Wendall and the carpenter frequently had quarrels during the passage, and at last when they arrived in port they had a fight. Each got pretty well bruised. The chief mate did not interfere, as he should have done, and Capt. Nash [had gone] up to the city. I do not think Capt. Nash liked Mr. Wendall, and when he returned he blamed Wendall, and said but little to the carpenter. The result was that Mr. Wendall left the ship. He and I got along very well together, although he was inclined to quarrel with all on board. When he left the ship, I was made second mate.

I met him in after years in New York. He was pretty well run down. He was a cartman in New York, said he had lost his horse, and was poor, but could support his family if his horse had not died. I gave him money to purchase another horse. Some years passed and I met him again completely run down, ruined by rum. I was instrumental in getting him into the Sailors' Home on Staten Island. I never heard of him afterwards.

WE DISCHARGED THE CARGO AND took another cargo of teas on board, keeping stones sufficient for ballast, as China ware was no longer shipped, the English ware having taken its place. The ship being loaded, Mr. Cushing ordered us to call at Cowes for instructions where to deliver our cargo. We weighed anchor and sailed down the river through the China Seas, passed through the Gaspar Straits [and] the Java Sea, through the Straits of Sunda, on our way to the Indian Ocean to the Cape of Good Hope, which we passed in sight, and experienced good weather. We had a good run through the trades, and nothing in particular occurring, we came to anchor in Cowes roads, where we laid some days before we received our orders to go to Boston. This was quite a pleasant surprise to me, as I had no doubt but that we should be ordered to some European port. I procured me a nice suit of clothes, coat, waistcoat, and pantaloons, being determined to go on shore looking like a gentleman. I thought much, how pleased my old father would be to know I was a mate, and to see me dressed like a gentleman.

When the vessel received orders to go to America, our English chief mate desired to leave the ship and go home to his family in London. He accordingly was discharged and I took his place, and became chief mate of an Indiaman. I was not quite twenty years old, and

probably the youngest man for the situation out of America. I naturally felt quite proud of my advancement, sailing from Boston as a
sailor, among entire strangers, and returning the chief officer.

We arrived in the afternoon at Boston, July third 1821, came to an
anchor in the harbour, furled the sails and got everything snug to haul
into the wharf the next morning. The Capt. went on shore leaving me
in charge. Towards evening a boat came alongside, bringing my
brother James, who was then in Mr. Willoughby's store. He went forward among the sailors enquiring for me. He was told I was aft. He
was quite surprised, as well as pleased, to find that I was mate.

After answering my various enquiries about the family, he told me
that our brother Dudley had just returned from Paris, where he had
been studying his profession in a medical college, and attending the
French hospitals &c., and that Mother was going to have a party that
evening as a kind of reception for him, and she did not want me to
come on shore that evening. Poor woman, I could not blame her as
she could not forget the disagreeable plight I was in when I returned
from Havana, but to me it was a stunner, as my mind had been
dwelling on the pleasure I should have in meeting them all, and in receiving their congratulations, for my advancement. I was terribly cut
down, and told James that I could not on any account leave the ship.

In the morning the ship was hauled in at the end of Central Wharf
and made fast, and the sails unbent and stowed away. All this was done
before eight o'clock in the morning and all the crew left. The owner's
ship keeper came on board, and I went up to an eating place and got
my breakfast. I came back to the ship, making up my mind that I
would not go home. I put on my best clothes, and stayed on board to
enjoy the Fourth of July, a very disappointed man. I saw Dudley who
had come down on the wharf, probably to see me. He had a quizzing
glass at his eye looking round the ship, but as he did not come on
board, I did not speak to him.

In the afternoon when there was hardly a person moving on the
wharf, all enjoying the gaieties of the day up in town, I espied my father coming down towards the ship. The sight of him changed my
feelings, and I run to meet him. He chided me for not coming up to

the house. I excused myself as well as I could, that I was left in charge and did not want to leave, but now as the ship keeper was on board I was going up. We walked up together, and called in to see Aunt Elliot on the way. She was the first lady that I had seen to speak to for the last two years, and as she was very cordial, I enjoyed that little visit exceedingly. It made a very good impression on my disturbed mind, and quite prepared me to meet all the family most affectionately.

I stayed by the ship until she was entirely discharged, keeping an account of the cargo as it came out. This is the duty of the chief officer, and it was noticed by Colonel Perkins, as the ship lay in front of their store. The ship's company were all paid off, and I hardly saw any of them again excepting Harry Neef. He became a master of a ship in Enoch Train & Co.'s employ and commanded one of their Liverpool packets. In after years, he lived in a cottage next to my house in Dorchester, having married a German lady, and had a small family. He unfortunately took to drink and run down. The last I heard of him his wife had taken charge of [a] water cure establishment, and he was in the country with her. Nat Carnes was a noble fellow and always a true friend to me in all difficulties on board of the ship. Poor fellow, he was lost at sea on his next voyage. Capt. Nash, soon after his arrival married a lady with money, and gave up going to sea.

Capt. Conant, I met in after years in Havana when I was there [as] Captain and owner of the brig *Eight Sons*. He seemed to be an unhappy man. I never saw him smile during our India voyage, and hardly ever heard the sound of his voice, and in Havana he was the same, never liked to allude to our voyage together. He then had command of a brig called the *Halcyon*. She loaded with a cargo of coffee for Antwerp, and for some reason put into Key West the second day from Havana, and there poor Conant took laudanum, and died.

6

Sharks, Monkeys, and Lord Byron

I REMAINED AT HOME five or six weeks, hoping to get a chief mate's berth. Messrs. Perkins & Co., having sold the *Houqua*, had no vessel then fitting out. An opportunity offered for me to have a second mate's berth in the ship *Heroine*, Capt. Charles Smith, bound to Philadelphia, South America, and Europe, and I was glad to take it as I saw it was impossible for me to get a chief mate's berth. I was considered too young.

My brother George had entered Harvard College. My brother Stephen had left Uncle Perkins's counting room, and was studying divinity with Bishop Griswold. Dudley was about going to study with Doctor Physick of Philadelphia, and James was in Mr. Willoughby's counting room on Long Wharf. My father was very much interested in getting up the new parish of St. Paul for Doct. Jarvis, and I shipped as second mate in the *Heroine*, a very good vessel of about three hundred tons. Capt. Smith was a very gentlemanly man of about sixty years. The first mate's name was Deveraux from Marblehead, an easy sort of man, somewhat advanced in life, and as far as I recollect about

Bahia X

the crew they were a quiet set of men. We sailed from Boston about the middle of August 1821, for Philadelphia, where we received a cargo of flour on board, and sailed for St. Salvador, generally called Bahia, in Brazil.

Mr. John Higginson Cabot joined the ship in Philadelphia as supercargo. He was a cousin of my mother's, a well educated man and very much of a gentleman, well informed upon every subject.

I continually felt that I was living among gentlemen, but I began to feel the want of an education. I had been going to sea for six years, and during that time I had not read a book, or given an attention to study of any kind excepting navigation. I often was shocked with myself for the many mistakes I made and deeply regretted that I had not studied when I was younger, and I commenced on that passage to read and study every spare hour I had.

I liked Mr. Cabot exceedingly. He was a most kindhearted man, he understood me perfectly, and felt an interest that I should improve in my conversation, and reading. He would set with me in my watch on deck and converse for an hour or two. He also lent me his books to read, and did what he could to improve me and make the time pass pleasant. What a contrast to my uncle John Higginson, from whom he was named.

We had a passage of about sixty days out to Bahia. We came to anchor in this most beautiful of all bays, from which the place takes its name. The entrance between high land is narrow, and forms into a large circular bay with the land very high all round. The city is built on the side of the hill opposite to the entrance, the streets running one above the other, the roofs of the houses being even with the basements of the houses in the streets above. The entrance from one street to the other was by a zig zag, rather steep ascent. The buildings were mostly white, being built of stone, and covered with plaster of lime.

There was a serious revolt at this time and fighting was going on among the Portuguese and Brazilians. Dom Pedro, the father of the present emperor, had declared himself Emperor, in the place of his father King John, who was emperor of Brazil, and king of Portugal, who had died, and the Brazilians were fighting for their independence from Portugal. Dom Pedro had come from Portugal to establish his rights, leaving his brother Dom Miguel his representative in Portugal. A few days after our arrival the fighting commenced in Bahia, and our ship was crowded with women and children who had sought safety among the shipping. One forenoon we witnessed a serious fight from the ship between the inhabitants and the soldiers, firing muskets from the windows into the troops, and they returning the fire. It lasted for some time, when all at once, everything was quiet. In a few days matters on shore seemed to be all right again, and the women and children were taken on shore, and business went on as usual.

The cargo of flour being all discharged, we made preparations to take on board a cargo of sugar. The sugar from Brazil is packed in large boxes weighing from eight hundred to one thousand pounds. They are very unwieldy things to handle, particularly in stowing them away in the ship's hold. The Blacks that work in the lighters and about the wharves are remarkable for their strength. I have seen them carrying barrels of flour on their heads from the landing up to the ware houses, in fact that seemed to be the only way. Two Negroes would take hold of each end of a barrel and lift it up apparently with ease and place it on the head of another Negro on its bilge and he would reach up his hands to steady it and trot off as unconcerned as any common man would with fifty pounds. Some of them were employed on board of the ship in hoisting the cargo out, and in.

I had the overseeing of the stowage in the hold. It was hard work, the weather being very warm, Bahia being in the latitude of twelve south. I felt the heat very much, but perspiring freely I threw it off, and in the afternoon after the work was done I was very glad to take a bath. There being many sharks in the bay, it was dangerous to go in swimming, so I used to go out to the end of the bow's studding sail boom and go down to the water by the rope at the end used to haul the boat to. I did not believe that sharks would come so near to the ship. Although I had been warned of the danger, I did not believe there was any fear.

One afternoon as I was holding on to the rope washing myself, a large shark came up to me. I did not see him until I felt him rubbing against me trying to bite me. Sharks' mouths are so under their heads that they must get their heads over the object they want to bite, and as I fortunately was hanging straight up and down, he could not get hold. Had he been along a moment before when I was kicking my legs out, he could easily have taken them in. He hung around the ship some time, and finally we caught him. He had a whole green hide in his stomach, which he had taken from some vessel that was soaking it by the side of the vessel. I forget the exact measure but he was over twelve feet long. He was very savage after we got him on deck. I struck him several times on his head with the axe trying to kill him. I afterwards put the axe in his mouth and he dented it with his teeth in biting it.

I saved the jaws of his mouth, which had six rows of teeth, and dried it. I could put it over my head easily although it was much shrunk in drying. He could have easily swallowed me. I kept that mouth for a number of years among the many curiosities I had collected. I finally gave my cabinet of shells and other things I had preserved, to the Newburyport museum, and the mouth of that shark with the rest. I never forgot the horrid feeling of that shark rubbing against me. I pulled myself out of the water quicker than I could have jumped had I been on land.

I purchased several small monkeys, of a different kind from those I had seen in the East Indies. They had rather pretty faces, surrounded with long hair standing away from the face. I also bought some green and yellow parrots that were easily taught to talk. These I took for my adventure, and it occurred to me that they would pay better than anything among the Italians, as the ship was bound to Leghorn with the cargo of sugar.

Brazil is famous for the variety of fruits to be found there, particularly in the northern parts, as it extends from five degrees north latitude, to thirty five south, taking in all of the south and part of the northern tropics, where all the varieties of tropical fruit can be found of other countries, and many that are found no where else, particularly the jack fruit, which somewhat resembles the West India sour sop, but is much superior. It is a large fruit with black seed of the size of kernels of corn, distributed through the pulp of the fruit, of a sweetish aromatic flavour, which is very agreeable. It grows on trees of immense size, and the tree is beautiful, especially when in full fruit, as it was when we were there.

We laid at anchor in Bahia a little over a month, and when the cargo was all on board, and the ship cleared, for Leghorn in Italy, we weighed anchor and set sail for Gibraltar. Nearing the western islands we fell in with a whaling brig, and spoke her. I do not remember her name, but she was from Nantucket, had been out some time, and had not been very successful. The Captain came on board of us. There being scarcely any wind, we kept along together. Whilst he was on board of our ship, there was a school of humpback whales made their appearance, coming towards the vessels. All was excitement with the Capt. and his boat's crew, for as he said, "That is what we have been looking for the month past."

The whaling boat is of a particular model, built sharp at both ends, with a curve in the centre, crescent shape. They are always kept ready to go in pursuit of a whale, and never leave the vessel without having all their implements on board, which are three or four harpoons, one or two spades, which are sharp, spear shaped instruments fixed on a wooden handle six to eight feet long. These and the harpoons lay handy in the bottom of the boat. In the bow of the boat is a round block of wood secured to the forward thwart called the drum head. A sharp hatchet is secured in a becket close by and the lines are nicely coiled in tubs in the after part of the boat, always clear for running.

The boat's crew consists of six, four sailors to row, an experienced steersman, and a harpoon man, which is the captain or one of the mates. A whale being discovered, the boat is manned, and gives chase. The lines are made fast to the harpoons, and a turn taken round the drum head, and the harpoon man, with a small coil of the whale line in his hand, and with the harpoon, stands ready in the bow of the boat, to throw it into the whale as he comes up to blow, or breathe, which he has to do every few minutes. The man at the stern of the boat guides her with an oar, a rudder is never used, and he must be an experienced steersman, as any mistake on his part would be the cause of serious consequences. Care must be taken to run upon the whale in such a way as to avoid its flukes (tail) as he moves it violently when wounded, and if it strikes the boat would knock it to pieces.

When the whale comes to the top of the water the harpoon is thrown with force, and away he runs. The line round the drum is held, and the boat is dragged through the water with great swiftness. The harpooner stands ready with the hatchet in hand to cut the line in case the whale sounds (that is runs down) so as to endanger the boat to be swamped. The whale seldom runs more than a mile or two before he slacks up to breathe, and then they haul in the line as fast as they can.

The harpooner has a spade fastened to a line all ready, as soon as they get near enough, to throw it into the whale, which makes a great wound, and the blood begins to flow. This is repeated several times until the whale dies from loss of blood. It then floats and is towed to the ship, when it is secured, and tackles from the fore & main yards are hooked in to the blubber, which in a common whale is from eight to ten inches thick, and as the man on the whale cuts with his spade the crew hoist it into the vessel, where in leisure time it is tried out in the large kettles carried by all whalers, and filled into casks.

There are several kinds of whales, and experienced whalers know them by their movements. The sperm whale is the largest, and spurts the water from the blow hole in the head (which all whales have) in a solid column. The right whale blows it up spreading out, by this means they may be known a mile or two distant. The humpback is known by its motions, and is much smaller than the others. As soon as the school of hump backs made their appearance the Capt. bid us good bye and jumped in his boat and went in chase of them. The mate also manned another boat and joined the Capt. It was not long before both boats were fastened each to a whale, and the way they were dragged through the water was a sight to us. The breeze springing up we soon lost sight of them.

WE HAD LIGHT WINDS AND CALMS, going up and our passage was rather lengthy. We at last arrived at Leghorn, a very ancient city, with high walls surrounding it. The harbour was made in to the Mediterranean Sea by building long curved break waters, which formed almost a semi circle. It was filled with shipping, apparently of all nations. A great number of Turkish vessels were there, the sailors of which struck my fancy by their peculiar dress. All of them wore turbans of different colours, loose trousers drawn in round the ankle, and very short waisted jackets. On Sundays there seemed to be flags of all nations flying. There was at that time no Italian flag. Italy was divided into dukedoms, and each duke had their flags. Leghorn was in the dukedom of Tuscany and the flag was blue and yellow.

The front of the city towards the harbour had a number of small piers projecting into the harbour, to accommodate the landing of cargoes. On entering the main gate, there is a small square, surrounded by large four story buildings of a light coloured stone. In the centre is the famous monument of the duke of Tuscany in white marble on high pedestals. About six feet from the base are found prisoners in bronze, chained at each corner, representing father and the three sons. These as well as the duke are of colossal size. They are said to represent four pirates, of great renown in former years, and were captured by the duke. They are most splendid pieces of statuary.

We commenced at once to discharge our cargo, and to take in ballast. During our stay I went up to Pisa, a city about five miles from Leghorn, famous for its leaning tower, cathedral, and cemetery. The tower is built of white marble, and leans at an angle of about 12° to 15°. Its form is similar to two tumblers one over the other, with a space of about eight feet or more, the inside wall is without an opening. The outer is divided into stories, having handsome marble pillars in a double row round each story. Between the two are steps of marble, so easy of ascent, that it is said men have rode up on horse back.

The object of this tower is for a belfry for the cathedral, and on the top are a number of bells of different sizes. Some are quite large and all have their dates when they were cast. I do not remember those dates, only that they were several centuries old. There is a good view of the city from the top, and looking down from the leaning side one feels as if he would fall to the ground. The inside is entirely empty. One can look from the top down to the bottom. There has been a question, and I believe it never has been settled, whether it was originally built at this angle, or by some other cause got this cant. It is over six hundred years since it was built.

I spent hours in walking about the city, and in the evening returned to Leghorn. When we first arrived in Leghorn, I had many enquiries for my adventure of parrots and monkeys. I found that they had come to a good market, and I held on for a good price. I do not remember the price I sold them at, but I got about two hundred dollars, for my twenty invested. I invested the proceeds in Leghorn hats, for my home adventure. Capt. Smith said it would have [been] better than sugar if he had filled the hen coops with parrots.

As Mr. Cabot took lodgings on shore as soon as the ship arrived I saw but little of him. He was a great admirer of Byron's poems, and as Lord Byron was in Leghorn at the time, Mr. Cabot made his acquaintance, and one day they came on board of the ship together. I was struck with his appearance, and rather disappointed, as on the passage I had read some of his works and formed a high opinion of him. He appeared to me as an ordinary Englishman. He was under size, and walked lame. His face was pleasing, with a high forehead and good shaped head. He wore a high shirt collar, turned over on the side and quite open in front, which was different from the fashion at that time, as gentlemen wore generally wide stiff black stocks.

When they went in the cabin, a set of his works lay on the table. I presume Mr. Cabot had them put there. Lord Byron said it was the greatest compliment that could be paid him. He was on board about half of an hour. Then he and Mr. Cabot went on shore. I never saw or heard of Mr. Cabot after that. He stayed in Europe after the ship left. Lord Byron was on his way to Greece. The Greeks were fighting the Turks for their liberty, and he felt sufficient interest to join them, and a year or two afterwards lost his life fighting in Thessalonica. I was in Boston when we heard of his death, and George Ticknor, who married my cousin Ann Elliot, delivered an oration on his life, which interested me much, as I had seen, and heard much of him.

7

Mutinies and the Mermaid

WE WERE GONE ABOUT TEN MONTHS. My father had just moved to Newburyport, with the family, into the old house, inherited by him from his mother. His sister, my Aunt Rebecka, had lived there since the death of her mother, which was about twelve years, she having died in 1810. She [Rebecka] not wishing to live with the family, after living so long an independent old maid, my father in conjunction with his sister, Mrs. Elliot, built a small house for her in the garden on The Street. I, of course, as soon as I got settled in with the owners of the *Heroine*, hurried down to Newburyport, and had a very happy meeting with the family.

My adventure in Leghorn hats did not turn out as well as my adventure from Bahia. I have always thought the purchaser took advantage of my ignorance of the article. I believe I did not lose by the operation. I passed about a month very pleasantly at home in Newbury.

I had called on the Perkinses, my former owners, asking for employment. The firm at this time consisted of the Colonel, his son in law Samuel Cabot, and his son Thomas. I understood that Mr. Cabot

had enquired about me of Capt. Smith, which gave me encouragement that they were thinking of me, so when I was in Boston I called
again. They had just bought the brig *Cadet*, and were glad to see me,
wished me to take charge of the brig, and have her overhauled and
made ready for sea. I of course was pleased with the opportunity, as
well as their confidence. I immediately had her hauled to the wharf
they designated, and employed men to overhaul the rigging, clean
ship, and have her painted. She was a good looking vessel of about
220 tons, and I was pleased with her. She had some new inventions,
which I had not seen before. One was patent iron trusses to the lower
yards, instead of rope, which had always been the custom. I did not
like them. They were Wells patent truss, too much clock work about
them, entirely different from the simple iron truss of the present day.

It was over a week before I got her ready to haul in to Central
Wharf in front of their store. She was armed with four six pound carronades, and two swivel guns. One of these carronades had the touch
hole stopped, and had to be sent to the South Boston iron works to
be fixed, and although I had put on relieving tackles and lifts on the
fore yard to hoist the gun into a boat alongside, the truss broke, with
the operation. It made some talk, and several masters, and others came
to look at it. They all agreed that I had put in sufficient relieving tackles, and there was no blame upon me. It seems this patent was just
introduced among the shipping, the *Cadet* being one of the first to
have them. The breaking of this truss injured their reputation with
masters & ship owners.

I got the vessel all ready, and in prime order. I felt that I was the
Capt., but I had noticed that Mr. Cabot had always said Mr. Tyng
when he spoke to me, which created a doubt, if I was Captain, or
mate. I had been placed in charge to get her ready for sea, and everything was done as I ordered, and I was called Captain by almost every
one, and I believe it was the intention of Colonel Perkins in the beginning that I should go as Captain, for he one forenoon, when on
board of the vessel, said "Our old Captain Magee wishes to go out as
the Captain of the brig, and I want you to go as chief mate." I told
him I did not care to go as mate. I was dreadfully disappointed, but after

some talk, he telling me that I should have the highest wages of any mate out of Boston, and putting me in mind of my youth &c., I consented to go as the first officer.

I had entirely forgot all about Magee's treatment of me in the *Cordelia*, in fact I had not heard or hardly thought of him since we parted, and when he came on board I should not have known him had I not expected him, he had altered so much in appearance. He had dark hair, and was tall and thin when I last saw him. He was now quite stout and fat, with hair almost white. He met me very cordially, and I had not the least ill feeling towards him. The thought of his ill treatment never came to my mind. A young man by the name of William Bowers from Providence was the second mate. He was recommended to the owners by Mr. Carrington, his uncle, who had lived sometime in Canton and was a friend of Mr. Cushing's. He was not much of a sailor, and by no means an agreeable person.

The vessel being ready for sea, a shipping master had the order to ship a crew. I was not consulted, and Captain Magee paid no attention to it, so that neither of us knew what kind of men we had for sailors. I was told one afternoon, that in the morning the crew would be brought on board, and to haul the vessel into the stream. Mr. Sargent, an old pilot, was sent on board in the morning to take her to the anchorage, and at about ten the shipping master brought the crew on board, about the roughest looking set of fellows as I had ever seen. There were eight of them. All of them had been drinking, and some of them intoxicated, feeling more ready for a fight than to work.

A kedge with the hawser had been run out, and the end brought to the Captain, the fastening to the wharf cast off, and the vessel swung off. I was forward on the bow. Mr. Bowers was aft with the crew at the capstan, to heave the vessel off. I heard Mr. Sargent calling me, and knew there was trouble aft with the crew, and did not at first pay attention to his calling. I felt more like running away than anything else, and believe if the vessel had not been cast loose from the wharf I should have done so, for I was fairly trembling with fear of these wild looking, drunken rascals.

I had to take notice, and asked Mr. Sargent, as if I had just heard him, "What is the matter?" He said "We can't do anything with those men." I jumped on deck, and went aft, and asked Mr. Bowers, "What is the matter?" He said "That fellow," who was sitting on the deck holding on to the hawser, with the turn round the capstan the wrong way, "will not take the turn the right way." I told him to take the turn the other way. He was very abusive and would not do as I told him. I took one of the capstan bars and knocked him over. Seeing that the rest came at me, and the biggest fellow among them, the nearest, with his fists (half as big as my head) doubled up, in the act of striking me. I swung my bar and he fell over, all of them cursing and swearing, and very violent. But seeing their leader fall, they hesitated, and I then told one to take the turn of the capstan and put it on the other way, which he did. I told the others to put in their bars and heave round. They obeyed and all was quiet.

The vessel was not more than ten feet from the wharf, and there were several standing there, among them Capt. Ben Rich, who had his store next to the Perkinses', and they were looking out of their windows, attracted by the noise of the men. Capt. Rich said it was the smartest thing he had ever seen, what appeared to be a serious mutiny quelled in a minute. The two sailors which were knocked over were put one side, and being pretty drunk, lay still and went to sleep.

There was no more trouble with those fellows afterwards. They saw & felt that they had a master, which is absolutely necessary with a new crew on board of a ship. They come together strangers to one another, and to the officers. Then is the time to impress them with a lesson for the voyage. Mr. Sargent, who had been a pilot out of Boston many years, told me after the vessel anchored in the stream, that he had seen many drunken crews, when they first came on board, but these were the worst looking fellows he had ever seen, and that he expected very serious trouble, and that few mates could have quelled them as quick as I did. They proved a good set of men, and very good seamen, and I had no more trouble with them during the voyage as I recollect.

We sailed for Batavia in the month of June 1822. Our ship's company consisted of Captain Magee, two mates, cook, and steward and a

carpenter, a crew of eight sailors, and two boys, sixteen in all. The two
boys were George Tilden, the son of Joseph Tilden, president of the
Columbian bank in Boston, and Joshua Lincoln, a nephew of Governor [Levi] Lincoln, both about fifteen years old, and their first voyage.
They were both good boys, and I never allowed a cross word spoken
to them, by any of the older sailors, or by any one else if I could help
it. I remembered my first voyage, and took much pains to make their
voyage pleasant to them.

The steward was a French mulatto, a half crazy fellow [who]
boasted of having been in the wars with Napoleon, [and] was very
careless, neglectful, and dirty. We had been out but a few days, when
he unpacked the crockery, putting it in the lee side in the cabin, plates,
dishes, cups, and saucers, in fact all the crockery on board. It was
blowing fresh, and the sea running high, and all the crockery piled up
on the lee transom, none of us knowing anything about [it]. The brig
was put in stays, and of course rolled very heavy, and the crockery was
thrown from one side to the other, until there was hardly a whole
piece left.

Here we were at the commencement of a passage to India, without
a tumbler to drink from, or a plate to eat on. The Captain scolded the
poor fellow, but it was of no use, our china was broken, and we must
get along as best we could. Between the carpenter and myself, we
manufactured wooden dishes, and cut bottles in two for drinking
cups &c., and got along as well as we could until we arrived in Batavia.

I had a great deal of trouble with the fellow. He cut up his table
cloth for wash cloths, he would kill a couple of chickens, and forget to
pick them. One morning I found two that had been laying in the long
boat for several days, and were putrid. I used to threaten to flog him,
but I never put my hand upon him.

One Saturday forenoon, when about half passage, Capt. Magee
wished the steerage to be thoroughly washed, and scrubbed out. The
two boys, the carpenter and the steward slept there. The chests of all
of them were brought on deck. It was my watch below in the
forenoon, and I was interested in a novel I was reading, and did not go
to sleep. I had been below but a short time when Capt. Magee called

me. I went on deck and found the Capt. in a great rage with the steward. Upon opening his [the steward's] chest, he found several of his bottles empty which were filled with cherry cordial, some of his private stores, which he had not commenced on. He wanted him tied up and flogged.

I tied him up to the rigging, and looked into his chest, and such a mess I never saw. He had made it a receive all for every thing. He had emptied tea leaves, and coffee grounds, and almost every thing else into it. I told Capt. M. that the man certainly was crazy. I begged him off from a flogging and got him to beg the Capt. pardon, and do so no more, which he did and the Capt. let him off. I then went down to my state room, and laid down in my berth, and as it was near time to take the altitude of the sun, I took my book to read, instead of going to sleep.

In the course of half an hour, the steward rushed into my room, with a large carving knife in his hand, his eyes glaring most wildly. He made towards me. I sprung up, reached my hand for my pistol. He seemed confused, evidently expecting to find me asleep. He went for the cabin door, but instantly turned and came to the door of my room. I pointed my pistol at him, he threw the knife down, and run up on the deck. At once there was the cry "A man overboard." I went up on deck and found that the steward had jumped overboard, and looked over the side and saw him about a fathom under water with his face downwards, his arms and legs stretched out, and without motion, sinking fast, so that it would have been useless to try to save him. I related to Capt. Magee what had just occurred in my room, and one of the boys then told me that he had threatened several times, that he would knife me, but he did not believe him, and therefore did not tell me. Capt. Magee said I had a very narrow escape. I found afterwards a pot half full of rum, which he had been drinking from, until he became frenzied, and produced that awful glare of his eyes, which I shall never forget.

We were then south of the equator, near the latitude of St. Helena, and we had a good run to the Cape of Good Hope, and when off the Cape we passed the body of a large whale floating, and hundreds of birds feeding from it. We sailed close to it, and saw plenty of sharks, as well as birds—which were principally Cape pigeons, about the size of the common fowl, black and white, all of the same colours, and marked alike, also many albatrosses, much larger than the Cape pigeon. We caught one, the wings measuring twelve feet from tip to tip. There were also hundreds of Mother Carey's chickens, which are seen all over the ocean. Sailors have a superstitious notion, that when [these birds are] seen following the wake of a vessel, it is a sign of a gale of wind. This probably was a body of a whale which had been cast adrift from some whaleman, after they had taken the blubber off.

We sailed on through the Indian Ocean, without anything of importance occurring. The monsoon being against us, we could not go through the Straits of Sunda, but had to go through the Gilola Passage, to the eastward of the island of Java, which made our passage longer, which was a little over one hundred days. We unfortunately run aground on entering the bay to Batavia on a shoal near a small island, about twelve miles from Batavia early in the morning. There being no pilots there, Capt. Magee had to trust to his book and chart. We at once took an anchor out a stern, and with all the purchases we could rig, were not able to start her. Mr. Bowers was sent up to the city for help with the boat, and Capt. Magee went on shore with the other boat and amused himself picking up shells. I remained on board with two seamen, and rigged extra purchases on the hand spikes so as to heave again at the windlass when we got help from the city.

In the morning the cook got us a good breakfast of coffee, bread, and lobscouse, a mess of beef and bread cooked together, after which we commenced to heave at the purchases on the cable again, having besides our crew, about eighteen others to help us. In the course of an hour we got her afloat, hove up the anchor, and by the middle of the afternoon was at anchor in Batavia roads, about half a mile from the landing. We soon furled the sails and got everything in order and the Captain wishing to see the consignees that night, the boat was manned and took him ashore.

The city of Batavia lies inward from the shore some distance, and a canal is cut from the landing up, and through the city, connecting with others, which like streets pass in every direction, on which there are ware houses to receive the goods from lighters, that are brought by the shipping. A little ways from the landing is a shoal which is the resort of alligators, some very large ones, and they come near the boats, which pass in and out of the canal. It is very seldom that they attack any one. There were some twenty or thirty ships and brigs at anchor there, besides several Dutch men of war, three American beside our vessel, the others mostly Dutch.

Batavia is in the latitude between five and six [degrees] south. It is of course very warm, and sickly in the city, but in the suburbs, and in the country quite healthy. All the foreign merchants that have their counting rooms in the city have their residence in the country, from one to three miles from the city. All keep carriages, and some half dozen of the little Java horses. All captains who live on shore are supplied with a carriage and two horses, which is charged in the disbursement of their vessels.

Our vessel was consigned to the house of Paine & Co., an American business house, at that time considered one of the highest standing in the place. There were one or two other American houses, one Messrs. Perkins & Co., he was a connection of our family, and through Capt. Magee, he invited me to come and see him. I went on shore and called on him. He was very cordial, insisted upon my going out to his house, which I did, and passed the night. He was going to dine with Mr. Paine our consignee, dinner hour 7 o'clock, [and] took me with him in his carriage. It was curious to see the styles, quite a comfortable carriage, with a pair of little Java horses, and a Javanese driver, with two runners going ahead with lighted flambeaux in their hands, one on each side of the road, keeping ahead of the horses to give light to the driver.

We arrived at the house, entered a long hall, with a table in the centre, on which was a decanter of brandy, and a pitcher of what should be water, but which was brandy and water mixed, and the light being at the further end of the hall, it was difficult to see how much brandy one poured in his tumbler without holding it up to the light. When getting the right quantity to suit his taste, he would fill up from the pitcher thinking it water and would of course get rather a severe dose. Mr. Perkins gave me the hint, and we both took a light glass from the pitcher. Mr. Perkins introduced me as his cousin, Mr. Tyng of Boston. Mr. Paine, a gross looking man of about fifty, received me very cordially, and introduced me to his partners, and several of the company, which were about fifteen, all jolly sort of fellows. We had a glorious dinner, of I don't know how many courses. Over the table hung a long fan, the length of the table, about three feet above, and was kept constantly swinging back and forth by two Javanese boys, one on each side, with cords in their hands.

Mr. Paine sat at the head of the table. Behind him stood a servant with a large fan, the handle resting on the floor, made of peacock feathers, which he kept twisting one way and the other, so that by both operations there was quite a cool breeze passing through the room. Wine passed freely of several kinds, and they all drank glass after glass. I was on my guard, for the little brandy and water I took when I first arrived was enough to warn me to take no more. My one glass was filled to drink Mr. Paine's toast, which was a health to us all &c., from which I took a sip, and let it remain. The eating part of dinner being finished, the cloth was removed, and wines, fruit, and cigars were put on, all of which found ready takers.

About ten o'clock Mr. Paine blew a whistle, which was a signal for his servants to take him to bed. He always knew when he was drunk enough. Two stout fellows came, hauled his chair back, he put one arm round each of their necks, and they with their arms round his waist lifted him out of his chair and took him to bed. Mr. Perkins told me that was his daily custom. He never drank anything in the way of liquor during the day, until dinnertime. They were all tremendous drinkers. Mr. Perkins was less so than the others. He had a very pretty cottage, surrounded by a neatly laid out garden. He had no family that I saw.

During the passage, Capt. Magee and I used to talk a good deal about the mermaid that Captain Eades of Charleston, Mass., had bought in Batavia, from the Capt. of the Dutch ship which came from Japan. It was at that time causing some excitement in England. The

Dutch government had permission from the Japan government to send one ship each year to Japan, for trade. No other foreign vessels were allowed to go there, until Commodore Perry opened the trade for America, and this vessel always came to Batavia from Japan, and all curiosities from that country were to be found in that city.

We believed that there were among the aquatic species, some creatures resembling the human, the same as the monkey and ape among the species of animals on the land, and upon enquiry Capt. Magee found there was one for sale imported by a Dutch merchant from Japan. Magee and I went to see it. It was nicely packed in a box, the same as when shipped from Japan. The top or cover of the box was taken off, and we were allowed to examine it as much as we pleased, but not allowed to touch it. The price asked for it was five hundred dollars.

After looking at it for a while, we concluded to buy it. It was a wonderful looking creature, three feet eight inches long, from the waist up a perfect resemblance of an aged female, from the waist downward of a fish, with the scales quite small at the waist, increasing in size downwards until they became quite large. The fins, and the tail, which turned, were quite natural. It had long hair hanging from the head over the shoulders, with the arms perfectly shaped, crossing over the breast, the hands partly open, the fingers and nails perfectly natural. The features were not bad, but like the body were shriveled, looking as if they had been dried or smoked. The body had shrunk showing the form of the skeleton, the paps like shriveled dried flesh, hanging slightly downwards, the whole having a dark brown mummified look.

As it lay on its back, we could discern no line of connection from the body to the fish. It looked perfectly natural, the skin and small scales meeting in the most regular manner. We wanted to look at the back, but the merchant said he could not permit it to be taken out of the box, as it was consigned to him from Japan, for sale on those conditions, for if one was allowed to handle it others would require to do the same, and it would soon get defaced and unsalable.

We agreed to buy it if the back was as perfect as the front, and that he should lift it out himself and we were not to touch it, as we did not wish to "buy a pig in a poke." This being agreed upon, we brought the five hundred dollars, and he lifted it out of the box, and all appearing in perfect order, we paid the money, and it was ours.

On the back was seen at the waist, where the fish and human appearance came together, where it had been cut open on one side of the back bone to take out the entrails, and was clumsily sewn up with coarse stitches. The back bone could be seen in regular form, from the ribs in the body, to the body of the fish. The flesh being dried, or smoked, seemed to cleave to the skeleton showing the form of the skeleton most perfectly. It was taken on board. One half was mine, the other half was Magee's.

There was when we arrived a Dutch ship chartered in Canton by Mr. Cushing, with a supercargo, and his clerk on board. I forget the name of the ship and of the supercargo. The clerk's name was Philip Dumeresque, quite a lad, and brother to the wife of Thomas Perkins Jr., a partner in his father's house in Boston, and owners of our vessel. He was a clever little fellow and I saw a good deal of him, as he was frequently on board of our vessel, not being contented with parties on the Dutch ship. He afterwards became a Captain in the Perkinses' employ, married a Miss Deblois of Boston, had quite a family of children. I met him in Boston some thirty years afterwards, then in command of a clipper ship bound to Canton. I afterwards heard that he jumped from a sound steamer coming from New York to Boston.

This Dutch ship was laying in Batavia waiting for our arrival. She was to take on board Bangka tin in blocks sufficient to load us— she was much larger than the *Cadet*—and then we were to go into the Straits of Sunda on the Sumatra side, and take the tin on board of our vessel, as the Dutch did not allow tin to be exported under a foreign flag. The Dutch ship was then to return to Batavia for another cargo to be taken to Canton. We were to proceed to the mouth of Canton River with our cargo and there wait for orders. When all was ready, both vessels sailed for the Straits of Sunda and came to an anchor near the Sumatra shore, opposite Angier Point.

The inhabitants of Sumatra were Malays, a very warlike race from

Malacca. They conquered and became in possession of all the sur-rounding islands except Java and Borneo. The inhabitants of Java are a very mild pleasant looking people, quite dark, with straight black hair, make most excellent servants. The Dutch had but little difficulty in taking possession of the island, and soon gained the good will of the inhabitants, and learned their language, so that all communications be-tween them is in Javanese, and the islanders never learn the Dutch lan-guage. They are a delicate race, and are poor labourers. The Chinese of which there are many, do most of the labour, on the sugar, and cof-fee plantations, as well as in the tin mines, not as coolies, but as free men. The Malays are different in every respect, a wild unconquerable race, pirates on the water, and robbers on the land. The Dutch have had several wars with them but never succeeded in getting possession of the island of Sumatra, or any other nation on the Malacca coast.

It is a splendid island, over six hundred miles long, running from the south east to north west, and in some parts three hundred in width. The land is high in the interior, and is in sight from Angier Point. There are several commercial cities on the island which are held principally by the Dutch, as Padang and Bangka. It is famous for black and white pepper, nutmegs, and other spices.

The second day after we were at anchor, two large proas came to anchor not far from us. There appeared to be but few Malays in sight on them, and at first we did not take much notice of them, as we supposed them to be trading vessels, as both piratical and trading proas look alike. Both have large coverings of bamboo the whole length of their vessels. These coverings are made so that one slips over the other, and the vessel is uncovered in a few minutes. For trading proas they serve to protect the cargo, and on the pirates to deceive, and cover the men.

Our suspicions were first raised by canoes from them passing round our vessels, and pointing to the quakers, or false guns on the *Cadet*. I had made on the passage by the carpenter twenty wooden ends, repre-senting carronades, like our four iron ones, which were fastened on the outside whilst we were in Batavia, and it gave her the appearance of a man of war brig. After consultation with the Dutch Captain we concluded it would be best to ascertain what they were before night. We manned a boat from each vessel, armed with muskets & pistols, and rowed along side of them, our vessels having their cannon loaded and pointed toward the proas in case they should show fight to the boats. I had charge of our boat with six men.

We soon made up our minds that they were pirates, as there were too many men on board for trading vessels, and probably more concealed under the coverings. In the Dutch boat there was a Malay sailor, who acted as interpreter. We told them to go away at once, that our vessels were armed, and if they were not off within an hour, we would sink them. They replied that our guns were wood and that they were not afraid of us.

We returned to our vessels, and fired a shot into one of them, which soon started them, and then fired several guns without shot, which let them know that all our guns were not wooden. We saw no more of them. The Dutch captain, who had been a trader in those seas for a long time, was certain that it was their intention to have boarded us that night. They probably had at least sixty men on board of each proa, and if they could have got along side, fifty of them would have jumped on board of each vessel (and with krisses, long crooked daggers, generally poisoned), they would most probably overcome the ship's company, and put them all to death.

There were a great many piratical vessels in those seas at that time, also in the China Seas, and it behooved us to keep a sharp look out, and always to be prepared for their reception. I at once had made a boarding net out of rattling stuff (a small hard twisted rope, used to rattle down the rigging), to go across the deck on the fore part of the main rigging fifteen feet high, from one side to the other, and on each side from the upper part of the cross net to the taffrail, and always kept two carronades aft, one on each side, loaded with grape, or cannister shot.

The boarding net was always kept handy, and could be triced up at short notice. The whole crew would be abaft of the netting, and the guns pointing forward, and in case they should attempt to board us, we would let them get collected on the deck, then fire one gun which would rake that side of the deck, and those not wounded would probably flee to the other side, and then fire the other gun which would sweep that side. We were always on the watch, and ready, but we had no further trouble. We heard of several vessels which were boarded and taken by pirates and all on board murdered.

In a few days we received all the tin on board from the Dutch ship, and she left for Batavia, and we sailed for Canton River. As it was about the change of the monsoons, which is every six months, from S.E. to S.W., it had been blowing from the east to the southeast, and now the S.W. were commencing, which would be fair to Canton, and during these changes the weather is very various—calms, gales, and sometimes severe typhoons. Now it was light winds and calms, and we had a long passage to Canton River.

One day when becalmed on entering the China Seas, we were surprised to see the water covered, as it were, with what appeared to be serpents, or a kind of eels. They were of all sizes from a foot, to six or eight feet long, with black and white rings round them. The colours were extremes, black and white, and all were alike. They seemed to be lying still on the surface. We caught several of them in a bucket alongside of the vessel. We could not make up our minds whether they were serpents, or fish. The water was covered with them as far as we could see.

On the passage, Capt. Magee got quite tired of the purchase of the mermaid. He evidently had been quizzed by his friends in Batavia, and he said a number of times it was a foolish purchase, and wished he had never seen it, so one day I asked him what he would take for his half. He named two hundred dollars. I told him I would give it, and the mermaid was mine. He appeared to be relieved.

WE AT LAST ARRIVED at Chinpee, an island off the mouth of Canton River, and came to an anchor, and Captain Magee went up to Canton. He was absent for a week, when he returned. I did not like the anchorage, as we were too much exposed to gales of wind, and I proposed to Captain M. that we should change to a roadstead more protected, near the island of Lintin, where were two country vessels laying, which we did. These country ships, as they were called, were English, belonging to Calcutta, and were there with cargoes of Patna opium, which were to be delivered to smuggling boats. Opium was contraband in China, and all that was used (and it was an immense quantity) had to be smuggled on shore.

The English East India Company by their charter held the right of all trade in the East Indies and China. No other English ships but theirs could go to Canton for cargoes. All their ships were very large, like the three decker war ships, and were painted like them, three wide white streaks with black port holes. They had their own colours, which were different from the English flag. They were manned with large crews, and officered like men of war, wearing the uniform of the company. These ships had to anchor some ten miles below Whampoa, on account of their great draft of water.

I found now that our vessel was to lay where she was for some time, how long was uncertain, as she was to receive the [Turkish] opium that the American ships brought from the States. These vessels when they arrived would discharge what they had on board into our vessel before going up the river, it being forbidden by the Chinese government and would be seized. We discharged a quantity of tin in each vessel, which answered for their ballast under their cargoes of tea. I had a very pleasant intercourse with the officers of the country ships. The Captains having their families on board made their company agreeable, and the time passed pleasant.

The Turkish opium was in round balls, the size of common cannon balls, packed in tin cases, about two feet long, and on end a half square, covered with a wooden box. These were sold in Canton by the consignee who gave the order for their delivery. A smuggling boat would come alongside in the night, and bring the order, and the boxes were delivered to them. They then would break open the cases and take the opium out, and put it in bags, about ten balls in each, so as to be convenient to run on shore.

It was the custom to pay a kumshaw to the vessel of two dollars for each case. This was for the Captain and me. The case and tins were for

Mr. Bowers the second mate. The smuggling boats, and government armed boats to prevent smuggling, were so much alike that we could not tell one from the other. Both had from thirty to forty oarsmen, fifteen to twenty oars of a side, and the government boats came as often for a load as the others, both being hired by the purchasers in Canton. We laid there about three months, when Mr. Cushing came down, and we made a trip over to Manila for a cargo of sugar. During the time we laid there, we received and delivered about one thousand cases of opium, so that my perquisites were about five hundred dollars.

Soon after our arrival, it was spread about that there was a mermaid on board, and all that came on board were anxious to see it. At that [time] the English had a disturbance with the Chinese, and all the English ships had to leave the river and came to an anchor, not far from where we laid. All these ships had physicians on board who were anxious to examine the mermaid, as they did not believe there was any such thing. A day was fixed when they all came on board, some of them bringing magnifying glasses.

I placed the mermaid on the cabin table, that they might examine it as closely as they were a mind to, with the condition that no one should touch it, that I would turn it or move it in any direction they wished. I should think they were near an hour examining and could not make up their minds whether it was natural or artificial. At first they thought it was an ape's body attached to a fish, but as an ape has no collar bone, which was plainly to be seen in this, and some other parts of the skeleton being different from any animal, they were in doubt, and went on board of their vessels, and made up a purse of six hundred dollars, to have it dissected. Mr. Cushing offered two hundred more, but as I had my doubts about it, I preferred not to have it cut up. One of their Captains who was about sailing for England offered one thousand for it, which I refused.

I had some time previously taken it to Macao, and had a handsome case made of glass in frames of camphor wood, so that it could be placed up right, and be seen on all sides, and no one could touch it, which was necessary as one would pull out one of the hairs from the head, or scratch off a scale, and in that way soon deface it.

Several American vessels arrived during our stay there, one that was commanded by Edward Cabot, a brother of Samuel Cabot, a partner of the Perkinses. R. B. Forbes was the second mate. His brother Thomas, who came out as a clerk to Mr. Cushing, had been a clerk in the counting room of Perkins & Co. He was lost overboard from his yacht, going from Canton to Macao a few months previous. They were cousins of Mr. Cushing, their mothers being sisters of the Perkinses, and were connections of mine, as well as Capt. Cabot. By that vessel I received a letter from my father informing me of the decease of my brother George.

When all was ready we sailed for Manila, Mr. Cushing as passenger, and a sociable pleasant person. A box containing a wedding cake was received just before we left by Mr. Cushing from his cousin Caroline Perkins, the daughter of the Colonel, who had married William Gardiner, the son of Dr. Gardiner, rector of Trinity Church in Boston. It was a good sized loaf and we eat it, on the passage. It was put upon the supper table until gone. Wedding cake and salt beef went well together.

We had a fair passage to Manila, [and] anchored at Casilda, where all vessels lay, about three miles from the city. Manila is pleasantly situated on rising ground, at the entrance of a small river. The original town, which is walled round, is called the *sitio*. In the centre is a fort, outside of the fort are fine stone buildings, the governor's palace, and government offices, and residences of the wealthier inhabitants. Outside of this citadel is a wide *paseo* used by the inhabitants as a riding ground, and every afternoon, just before sundown, it is filled with carriages. The largest proportion of the inhabitants live outside of the citadel, in stone houses, on well laid out streets.

Manila is on the island of Luzon, one of the Philippine group, lying between the latitudes of ten and twenty degrees north. They were conquered by the Malays. The original inhabitants were black with woolly heads, and are often seen in the streets. They do not mix with the Malays, but live retired in the mountains. Some of the Malays are good looking, but generally they are a puny looking race. I saw some of the women with long black hair, reaching to the ground. They are great smokers of cheroots, made purpose for them. They are about the size of a common broom handle, and about a foot long, worked over with coloured silk floss. The Indian women may be seen at all time of the day with these large cheroots in their mouths.

Our vessel was consigned to Baretta & Bros., Black merchants. I was invited to dine at their house, and was very much pleased. The elder Baretta was a very gentlemanly man, of about fifty five. His hair was curly, but grayish. The top of his head was bald, he had white whiskers. His brother was younger. They were both handsome looking gentlemen, and had more polished manners than those I had met before. Mrs. Baretta was a delicate looking white Spanish lady. There were three or four children, of mixed blood.

The dinner was more in style than I had seen before, servants in livery, with white gloves, and a great display of silver dishes, a glass of Rhenish wine with dinner, which was of various courses. The cloth removed, fruit of various kinds and cake was placed on the table, also one or two decanters of wine. Mrs. Baretta poured out the coffee in small cups, which was served on silver waiters, with sugar, and no milk. After taking coffee they all rose, [the gentlemen] bowing to Mrs. B. and her daughters, she returning the salute, and [the ladies] retired to the parlour.

The gentlemen again seated, the wine was passed round, and a large smoking instrument called a hookah was placed in the centre of the table. It was of silver, the lower part shaped like an urn. This was filled with aromatic water, and from the top rose a bowl the shape and size of a common coffee cup. This was filled with tobacco, and lighted by a live coal on top, the pipe passing through into the water. From above the water projected elastic tubes long enough to reach to any part of the table. These were handed to each individual. A small saucer, with amber mouth pieces was also passed round, for each one to choose one to screw on to this tube. Then we all commenced to smoke from the same pipe. A very little wine was drunk, and I could not help to compare in my mind the great difference between the dinner in Batavia with white gentlemen and the dinner in Manila with Black gentlemen.

We took on board a cargo of sugar in small mat bags, and got ready to return to our anchorage at the mouth of Canton River. I had bought an adventure of birds' nests, and pearl shell, for the Canton market, the first an article much esteemed in China for soups, and the pearl shells, which were larger than a common plate, and flat like a plate, are used for making fancy articles. I gained money on this adventure. We had a short and pleasant journey back to our old grounds. As ships arrived we put on board of them sugar enough for ballast under their cargoes of tea. We received chests of opium, as before.

Whilst we were absent the country ship had been ordered away by the Chinese men of war, and gone out side for awhile to return again. In a short time after we arrived they came back, and soon several war junks came down upon us and ordered us away. They kept up a terrible pounding on their gongs. I hoisted our American flag and fired a couple of guns as a salute. Our comprador came on board very much agitated, afraid the men of war would sink us. Captain Magee went to the city with Mr. Cushing. When we arrived, I told the comprador to go to the Chinese commander and make him understand that we were Americans, and it was our custom to salute the admiral's ship, that we would go to sea.

I got the brig underway and went outside a little distance, altered the brig so that she would not be known as the same vessel, by painting a canvas cloth white and putting it round the waist, which was painted black, and rigging up a long spar which we had on board for a mizzen mast, and thus making her appear as a ship. We returned after three days, and came to anchor in the same place, and were not troubled any more. The admiral no doubt reported to his government that he had driven the barbarians away.

After laying a month or six weeks, we again sailed for Manila. On our passage we encountered a furious typhoon, which carried away our fore yard and broke some other spars. We however weathered the gale and arrived safely at Casilda, the anchorage place of Manila. After laying here a short time, the brig was sold to George Hubbell, the American consul, and all on board were discharged and paid off their wages. Mr. Hubbell wished me to remain and take charge of the vessel as Captain, for a voyage to Valparaiso. All the rest went back to Boston, excepting the carpenter, cook, and a mulatto boy who was shipped as steward when we arrived in Batavia. He agreed to stay if I would let him go as one of the crew, which I did.

I never saw any of them afterwards as I recollect, excepting George Tilden, whom I met many years after in Boston at the Club, one evening. He told me he never made another voyage, his father having died soon after, leaving his children ample fortunes. Mr. Bowers became a Captain and sailed from Providence for some years, and then kept a ship chandler store there. Capt. Magee had married Miss Louisa Deblois, some years before he joined the *Cadet*. He never went to sea again, but died soon after.

There were several American vessels loading for the States when we arrived, and the crew were distributed among them. The *Cadet* was soon loaded with sugars, white wax, and Manila goods in general. I had much difficulty in procuring a crew, sailors being very scarce, when one forenoon I got a note from Mr. Hubbell requesting me to come up [to] the city, as some men had offered as sailors, and he wished me to see them and ship them. There were four fine looking men and they signed the articles and came on board. A very good man by the name of Richards was shipped as first mate, and a young man by the name of Ripley, who had been a voyage or two as a sailor, but was then a clerk in Mr. Hubbell's counting room, wanted to go as second mate. A very pleasant man by the name of Bennit was supercargo, and a young brother of Mr. Hubbell was his clerk. The ship's company consisted of Captain, two mates, supercargo and clerk, carpenter, cook, and steward and nine sailors, seventeen in all.

I had been trying to dispose of the mermaid, but could not get a price to suit me. Finally I made a sale to two American Captains in this way, valuing it at one thousand dollars, I retained one half interest and they each one quarter. A written agreement was drawn up, each having a copy. The vessels were bound to Boston. The mermaid was to be exhibited as a show, each sharing according to their interest, in the net profit. I never saw the Captains or the show afterwards, but I heard they exhibited it in Boston and about the country. A cousin of mine went to see it whilst it was exhibited in Boston, and was surprised by being told by one of the Captains that he bought it from the man who caught it, Capt. Chas. Tyng. I never knew what became of it, or the Captains. I received two hundred and fifty dollars from each of them, for their shares, but never saw any profits.

In my agreement with Mr. Hubbell, I had the privilege of two tons measure in the hold of the brig for my adventure, and one hundred dollars per month wages. I invested my money in Manila goods, such as hats & cigar cases made of straw, mats, and wax, for my adventure, amounting to about one thousand five hundred dollars.

Everything being ready, I received my instructions from Mr. Hubbell to proceed direct to Valparaiso in Chile, and to be governed by Mr. Bennit in all things connected with the disposition of the cargo and the vessel after our arrival. Nothing more occurring, we got under way and sailed for the Straits of Sunda.

I came to anchor at Angier Point and filled up my water, as I had a passage of about nine thousand miles to make. To avoid the southeast winds which prevailed in the Pacific at that season, I had to run south of them, to find westing winds. I therefore run south of New Holland now called Australia, and further south of the New Zealand Isles, which lie nearly fifty degrees south.

We experienced a terrific gale going round Van Diemen's Land. The wind was so violent, and the seas run so high, I was obliged to send the vessel under bare poles, and during the night a heavy sea boarded us over the stern, washing the helmsman away and breaking his leg. The vessel swung off in the trough of the sea. I run forward myself to let the lee braces main go, trusting that I might lay her to. As I was abreast of the cambose a heavy sea came on board and washed me through the cambose house, which no doubt prevented me from being washed overboard. Fortunately, no one was lost, and the vessel laid to like a duck until the gale was over. We passed to the southward of New Zealand, and Antipodes Islands, finding good westerly winds and fine weather, when we had been out one hundred days.

One Saturday forenoon just after breakfast, as Mr. Bennit and my-self were standing by the capstan, the lad Dimpsey came aft, and wanted to speak to me, but did not wish to say anything on deck. I told him to go down in the cabin, and Mr. Bennit and I went down. He told us that in the night, he overheard Horseman, and George, planning a mutiny, that Luis and Williams were with them. They were to attack Mr. Ripley in his watch on deck when the rest were asleep in the cabin, knock him down with a handspike, and throw him overboard, then kill me, Mr. Richards, Mr. Bennit, and young Hubbell, and take the vessel into Chiloe.

I did not at first give any credit to this story, told him he had been dreaming. Mr. Bennit questioned him very closely, and from something he had noticed among the crew had some suspicions that there was something wrong. I did not, neither did Mr. Richards, who was called into the consultation. We had always found the crew as good as any that we had ever sailed with. Dimpsey was very much alarmed that they would kill him.

After talking the matter over for sometime, we finally decided that it was necessary to take some steps to ascertain the truth, and the first thing was to see to our arms, to examine and load our pistols. I felt certain of the correctness [of] all but those four who Dimpsey named. They were the four who offered themselves to Mr. Hubbell, who sent for us to see them and ship them. They had given me no cause to suspect anything of the kind during the voyage. I sent for the carpenter, in whom I had the utmost confidence, and questioned him. He was an American and had been on board since we left Boston. He had no confidence in those four men, and agreed with us that something should be done.

It was Saturday forenoon, and one watch below, and they were cleaning out the forecastle. The other watch were employed in jobs about the rigging. I told the carpenter to get the irons ready, in case they should be needed, and sent Mr. Richards forward to watch the forecastle. He had his loaded pistols in his pockets, ready to shoot in case they attempted to rush aft. Mr. Ripley was ordered to send Luis down in the cabin to move some trunks. He was a huge rough looking fellow, a Spaniard, and one of the four who were suspected, and it was necessary to secure him before we took any further steps. As soon as he came down, I took him by the collar, and ordered the carpenter to put the irons on him, and to my surprise he made no resistance, which I had expected. He seemed perfectly overcome, not saying a word. He was secured to a staple in the cabin floor. Young Hubbell was to remain in the cabin, on guard and to look out for the loaded muskets, which we had put in the state rooms to be ready in case we should require them.

I, Mr. Ripley, Mr. Bennit, and the carpenter went forward to the forecastle. Mr. Richards was there on the look out. I called Horseman up on deck. He was an Englishman, the largest man on board. I told the carpenter to put the irons on him. He became very violent, said no man should put irons on him. He dared me to shoot him, and was in the act to spring on me, when both the carpenter and Mr. Richards sprung upon him, and I striking him with my sword at the same time, he was overpowered and secured in irons. The others were called up one at a time, and put in irons. They saw that resistance was useless, and made none. I had only the four named secured in irons. Horseman's arm was badly cut by my sword, which I attended to as soon as he was secured. We then had their chests brought up and examined. We found arms of some kind or other in each of their chests, mostly Malay krisses, a crooked dirk, or short sword, generally poisoned on the point. In Horseman's chest we found the log book of the English brig *Elizabeth*, of Hull, England, of which he was captain, and some letters.

I then took George, who was a young Englishman, one side, and with Mr. Bennit cross questioned him until he confessed the whole plot. It seems that Horseman, that was not his right name, was the leader, that he had been captain of a vessel, which he sold at the island of Chiloe, and that he arranged the plan in Manila, before they shipped, to take possession of the brig, and carry her into Chiloe. We made him tell the story over in the presence [of] all of us, so that in case it was necessary, we all could be witness.

We were then some three hundred miles from Valparaiso, and the weather became stormy. We were extremely puzzled what to do with the prisoners, as the vessel was stowed full of cargo, there was no space left open below, excepting the cabin, and the forecastle, and we had no place to put them, but had to confine them in some way on deck. We took a chain that was used to secure the anchor (called the shank painter) and secured the two ends to the waterways across the after part of the deck, and then put the bolt of the irons through a link of the chain. This secured them thoroughly. We then arranged to keep our pistols always with us loaded, and made them understand that if they made any attempt to get loose they would be shot. We also had to watch sharp four of the others, as of course we could not tell how far they were implicated, or how much they sympathized with the prisoners.

It was over a week before we arrived at Valparaiso. We had a miserable time of it, as we were all obliged to keep a strict watch night and day. We came to an anchor too far from the shore, although it appeared to us that we were near the other vessels which were at anchor there. We could get no pilot, and [had] to do the best we could without one. I did not know that the bottom of the harbour run off from the beach at an angle of about 35° and when my anchor was down I sounded and found there was near seventy fathom.

As soon as we were anchored Mr. Bennit and I went on shore, he to the consignees, and I to the American consul, as he was called, for there was no American consul at that time to any of the Spanish colonies. He was an Irishman with a wooden leg, having lost his leg in the war of 1812. I related to him the circumstances of my situation, and desired him to have soldiers sent on board and take the mutinous sailors and put them in prison. He said that was impossible, as there had been an earthquake a short time before, which had broke the prison down, and all the prisoners were loose about the city.

I told him something must be done as they were confined on deck, having no room below, and as they spoke Spanish, they were in communication with boats alongside, and that we were in fear that they might be liberated, and some of us lose our lives. He sent one of his clerks with me to see the governor of the place. We found him in the navy yard, a very ordinary looking fellow dressed in sailor's clothes, looking at the workmen caulking the frigate *O'Higgins*, which was fitting out as a Chilean frigate. The Chileans were then fighting for their liberty from the Spanish government, and Admiral Cochrane was expected there to command the Chilean squadron. He said he could do nothing, but if they would ship on board the frigate, they might.

We went back to the consulate. He seemed angry that the vessel was not consigned to him. I told him I had nothing to do with the consignment of the vessel or cargo, as Mr. Bennit was the supercargo, and had all to say about that. He said he did not see how he could help me, but that the *Franklin*, man of war, Commodore Stewart was daily expected, and that I must keep them until her arrival, when they should be put on board, and taken to the United States for trial.

I then went to the ship chandlery store kept by a Mr. Mackay, an Englishman, a very good man, and had some talk with him. He said it was impossible to do anything with them on shore, as it was as the consul said, but there was an English man of war in the harbour, and advised me to go on board and see the Commander, as he thought he would take them on board and keep them until the *Franklin* arrived. I then went on board of this man of war, [and] saw the Commander. He said he could not take American sailors from an American vessel. I told him that they were Englishmen. He said if they would ship on board the vessel he would take them, otherwise he could have nothing to do with them. I then went on board, as it was towards evening I could do no more.

We kept a good watch that night, and in the morning a Captain of an English schooner came on board, was told by Mr. Mackay that we had some sailors to be discharged, and [said] that he was in want of men and would like to ship them. Of course I could do nothing then, but after he left, I had a talk with the prisoners. I told them the *Franklin* 74 gun ship was daily expected, and that I could put them on board of her, and that they would be taken to the United States and tried for mutiny, and that I had proof enough to hang them in any court, but I had saved our lives and brought my vessel safe in port, and owed them no ill will. It was no object for me to have them tried, and if they would ship on board of the English schooner, and go away, I would give them their liberty, and the wages due them.

They seemed very grateful, and promised me most faithfully that they would do so. I then let them out of irons, gave them their money, and they left the vessel, seemingly full of thanks and gratitude.

SOME THREE OR FOUR DAYS HAD PASSED since I had got clear of the mutineers, and as I had not seen or heard anything about them, I supposed they had gone off in the English schooner, when one morning, as the mates and crew were at work in the hold breaking out cargo to be ready for the lighter when she came alongside, and I was walking the quarter deck, I heard a boat row up to the gang way. I looked over the side to see what it was, and there saw two of the fellows in the boat, George and Williams.

I asked them what they wanted. They replied that they heard the carpenter was sick, and came off to see him. I knew that was a lie, but as I had parted with them in peace, I thought it not worthwhile to make trouble with them, and turned round and walked again, thinking they would go forward to see the carpenter, but when I turned to walk forward again, I saw them still standing at the gang way. As I stepped up to them I asked them, "Why don't you go and see the carpenter?" George sprung towards me with doubled fists, saying, "It is not the carpenter we want to see, but you." I received his blow with my left arm, and with my right knocked him down on the deck. The cook who was standing near the cambose with an iron ladle in his hand, seeing George attack me, sprang aft, and at the same time struck Williams a stunning blow with the ladle which put him down. We then drove them into the boat.

George, when he got down in the boat, was extremely overbearing in his language, making threats what he would do with me. I told him to shove off at once, and as he would not obey me, struck him with the man rope which was hanging down the gangway. It hit him on the cheek, and made quite a cut in the face, which bled down over his shirt and trousers, which were of light colour, giving him a bloody appearance. They then went on shore, to the Captain of the port, to make a complaint of the ill usage of their Captain.

The Captain of the port sent for me to come to his office. I went on shore to get my friend Mackay to go with me. As I went up the steps from the boat I saw in front of me a stranger beckoning to me to go with him. I did not, but watched him, till I saw him go into a drinking place where sat Horseman and Luis. I found Mr. Mackay in his store, and asked him to go round to the Captain of the port with me, which he willingly did. When we got there, George and Williams were there, the former covered with blood.

The Captain of the port being busy, we had to wait a little while. Soon a young Chilean naval officer commenced a conversation with me in good English, told me he had been educated in New York & asked me what was the matter. I related to him the affair. He said he would go in and see the Capt. of the port. He soon came out and told me to go on board of my vessel, that the Capt. of the port said, if these fellows were not gone in 24 hours he would put them on board of the *O'Higgins*. This was told to them.

As Mr. Mackay and I were walking up the beach to the landing place, these fellows followed us, swearing and threatening what they would do. When they came pretty near, evidently with the intention of attacking us, as they were under the influence of liquor, I turned round, drew my pistol, and pointing it to them, told them if they came any nearer I would shoot them. This kept them away from me until I reached my boat. I did not go on shore again for several days, and never saw them afterward. Mr. Mackay told me they shipped on board of a whale ship that had sailed.

About a year afterwards I read in a newspaper of the trial and hanging of two men for the mutiny and murder of the Capt. and officers of the whale ship *Globe*, relating the whole story about as follows. Four men shipped on board the ship *Globe*, a whaler in Valparaiso. After being out a few weeks, they rose upon the Captain and mates, took possession of the ship, went to an island in the Pacific ocean, and went on shore. In a short time after, these mutineers being on shore, the original crew cut the cable and made sail, for a port in South America. As soon as the owners heard of it, they petitioned our government to send a vessel for them. The U.S. schooner *Dolphin*, which was on the

Pacific coast, was sent for them, and brought two of them, the other two had been killed, to Boston.

I FOUND A READY MARKET for my adventure, selling all that I had at an immense profit, on board of the vessel, the purchasers coming on board and taking them on shore, paying cash as they received them. We stayed there about a month, the cargo being all landed, and a good opportunity offering to sell the brig, and Mr. Bennit having a power of attorney from Mr. Hubbell, he sold her to the Chilean government. He took good care of Dimpsey, as he considered that he saved his life.

The *Franklin* 74 gun ship, Commodore Stewart, which had been on the Pacific station for three years, was now relieved by Commodore Hull, and bound to New York, from Lima, stopped at Valparaiso on her passage. I applied to the Commodore for a passage. He said that the government ships did not take passengers, but if I could arrange with any of the messes, he would have no objection to my going. I arranged with the sailmaker to join his mess, all the other messes were full. The mates and crew were discharged and paid their wages. I parted with Mr. Bennit and Mr. Hubbell at the hotel where they were staying, and took my things on board of the *Franklin*.

THE *FRANKLIN* WAS A SPLENDID SHIP, with a crew and officers all told, of about five hundred persons. I found I had got in a very good mess, the sail maker a young man, and very pleasant in his manners. He had a large room on the lower deck. The vessel had three decks. I had a very good berth. I do not remember his name. His wife was with him. She seldom came below to the room, as they had a room on the gun deck which she liked better. Our mess consisted of the petty officers, sail maker, boatswain, armourer, & carpenter. I paid my share of the expense of the mess. They were all good fellows, and I had a good time.

The upper deck was called the spar deck. On the after part was the poop containing the Commodore's rooms, and office. He had his

family on board, Mrs. Stewart, and two children, who had their rooms
on the next deck below, called the upper gun deck. On the next deck
below called the lower gun deck was the ward room, or cabin for the
lieutenants, and the deck below was called the orlop deck on which were
the midshipmen's quarters, or mess rooms. All these rooms were in the
after part of the ship. The petty officer's rooms were in the forward part.
The hospital and surgeon's room was on the upper gun deck forward.

The crew was divided in watches, the same as on board of merchant
vessels. They slept in hammocks on the gun decks amidships. Every
morning they were laced up and taken on deck and put into the ham-
mock nettings, on the rails each side. In the evening at eight o'clock
they were piped down. All orders to the crew were given through the
boatswain mates, with their pipes or whistles.

The sailing master and surgeon messed in the ward room with the
lieutenants. The first lieutenant was named Hunter. His situation on
board was similar to a Captain of a merchantman, has all to say respecting the management of the ship, does not stand a watch. The sailing master, whose name was Peck, has all to do with the navigation of
the ship. There were eight or ten lieutenants, and about a dozen midshipmen. I do not remember the names of hardly any of the officers.
Goldsborough was fourth and Sands was fifth. As Goldsborough and I
were school mates when boys, we renewed our acquaintance, and had
pleasant conversations of old times. In the ward room was a passenger,
Captain Borroughs. We used to be together a good deal of the time,
and we were company for one another.

We sailed from Valparaiso, & had a good passage round Cape Horn.
We had not been out long before Mrs. Stewart heard that I was on
board, and sent for me. I went up to her cabin, and sent in my name. It
was a curious meeting. As I entered one door, she was standing in the
door opposite. I bowed, and she bowed. We stood there some time
bowing. She finally advanced, and asked if my name was Tyng. I told
her yes. "The son of Dudley A. Tyng?" I said, "Yes." She then gave
me her hand, and showed me to a seat, said she knew my family very
well, and always felt under great obligations to my grandfather Higginson and his wife, who took charge of her in England and brought her

home. She was the daughter of Judge Tudor. They lived in Belknap St., not far from where we lived before we moved to Cambridge. I remembered her, or of hearing about her when I was a boy.

Mrs Stewart was always very kind to me. As it was not prudent that I should go to her cabin, I did not see her again, but most every day I had something sent to me from her table, and she sent her two children to see me. They were very interesting children, Delia, a very pretty little girl about ten years old, and Charles, a smart little fellow of about seven. They used to come down in my room, almost every pleasant day, and I used to amuse them telling stories. We got to be the best of friends, often brought me pleasant messages from their mother. I was on very good terms with most of the midshipmen, and of course some of the lieutenants, and my time passed very pleasantly.

There were several curious occurrences on board during the passage. One clear bright night, in the second lieutenant's watch on deck, we collided with a merchant brig, striking her in the stern. She swung alongside, and got foul of the rigging, and an amusing scene occurred on board of her. The Captain was very angry, called the mate, and ordered the boat cleared away, as he thought she was sinking. The mate, called up out of his sleep, could not well take in the situation, looking up to the high sides of the *Franklin*, asked the Captain "What is it, land?" "No, you fool, cut the boat adrift," and the mate having the axe in his hand to cut the lashings, in his excitement struck the side of the boat, and stove a hole in her. Then there was a funny conversation between the Captain and mate, which caused much amusement to the midshipmen and others on board. She was soon got loose, and floated off.

The *Franklin* was stopped and a boat sent on board. The officer found the captain an old man, very much excited. He wanted to know who commanded that ship. He was told, "Commodore Stewart." "Well, I will tell Congress as soon as I get home, it is a pretty how to do, that a commodore can't keep a better watch in the night, than to run into my brig." Carpenters, caulkers, riggers, and sailmakers were sent on board, and by daylight all was in order, and she proceeded on her voyage. The amusing sayings of that night, were bywords during the rest of the passage.

The *Franklin* was a fast sailer. I had some discussions with sailing master Peck one day about her sailing, when he hove the log, and she run off twelve knots with ease. Nine miles the hour had been the fastest I had ever seen a vessel go before. We had a pleasant run up from the Cape to Rio de Janeiro in Brazil, where we ran in and came to an anchor. As it was supposed the ship would lay there ten days, to fill up the water and provision the ship &c., Captain Borroughs and I concluded to take up our quarters on shore instead of remaining on board during the time. We took a suite of rooms at the Braganza Hotel, and as it were, kept open house for the officers of the ship.

During our stay in port, Admiral Cochrane came on board to visit the ship. He was received in true style. The sailors manned the yards, a salute was fired, and the marines in full dress, with the band playing, received him at the gang way. The Admiral was on his way out in a frigate he had fitted out in England at his own expense, to help the Chileans to gain their independence from Spain. He was an ordinary looking man, middling size, sandy hair, and dark eyes which is generally a good index of a strong character.

Rio is a fine looking city, situated on an inlet from the ocean, about twelve miles inland, on ground a little rising from the shore of a magnificent bay large enough to hold all the navies of the world. There is a peculiar looking hill at the entrance of the harbour called the Sugar Loaf, as it resembles the old fashion sugar loafs. It is not far from the city. Although the sides are steep, it is cultivated on terraces formed from the sides, and is a very pretty sight. We made several little excursions to the interior, visited the tea gardens where the Brazilian government were introducing the tea plant. We visited several coffee estates, and had a good time generally.

The ship being ready, we went on board and sailed for New York. We had rather a funny time when we got up in the vicinity of the West Indies. The officers had been anxious to speak some vessel out from the States, to hear the news, particularly who was the president of the United States. So one day a schooner was seen on the horizon, standing south towards the West Indies. Mr. Peck persuaded the Commodore to let him run the ship down to speak her, which he at first objected to, as the wind was fair for home, but her course was altered towards the vessel and after a chase of two hours, she was overhauled, and hailed.

Everybody was on deck to hear the news. Mr. Peck, with the speaking trumpet, after asking him where from and where bound, asked him who was president of the United States. The Captain was a little confused, and after taking of his hat off & scratching his head, had some conversation with his mate. The Commodore was getting rather impatient waiting for the answer, when the Captain said, "I don't know, the last man I heard of was General Washington." Most of the officers burst out in a roar of laughter, but the Commodore called him a fool, and was mad enough. [He] ordered the course changed, feeling that we had lost some twenty miles on our way home.

In those days there were but few newspapers, and the common people's politics did not reach beyond their own state, and there were no such thing as mails to the Pacific coast, excepting round Cape Horn, and that very seldom, and it was about eight months that the officers were without a word of news, and of course anxious to hear something about home affairs.

We at last arrived on the coast off New York, and took a pilot on board, who gave us all the news, and we soon sailed up the bay and came to an anchor off the battery in New York harbour. I and Capt. Borroughs called upon Commodore Stewart, and thanked him for our passage. He shook hands with us, and wished us success. I had no opportunity to say farewell to Mrs. Stewart, or the children, which I much regretted, as she had been very kind to me, and the children I became very fond of, and they had added much to my pleasure during the passage of about one hundred days. I never saw any of them afterwards, excepting the officers I have mentioned.

I stayed in New York but one day, to get my baggage on shore, and then went on to Newburyport. It took me three days to reach home from New York by the stage route, there were no other ways to travel but by the stage, and that was very slow, as they laid by in the night time. I was received very affectionately by all the family and friends, and it really seemed good to get home after an absence of over two years.

8

The Schooner Zephyr

I N THE COURSE OF A MONTH or six weeks, I called upon the Messrs. Perkins & Co., my old employers, to see if they had any vessel for me. The Colonel was glad to see me, and said they were building a little brig to be called the *Greyhound*, to be employed in the Canton trade, on the coast of China, and he thought they would like to have me take command of her. I liked the idea very much, and went over to Medford where she was being built, to see her. I found that her frame was but just put up, and that it would be two or three months before she could be launched.

I then went home & spent my time pleasantly, as I had purchased a horse and chaise soon after I got home, and could ride about as I pleased, with my sister Mary or any one else. It was in the winter time and we had many good sleigh rides. I occasionally rode up to Boston, and stopped at my grandfather Higginson's, where it was convenient to put up my horse in his stable, and my grandmother particularly requested me to come there and stay.

I used to go out to Medford every week or two to see how the

Greyhound got on, and about the time she was newly finished I happened to meet the Colonel's son Thomas on change. I asked him when the *Greyhound* would be launched. He asked me why I was troubling myself about the *Greyhound*. I said, because his father wished me to go in her. He replied, rather curtly, that his brother [in law] Philip Dumeresque was to go captain of her. I said no more, but was somewhat disappointed.

I remained at home a month or two longer, waiting and hoping for some chance to get a vessel. I felt willing to go even without pay if I could get command of a good vessel. I had frequently cried myself to sleep, after I went to bed, I was so anxious to get employment as a Captain. I sometimes thought of going mate again, but I could not bear the idea of going backwards. About this time, when I was staying at my grandfather's, who seemed to put confidence in me, by letting me do many little things for him, my uncle Stephen Higginson [Jr.], who was there, asked me if I was going to remain idle all summer. The question almost suffocated me. I could make no reply, I was so completely overcome.

I had been at home nearly six months, and it was now the last of May 1825. When I was walking down on the wharves, I saw a fine looking schooner, that I fancied, and the thought came into my mind to enquire if she was for freight or charter. I found that she was for charter. She was called the *Zephyr*, and was one of the old fashioned Boston rigged schooners having standing royal yards, of 160 tons burden, a rig unknown to navigators of the present day. I chartered her of the owners, Bixby & Valentine, for $240 per month, $1.50 per ton.

I decided to lay her on for Amsterdam, as there had been a great inundation owing to the breaking away of the dykes in that vicinity. There were several towns under water, and an immense quantity of merchandise and provisions were destroyed. I advertised the vessel for that port, and soon had more applications for freight than the vessel could take, so that I had my choice, and took none that was not consigned to me.

The vessel was soon loaded. She lay at Central Wharf, opposite the Messrs. Perkins & Co. store, and at that time they had purchased a new ship that was just launched, and they were in a hurry to send her out to Canton. Mr. Samuel Cabot, one of the firm, came on board of the *Zephyr*, and offered me every inducement to take command of her. I told him I was sorry not to be able, but my engagements were such that I could not. He offered to take charge of the business of the *Zephyr*, and that I could put in whoever I was a mind to for Captain. The offer was very tempting, to be captain of a fine ship in their employ, to China, and I would have jumped at it a few weeks before, but now I was both captain and supercargo. I had the satisfaction of telling him the reason I gave up the idea of going in the *Greyhound*.

On the 10th of June 1825, the crew on board, and the vessel all ready for sea, we made sail for Holland. The mate was a man of about forty-five years, a good natured sort of a man, but full of the superstitious notions of old sailors in those days. The crew were a mixed set of various nations, and most of them were under the effects of intoxication, and disposed to be unruly, so much so that I hesitated to go to sea with them in that state, but my mate seemed to think there was no risk, so I kept on. By the time I got off Cape Cod, it commenced blowing a gale of wind, and we had to shorten sail. I found my men in such a state, that we came near losing our masts and all our sails before I could get the vessel under snug sail.

There was nothing particular occurred after getting the crew into a healthy condition until we arrived in the English Channel, when off the Land's End, in a very thick fog, between one and two in the night, we collided with a Dutch brig which was bound out of the Channel. It was blowing a fresh breeze, and both vessels were going pretty fast, head on, one towards the other. We just grazed one another, carrying away some of our forward bulwarks, and doing some injury to the other vessel. Had we struck one another squarely, which we should have done, had either vessel been a few feet from the course they were steering, both vessels would have been stove to pieces, and probably everyone perished.

We finally arrived off the coast of Holland, and took a pilot into the Helder, which is the sea port of Amsterdam. We had a passage of about forty days, upon the whole a rather pleasant one. The Helder is situated on a small arm of the North Sea near to the coast. This entrance continues up several miles until it enters the Zuider Zee, a large inland lake, or sea, on which the city of Amsterdam is situated. All vessels had to go round through the Zuider Zee, to get to the city. This was a circuitous, as well as a long difficult passage between seventy and eighty miles, from the Helder to Amsterdam, and sometimes vessels were weeks in getting up. There were no such thing as a steam boat to tow vessels in those days.

The Dutch government had been some years in constructing a ship canal from the city to the Helder, which was just finished, and a government vessel had come through a few days previous to our arrival. This canal shortened the distance more than one half from the Helder to the city. I got permission, after some trouble, to go up with my vessel to the city through the canal. I was strongly opposed by the board of pilots, as they saw the canal would ruin their business and they could not well think that an American vessel should be the first merchantman to break their rules of pilotage. But by the good management and influence of the agents which I had employed on my arrival at the Helder, my vessel was permitted to go up. One of the conditions was, that I was to employ one of the Zuider Zee pilots, and pay half pilotage to him. I supposed this was to pacify the board of pilots. I believe this established the rule which has been kept up to the present day.

Although he had nothing to pilot, as he knew no more about the canal than I did, yet he was very useful as an interpreter, as I did not understand a word of Dutch, and he managed about the horses, and the tow lines much better than I could have done, and steered the vessel through the draws at the bridges, of which there were more than thirty. I had the honour of flying the first American flag through that canal. It is a superior piece of work & passes through a thickly populated country. We passed through a number of villages, and one large town called Alkmaar, besides many farms, with the farm houses near the bank of the canal.

The great numbers of bridges we had to pass through made it slow and tiresome work, but the whole thing was so novel, to be drawn through the water by four horses, and the passing through the populated country made it so extremely interesting and pleasant that we did not mind the work or trouble. It was very amusing to see the inhabitants crowd the sides of the canal, to see an American vessel pass their houses, and to be so cordially greeted by all, old and young, the young men and maidens standing on the banks, swinging their hats & bonnets bidding us welcome. They had never seen the American flag before. When we stopped, as we had to several times for other small craft passing through the draws, or [to] tie up for the night to the banks of the canal, they would come on board and bring pails of sweet fresh milk, which was a great treat to us, after a long passage on the sea, also fruit and bread, for which it was difficult to make them take any pay.

We were the best part of two days, getting up to the city of Amsterdam. Several of the bridges were damaged by striking the sides when going through the draws, and a big bill for damages was presented, but was not paid, as it was decided the vessel was not responsible. The harbour was pretty well filled with vessels, several American amongst them, who hoisted their flags, giving me a good reception. They all congratulated me on coming through the canal, as they had been told that the canal was only for men of war, and that foreign merchant vessels would not be permitted to go through it.

We soon got our little vessel safely moored, and we were boarded by all kind of tradesmen, handing their cards and urging us to employ them when anything was wanting in their line. I engaged a boatman. He was an oldish man, and attended on the American vessels. He spoke English, and proved to be very serviceable, as all vessels are moored to dolphins, some ways from the shore, and require a boat to go to and from the vessel.

All captains lived on shore at the hotels and boarding houses in those days. I took lodgings at Madam Kurtz, where the Americans generally stopped. Mr. Nathan Bridge, a merchant in Boston, shipped a large portion of the cargo, on condition that I should consign the vessel to his friends Messrs. John Hodshon, & Co., when I arrived in Amsterdam. He gave me a letter of introduction to them, which I presented as soon as I arrived at the city. I found Mr. Hodshon an elderly gentleman, who received me most cordially. His son was in partnership with him, a young man, a few years older than myself. I handed them all the letters and invoices of the cargo which I had brought.

My adventure was tea. Mr. H. told me I could not have invested my money in anything which would have paid a better profit. We talked over business matters for some time. I told him I wished for the greatest dispatch, as I was paying for the charter of the vessel by the month, and to advertise her for freight to Boston. They made prompt arrangements for discharging the vessel, and to procure another cargo back to Boston.

During my stay in Amsterdam I had an exceedingly pleasant time, being invited several times to dine at Mr. Hodshon's, whose family were extremely pleasant, enjoying all the luxury and elegance that wealth could procure. The family consisted of his wife, a very refined and handsome old lady, and several sons and daughters, most of them married, and with families of children who used to join in the dinner parties.

They were all highly educated, speaking English, and various other languages. They had a high opinion of Americans, and knew much more of their history than I did. Mr. Hodshon told me that he had followed the practice from their childhood, to cause them to speak a different language each day at the dinner table. One day all must speak English, another day French, Italian &c. It was very amusing to me, to witness the excitement particularly among the younger members, whilst going through the conversation, of asking a question in one language and answering in another. It was surprising how perfect the young children spoke English. Of course I could not form any opinion of their proficiency in the other languages, but had every reason to think them very expert, as they seldom required correction.

I made the acquaintance of Mr. Nathaniel Tucker, who was super-cargo of the brig *Eight Sons*, from Boston. He was a much older man than me, and a brother of Mr. Richard Tucker of Boston. I used to meet him most every day whilst the vessels lay in Amsterdam. Mr Tucker was procuring a cargo for the brig to Boston, and felt a little opposed to my advertising the *Zephyr* for the same port. I asked his opinion of what was best for me to invest the proceeds from my adventure of tea in. "Oh," says he, "in seltzer water by all means." I asked him if he was buying any for his cargo. He evaded answering direct, by saying that he had not began to purchase yet. I mistrusted his advice and luckily did not buy any. In a few years after, his son was a mate with me in the *Bashaw.*

I consulted Mr. Hodshon about my investment. He thought the most sure thing was linseed oil, as there had not been the usual quantity shipped to the United States of late. I then requested him to invest the proceeds from my tea, and the balance of the freight money, after all port charges and disbursements had been paid, in good linseed oil, which he did. In about three weeks after my arrival, my business was finished, the vessel being loaded with a full cargo at a very good freight, one third of which was linseed oil. All but mine was to Nathan Bridge & Co. Mr. Hodshon did not charge me any commission on the sale of my tea, and when I spoke about it, he said they never charged a commission on a Captain's adventure.

The vessel being loaded, and everything being ready, a pilot came on board and took her over to the entrance of the canal, ready to go down to the Helder. I called on Messrs. Hodshon & Co., for my papers. All was ready, and I took leave of them, thanking them for their great kindness to me during my stay in Amsterdam. We passed through the canal to the Helder, [and] had a very pleasant time. Several of the farmers who lived on the banks recognized me and the vessel, and with their families bid me good bye and wished me a pleasant voyage. All this was very agreeable and left a very happy impression on my mind.

We sailed out from the Helder into the North Sea, through the English Channel, into the Atlantic Ocean, having a fair wind and fine weather. Nearly all the twenty four hours it was light, as the sun in that high latitude rose in the morning about 3 o'clock and set about 9 in the evening. We sailed along towards home with a fair wind and good prospects of a short passage. When about mid-passage, I was called up between one and two o'clock in the night by the mate, the air having become quite cold. I tried the temperature of the water with my thermometer and found the water several degrees colder than the atmosphere. I at once suspected that we were in the vicinity of ice, and as it was quite thick and foggy, I thought it not prudent to run, and turned round, and stood back the way we had come, as I considered that the safest, as I could form no idea which way the ice was from me.

At daylight I turned the vessel back again in the course we had been steering, and in the course of an hour, we discovered an immense ice berg, which proved by measurement with the quadrant to be over one hundred feet in height, and as near as I could judge, about five miles in circumference, and as ice floats four fifths under water, and one fifth above, it must have been about six hundred feet in thickness, and at the time we turned about, we could not have been more than a mile from it, steering right towards it, at the rate of about six miles the hour, so that we should have been dashed to pieces in a few minutes had we not turned the vessel round at the time we did.

It was a most magnificent sight. I sailed by it, giving it a berth of between two and three miles, and when about abreast, the sun shone out clear, giving us one of the most gorgeous sights imaginable. With my spy glass I could see streams of water rushing down the sides into the ocean, and the appearance of castles, and turrets, of all imaginable shapes, with the bright sun shining upon them, was wonderful, and beautiful in the extreme. It was about in the latitude of 51° north and 40° west longitude. It must have been of immense size when it first left the Arctic Ocean, some months previous, and as it was in the direct track of vessels passing from Europe to America, there may have been some vessels not so fortunate as we were, to discover its vicinity in time to escape shipwreck.

We arrived all right in Boston, having had a very good passage of less than the usual time from Amsterdam. The vessel was entered at the custom house, and the crew were discharged and paid their wages. The old mate, I do not remember his name, I met some twenty years afterwards. He had an oyster stand in front of the Quincy Market.

It was the custom in those days, to enter on a book at the news room, the arrival of all vessels from foreign ports, and a list of the cargo, and the names of the consignees, so that all the merchants might see what had arrived, and who had the articles for sale, and of course my adventure of oil consigned "to the master" was on the list. I found that Mr. Bridge seemed much interested about my affairs. He told me that he and myself had all the oil there was on board, and that the article was very scarce, and that we must not sell under 80 cents the gallon, and that he should put his into the store and hold for that price.

I made the calculation for what I could sell mine for. I found I could sell at about 60 cents and lose no money, and I was determined to sell. Several asked me what I asked for my oil. I said 80 cents the gallon. They turned away. Mr. David Henshaw met me on change. He was a large dealer in drugs, oils, and other articles. He had been trying to buy Mr. Bridge's lot. He asked me what I would take for mine. I told him 80 cents. He said, "I will give you 78 cents cash the gallon, and receive it from the vessel, on the wharf." I at once closed, as I saw it would net me more than 80 cents, as I would be saved the expense of storage, cartage, leakage, and other expenses. The vessel was soon discharged of her cargo, the various freights collected, and Messrs. Bixby & Valentine was paid the amount of the charter. They offered to sell me the *Zephyr*, for $1000, and I thought seriously of purchasing her, as I found I had more than that amount by the voyage.

9

More Pirates and a Sudden Squall

JUST AT THAT TIME the *Eight Sons* arrived from Amsterdam. She had on board a large invoice of linseed oil consigned to different persons. Mr. Bridge was rather annoyed when he found I had sold to Mr. Henshaw. I found he had depended upon him as a purchaser. He had heard that I was in treaty to buy the *Zephyr*. He proposed to buy half of a larger vessel with me, and desired me to look out for one.

I fancied the brig *Eight Sons*. She was three years old, coppered, built in Duxbury by Mr. Sampson, a well known ship builder, who had eight sons, and named the vessel for them. She was 220 tons measurement, which in those days was considered a good sized vessel. I proposed her to Mr. Bridge, who thought well of the idea to buy her, if she could be purchased at a reasonable price. We found that $8000 was the lowest she could be bought for, and we finally bought her, one half in the name of Nathan Bridge & Co. and one half in my name, and I took charge of her, as soon as her cargo was discharged.

About this time a fast sailing ship belonging to Theodore Lyman & Co., arrived from Amsterdam, with a large portion of her cargo in linseed oil. This vessel had not arrived in Amsterdam when the *Eight Sons* left there. She had a remarkable short passage, and was but a short time in Amsterdam. She was commanded by Capt. [Abel] Coffin, who afterwards brought the Siam Twins to this country. He was noted for making short passages. These arrivals of oil had the effect of reducing the price of the article. Mr. Bridge had put his into the store, and had kept it several months before he was able to sell, suffering leakage, and many other expenses, and then having to dispose of it at a serious loss.

The *Eight Sons* proved upon examination after her cargo was discharged a superior vessel, being double decked, and well found in sails and rigging, and we fitted her out for a freighting vessel. I had made several short visits to Newburyport. The family were all well, and glad to see me. My old father in particular rejoiced with my success, and began to think that I would be something, although I had not gone through the Harvard University.

About this time we heard of the murder of my friend Captain Selfridge, on board of a brig he commanded bound to Europe, by his mutinous crew. This caused great excitement in Boston where the vessel belonged. We had just got the particulars before I sailed, which were as follows. The vessel was on her way, about half passage, when two of the crew came down in the cabin, and finding Capt. Selfridge in his berth, asleep, they struck him with the cook's axe several blows until they had killed him. This was in the afternoon when he had gone below to get a little rest. They had killed the mate and thrown his body overboard, before they went down the cabin. They then run the vessel in near the land off Halifax, took the money out, some $25,000, and put it in the boat. They all got in the boat, having previously scuttled the vessel, so that she sunk, and landed near Halifax. In a few days, they were taken up by the authorities, and one of them turned state's evidence, and gave the above particulars. This made a deep impression on my mind, as Selfridge was about my age, and I was well acquainted with him.

I at once had my state room in the *Eight Sons* so fixed that I could fasten the door, which was on the slide, without entirely shutting it, so as to have the air, and to prevent anyone coming in without waking me up, and I always kept a good pair of pistols in cleats at the head of my berth, and never went to my room, either night or day, for a nap without fastening my door.

The brig being ready with a crew shipped, we sailed in ballast for City Point on James River, for a freight of tobacco to Europe. The chief mate's name was Libbey. I thought he was a first rate man, and put confidence in him, but he proved to be a great villain. The second mate was an inferior man, and the crew of eight men were ordinary. I soon lost confidence in all of them. We arrived off the capes of the Chesapeake in about a week, and I took a pilot for Hampton Roads, and there took a river pilot for City Point, which is about fifteen miles from Petersburg, and about twenty five from Richmond.

I took lodgings on shore at Mrs. Wood's, who kept a boarding house. I there met Mr. George Delius of the firm, Gavecoot & Delius, German merchants established in Petersburg. He offered me a freight to Bremen of tobacco stems, which I at once accepted, as it was a little above the quoted rates, although on account of the large hogsheads in which the stems were packed it did not prove so good as I had calculated, for they made bad stowage, and I could not stow as much as I expected.

I found several Newburyport vessels laying at City Point loading cargoes for Europe. There was Capt. Micajah Lunt in his father's ship the *Golconda*, Mr. Francis Tod's ship the *Allioth*, old Captain Graves in command. Mr. Edward Rand had a ship there, Captain Clarkson, so that I found many of my townsmen, for company. I was there about a month before the vessel was loaded. This was in the fall of 1825, when I sailed for Bremen.

Nothing particular that I recollect occurred during the passage across the Atlantic or through the English Channel and North Sea, until we got off the Helgoland island, where I expected to have found a pilot for the river Weser, the entrance of which was about fifteen miles. The wind was blowing a gale, constantly on the increase, and the seas were running high. We saw the low land ahead, and as the wind was blowing towards it, there seemed no escape from ship wreck, when most fortunately I discovered the pilot hoy at anchor right

lee shore

ahead. I run for her, under bare poles, and hailed her. The sea was running so high that they could not put a pilot on board, but gave me the course to steer, which I followed, and brought my vessel to anchor just within the entrance of the river, where I found the water smoother. The seas had been rolling in on both sides filling the decks, and it was a great relief me to find myself safe at anchor. Soon after a pilot came on board, and expressed his surprise that I could have brought my vessel safely in.

We weighed anchor, and sailed up to a town on the river called Brake. This was about fifteen or twenty miles from Bremen, and as far as loaded vessels could go, and about twenty miles from the entrance of the river. There is now a fine harbour made at the entrance of the river called Bremerhaven. There were a number of vessels moored to the banks of the river at Brake, among them several Americans. After my vessel was well secured with her anchors, and other fasts, I took the first opportunity to go up to the city of Bremen, to call on the consignees, Messrs. Everhard Delius & Co., which was in a small steamer, which left Brake the following day after I arrived.

I had never heard the German language spoken before, and was much amused to find it corresponded with English backwards, in many of their phrases. For instance, to make fast a rope, they would say "fast making," and to haul in a rope, "inhauling," and several other similar expressions. On the steamboat, I noticed a number eating their breakfasts, and as I had not eaten any, I felt hungry and asked the steward to bring me something to eat. He did not seem to understand, when after thinking a moment, I thought I would adopt the English backward plan, and asked him for a steak beef. He at once understood me, replying "steak de beefen" and immediately brought me a nice beef steak, which I relished exceedingly, after living on salt beef for six weeks.

As soon as I arrived to the city, I went to the counting room of the Messrs. Delius & Co. and delivered my letter of introduction. I found Mr. Everhard Delius, the head of the house, a man of about sixty years, and of very pleasing manners. I gave him the package of letters, invoices of the cargo, and other papers which Messrs. Gavecoot &

Delius had given me when I sailed from City Point, and whilst he was looking over them I had an opportunity to look round the counting room, which was more extensive that any I had seen. It appeared more like a school room. There were some twenty five or thirty clerks, sitting at desks, all of the same patterns, and in rows, like school desks, and all seemed to be busy writing.

It was in the fall of the year, and the farmers were still busy getting in their crops. I noticed that the women worked the same as the men at out door work. I quite liked the German country people. They seemed very industrious & good natured, always cleanly and tidily dressed, particularly on Sundays. The meeting house was a good sized wooden building with two steeples exactly alike, which to me had a very curious, as well as antique look. It was called the two sisters. I was told that it was built by two sisters in memory of their parents who were lost at sea.

Business was very dull in Bremen at that time, and no freights offering. All the vessels consigned to the house were discharged, and the Captains were anxiously waiting for some thing to turn up to give them business for their vessels.

Every morning we used to go, all together, to the counting room, and take our seats in a row of chairs set out for us. We generally marched in, one after the other, the oldest first. He would sit down in the furthest chair from the door, and each one would take a seat in the order they entered. I always managed to be the last, as I saw Mr. Delius did not like it. After sitting a little while, the first Captain would go up to Mr. Delius, and ask him if there was anything offering for his vessel. Mr. D. would say "No, Captain, not yet," or some such answer, and the Capt. would return to his chair, and the next would go up, and so through the whole of them. I would not go up, as I knew that as soon as there was any employment for my vessel he would let me know.

Something like four weeks passed, when Mr. D. sent for me and offered me a charter, from La Guaira, in Venezuela, back to Bremen with a cargo of coffee, at a very fair rate, amounting to something between six and seven thousand dollars, the charterers having the privilege of putting on board what they chose for the outward cargo, without freight, which was to be bales and boxes of dry goods, the lay days in La Guaira to be forty. I thought this very good business, and at once accepted the charter, which was drawn up, and signed by both parties.

I then went down to the vessel, and got everything ready to receive the cargo, which very soon began to be sent down. I did not find every thing in such order as I had expected on board of the vessel, and I lost much confidence in Mr. Libbey the chief mate. The second mate got drunk and I put him forward in the forecastle with the crew, and took a young man from the crew and made him second mate. His name was Bixley, an American, a good sailor, and a promising person. If I could have found a good man to take Mr. Libbey's place, I would have discharged him, but as I could not, I made up my mind to get along with him as well as I could, a great mistake as the sequel will show.

The vessel was finally loaded with a full cargo of manufactured goods, instead of a part of a cargo, as I was led to expect, and most of the goods being linen. It was valued at something like one hundred thousand dollars, and had the current rate of freight been paid, it would have amounted to six or seven thousand dollars, so that my charter was not so good as I had thought when I took it, as I had to pay the expenses of receiving and discharging this large cargo of boxes and bales, and carry it to La Guaira for nothing. There was a German, a middle aged man, I forget his name, who seemed to have something to do with the cargo, wanted to go as a passenger. I took him, although it was against my general rule to take passengers.

On receiving my papers and dispatches from Mr. D., I took my leave of Mrs. D. and others whom I had become acquainted with in Bremen, and sailed for La Guaira. It was about the middle of January 1826. I soon found my passenger to be a very disagreeable fellow. He and Mr. Libbey became very intimate, and the crew were unruly, and I made up my mind that I was to have a troublesome passage.

The brig was well armed for a merchant vessel, as all vessels were required to be by the policy of insurance, as in those days there were piratical vessels about the ocean. She had four six pound carronades, twelve muskets, twelve large pistols, besides cutlasses and boarding pikes. I had all the small arms packed away in my state room, which was always locked, so that no one could enter, whether I was in the room, or on deck. I had sufficient warning from my friend Selfridge's fate to be constantly on my guard. As we proceeded on our passage, I felt it necessary to keep my pistols about my person, loaded, for I was in constant fear that something would take place, when I might require to defend myself.

We had got about half passage when we found the water in the hold had slightly increased. We always, every day, sounded the pumps, with the sounding line. Finding that she did not leak, we had not used the pumps, since we left Bremen. I ordered the vessel to be pumped out, and when they commenced to pump, it was found that something was the matter with the pump boxes. They were drawn, and it was found that owing to their remaining so long in the pump, the leathers had become rotten. I spoke to Mr. Libbey about it. He became very insolent. I ordered him off duty, and to go to his state room, which he reluctantly did. It was about twelve o'clock, mid day. The passenger, who was on deck, made some impertinent remarks, so that it was necessary for me, to make him understand his position on board the vessel, as well as mine, and that he must be on his guard, and not interfere by word or act, in the affairs of the vessel, which I had noticed that he was inclined to do.

Mr. Libbey put on his best suit of clothes, and [was] playing the gentleman. I had sent him to his state room as punishment, and I had placed a board over the light in the deck to his room, so as to make it dark, that instead of reading his novel, he could reflect upon his conduct. He came on deck and violently kicked it off. I then called the carpenter, and ordered him to nail up the door of the state room. This of course was resisted, but he saw that I was determined, and he gave up. The next morning, he sent for me and apologized for his conduct the day before, and promised if I would put him on duty, he would do so no more. I therefore had him let out. I found that this little lesson was of great use both to the mate, and the passenger. I made up my mind that I would part with him, when I got into La Guaira.

AFTER BEING OUT ABOUT THIRTY DAYS, we made the island of Barbados, one of the British West India islands, and passed to the north of it, and to the south of St. Lucia, into the Caribbean Sea. We soon after made the Roquillos, which are high rocks, laying about one degree to the north of La Guaira. There are no pilots, and I had to find my way to that port as best I could. I finally saw some vessels at anchor, and steered in for them, and let go the anchor.

La Guaira is the sea port of Caracas. It is an open roadstead, entirely exposed to all gales of wind from the sea, and there is constantly a swell from the ocean rolling in, which keeps the vessels always in motion, so that it is necessary to lash the yards to the masts, and makes it very dangerous for [row] boats to come alongside, which have to be hauled out to the boom, as soon as they are out of use, or they will get swamped by the rolling of the vessel.

There were no wharves or landing places on the shore, and all boats had to take the chance of being swamped in the surfs as they landed on the beach. I frequently had my boat capsized and the boat's crew, as well as myself thrown into the rolling waves. We however soon learned how to manage the boat without much danger in landing, as the rollers run pretty regular. After every three large ones, comes a little smooth water, and the art is to row the boat on the third roller, as it rolls up the beach, and the moment the boat strikes the sand, the boat's crew must jump out and haul the boat up on the beach. If the boat is allowed to swing round either way when going in on the wave, which they are apt to do, if not carefully watched, she is sure to capsize, and often times lives are lost.

By the conditions of my charter party I was to consign the vessel to the house of William Ackers & Co., an English house. I therefore as soon as I landed inquired the way to their counting room. I found that Mr. Ackers had gone to England, and that a young man, a native of Colombia who was a partner with Mr. Ackers, represented the house. I do not recollect his name. He spoke English. I handed him the papers and letters given to me by Mr. Delius. I thought he received me rather coolly, and by the questions he asked me about the size of my vessel &c., that he doubted if he could get coffee enough to load the vessel, and that the charter was rather high. I then went to the American consul's, & found that he had died a short time before. There was a young man, who was his clerk, acting as consul, until another could be appointed.

Lighters were sent off to the vessel and we began to discharge the cargo. There was a custom house officer put on board when we arrived, who took account of every box and bale that went over the side, and he gave to each lighter man a list of marks and numbers of each bale and box.

We had been there about two weeks, and the vessel was about half discharged, when Mr. Libbey one afternoon asked me for the boat to go on board of a vessel, to see an acquaintance and to get some tobacco. I told him he could take the boat, but to be careful that she did not catch on the side of the vessel, as they were all rolling a considerable, and to be sure to be on board again before dark, which was between seven and eight, all of which he promised to do. I waited patiently until it became dark, when I began to fear some accident had happened. At eight, I found that he had taken the first and second watch with him in the boat. I told the men to go below, that I would keep the watch until the boat returned. Mr. Bixley the second mate was not well, and I told him to go below and get some rest, as he had worked hard, as well as the crew, in discharging the cargo. I walked the deck until eleven o'clock, and had about given up the boat, when I heard her coming.

Mr. Libbey came on board. I saw at once he was intoxicated, and told him I was sorry he had disobeyed my orders, and that he did wrong in taking the seaman who had the first watch. He made an insolent reply, which I was not disposed to take notice of, as I should discharge him the next day. He kept on, and asked for his discharge. I told him he was discharged from that moment, and to go below, and go to sleep. He became very abusive, and as the crew were aroused by his noise, and on deck talking in a mutinous manner, I went below and armed myself with my pistols and sword, and came on deck again, as I thought it not prudent to retire to my state room.

Mr. Bixley had gone on deck, and Mr. Libbey was very noisy, and had armed himself with a stick of wood, and was approaching me. I stepped up to him, and ordered him to put down the billet of wood, which he refused. I then struck him with my sword, which was in the scabbard. He grabbed it, and the scabbard came off, and he threw it overboard, thinking he had thrown the sword overboard, and came at me again. I then struck him on the neck with some force, with the edge of the sword. His neck handkerchief prevented serious injury but as he grabbed the sword, which was sharp, his fingers were badly cut. I then collared him, and with the assistance of the second mate tied his arms behind, and afterwards put the irons on his wrists, and pushed him below. I told Mr. Bixley to go down and bind up his wounds, whilst I would go forward and quell the crew, who were greatly excited by an Irishman who was trying to persuade them to go aft and relieve the mate.

As it was dark, I got forward amongst them without their seeing me, and at once seized the Irishman by the collar with my right hand, and with my left pointing my pistol to his head, and threatened to shoot him, if he uttered another word. They were completely overcome with fear, and jumped below as soon as they could. I gave the Irishman a piece of my mind, and as he was very penitent, begging my pardon, and making many promises for his good behaviour for the future, I let him go below.

I then went aft and found by Mr. Bixley's account that Mr. Libbey was only wounded in his hands, and that he had bound them up with linen from the medicine chest. Mr. Bixley insisted upon staying on deck to keep the watch, as he had some sleep and felt rested, and that I should go below, which I did for a couple of hours, and then went on deck and stayed until morning. On the following day I discharged Mr. Libbey, paying him his wages at the consul's office.

We continued to discharge the cargo without further difficulty with the crew. When on shore a few days after, I saw Mr. Libbey, the passenger and the partner of Mr. Ackers together. They did not see me. I suspected something, but could not see that they could injure me, but I soon found that there was a conspiracy brewing that if [it did] not ruin me, would be of great injury to me.

One day when the cargo was about two thirds discharged, the custom house boat came alongside with a demand, that I should immediately come to the custom house. Not expecting anything wrong, I at once went with the officer to the custom house. I was taken into a private room by the collector, and an interpreter sent for, as the collector did not speak English, and I did not understand Spanish. He then showed me the mate's cargo book, in which were the marks and numbers of all the cases and bales of goods that had been sent on shore, which agreed with the custom house officer who was stationed on board, also a long list of marks of his own fancy, mounting to some twenty or thirty packages, which he under oath swore I had smuggled on shore. The collector seemed to believe the mate's statement. I stated to him the manner the mate had conducted [himself], which caused me to discharge him, and that this was entirely a false accusation, that there was no such packages ever on board the vessel, and that I had never smuggled a single thing from the vessel, and that I had nothing in the way of merchandise to smuggle. I then demanded that my consignee should be sent for, which was done.

After some time he came, and appeared to be surprised, that I should be accused of smuggling, and had quite a long talk with the collector, which of course I could not understand, but resulted in my being permitted to go on board, and we went out together, my consignee pretending that the collector was a fool, and told me not to be worried about it. I somehow mistrusted him, as he did not seem to think it a serious matter. When I went on board I found another officer on board, who proved to be one of the most rascally little scoundrels I ever met. He spoke a little English, and said and did everything he could to annoy me. He carried with him a sword cane, which he would show once in a while.

I found that I had no one to consult with excepting Mr. Bixley, who was the only one that was true to me. I had made the acquaintance of a Mr. Anderson, a Scotchman, who had been a merchant in La Guaira for some years, and who spoke the language perfectly. He also had a business house in Caracas. He proved to be a good friend to me. I frequently consulted him about my business.

The day following the one that I was at the custom house, my vessel was seized, and a guard of soldiers put on board, consisting of a sergeant and six men. I went on shore, and saw the consignee. He pretended to think it a strange proceeding. I went to the American consul's office, and made a protest. The young man who was acting consul could give me no assistance, but said he would do anything I wished in the way of his official duty to assist me.

I saw Mr. Anderson. He recommended me to protest and abandon my vessel, and look to my government for redress from the Colombian government. He thought there was a conspiracy, and that my consignee was at the head of it, to get clear of the charter, as they had got a large cargo of goods brought to the market, free of freight, and that they could not procure a cargo of coffee back to Bremen, and that it was their determination to get clear of the charter, and had not this opportunity with the mate offered, they would have had to compromise by paying a portion of the freight.

I had some suspicion soon after I arrived that there was some doubt about my having a return cargo of coffee, but I of course in that case should have the penal sum which was five thousand dollars. I was not inclined to follow Anderson's advice, as I should not only lose my charter, but also my vessel. I had not much confidence in the American government, and as for the Colombian government, it was uncertain, as they were not acknowledged, and were still fighting for their independence from Spain.

I returned to the vessel, to worry over the matter. I felt extremely vexed to have the guard of soldiers on board. They were the ugliest set of ragamuffins I ever saw, a mixture of Indian and Spanish, most of the Indian, miserably clad, and shoeless. I was told that they were put on board to guard the vessel, to prevent me from running away with her, and that they were ordered not to leave the deck to go below.

I had some days previous covered the decks with turpentine to preserve the wood, as the hot sun was producing a bad effect on them, and had taken the awnings down, that the turpentine might harden & dry. In the night the soldiers lay down on the deck to sleep, and in the morning they found that their clothes, and hair stuck in the turpentine, and they had difficulty in getting up. This was reported to the colonel, that I had put sticky stuff on the decks, to annoy the soldiers, and had taken the tents down. I was told that the colonel was very angry and would make me repent of it.

In a few days the cargo was discharged, and I gave notice to the consignee that I was ready to receive cargo. I did this in writing, and sent it to them through the American consulate. No notice was taken of it.

The custom house officer who was put on board was very troublesome, and one evening after he had been on board a day or two, I had occasion to go to the medicine chest, and the supper table being laid, and the cups of tea being filled, I took a vomit powder from the medicine chest, and put it in the cup for the officer. He took his tea with Mr. Bixley and myself, and about half an hour after the officer went to his berth, feeling sick, and soon the vomit [powder] began to work. The poor fellow vomited rather hard, sighing out "Oh, Captain, put me on shore, I die." He went on shore and reported to the collector that I tried to poison him. So now I had the collector as well as the colonel against me.

It seems a sort of trial had been going on, and I was cited up to the court, and Mr. Ackers' partner went with me. He endeavoured to persuade me that the whole thing was wrong, that they could do me no harm &c. I was asked a few questions, through the interpreter, which I answered. I was prevented from stating my case, which I tried to do, but the interpreter was stopped, and Mr. Ackers' partner undertook to state it for me. I was annoyed at this and said something which offended the court and was ordered to hold my tongue, and that I could go.

I went immediately to see Mr. Anderson, and told him what had occurred. He said that he had spoken to several of the foreign merchants, and that they all considered it a great outrage, also that he had talked with one of the first lawyers of the place, who said it was not a court but a custom house committee that was examining the case, and that they had no right to use the military to detain the vessel &c., and that the custom house, not having found any goods that had been smuggled, had no right to seize the vessel on suspicion &c. and advised me to appeal, to the court in Caracas, and to demand the papers, or a copy of them, and proceed at once to Caracas.

I then went with him to the lawyer's office, and had a long talk with him. He stated to me the same as he had told Mr. Anderson, and seemed to take a great interest in the case. He at once wrote a paper of some length, addressed to the custom house committee, for me to sign, and at once present it to them, stating that I had appealed to the high court in Caracas, and asked that all the papers, or a copy of them, be given to me, to be taken up to Caracas. He said he would present the document himself.

I had taken a room at Madame Rouilee's boarding house, as I found it so uncomfortable on board of the brig. The second or third day after I was at the lawyer's office, Mr. Anderson brought me the copy of the papers and a letter of introduction to a lawyer in Caracas, and as there were some gentlemen of his acquaintance going up to Caracas that afternoon, advised me by all means to go up with them. He also gave me a letter to his partner, and advised me to call upon the lawyer as soon as I got to the city. I forget the names of either of the lawyers.

Caracas is on the other side of a mountain, between five and six thousand feet high, which we had to ascend on mules. Our party consisted of four besides myself. All were English or Scotch. I was introduced to them by Mr. Anderson, and found them very pleasant. They were all connected with business houses in Caracas, and La Guaira. The road had been made many years before by the viceroys of Spain. It was zig zag in its ascent, and in some places quite steep, cut out of the solid rock. We could occasionally get a glimpse of the ocean, and of the vessels at anchor in front of La Guaira. They looked like small boats.

We left La Guaira at four in the afternoon, and got to the half way house, as it is called, at seven o'clock, at which time it was getting quite dark, and as it was dangerous to travel in the dark we stopped at this house until morning. There were occasionally robbers on the road, and we all went armed. It was customary for several to together, on that account, and the heat being so great that they could only travel late in the afternoon, or early in the morning. We had a jolly time in the evening, talking, smoking and playing cards until bed time. Early in the morning our mules were ready, and after a good breakfast we were on our way to Caracas.

Soon after leaving the house we crossed an immense chasm, apparently a split in the mountain, caused by an earthquake many years previous. It was about three rods wide, and of uncertain depth, as no bottom could be seen, probably several hundred feet. This was crossed on a bridge made of rope cables with planks laid across, about fifteen feet, or less, in width, with no protection on either side. It was about as dangerous [an] affair as I had ever seen. We passed over one after the other, one at a time. The mules seemed accustomed to the passage and did not mind the swaying motion of planks under their feet.

We soon after found the highest point of the road, and began the descent to the valley where Caracas was situated which was about two thousand feet below, and as it came into view, it formed one of the most beautiful sights I had ever seen. The valley was very level as far as we could see, and appeared under good cultivation. There were a number of cocoa plantations in sight. The city of Caracas spreads out largely from the centre, where the cathedral and public buildings are situated, which look very large in comparison to the houses, which are mostly of one story, white, with red tile roofs, and as the sun which had just risen shone upon the city and valley, it gave us a sight long to be remembered.

The descent to the city was steep, and the road zig zag, the same as the ascent on the other side. I got to the hotel in the forenoon, and as soon as I could, I was shown to the office of the lawyer to whom I had a letter of introduction. I found him a pleasant looking gentleman of about fifty. He spoke a little English, so that I could understand him. He took the papers which were given to me in La Guaira, and read them over, and asked me many questions. He seemed to be surprised that the military should have taken possession of the vessel. He said if they had not taken any goods, which had been smuggled, the custom house officers could not seize the vessel on suspicion. He told me to leave the papers for him to look over more particularly, and to come round the next day.

I explained to him how important it was to me to have this business attended to, at once, as the forty days in the charter party were nearly expired, and if the vessel could not be cleared before that time I was afraid the parties would protest and throw up the charter party. I went back to the hotel feeling tired, and sick.

The next forenoon I called round to the lawyer's office. After waiting some time he came in. I noticed he was not so cordial as he was
the day before. He said he had looked over the papers, and found the
case not so clear as he had thought, and that it could not go up before
the court until the following week. I was dreadfully disappointed. In
vain I entreated him to try to see the judge, and get some positive answer to the documents I had brought up. He still insisted that it was
impossible, and as I knew no one else I could employ, I returned to the
hotel.

That night I became quite sick, and sent for a physician. He said
that I was feverish &c., gave me medicine. What, I never knew, but for
three days I was delirious, and considered a very sick man, among perfect strangers. Ten days had passed before I was able to go to the
lawyer's office. I found him quite affable. He seemed to regret that I
had been sick, said that he had laid the case before the court, and had
procured a document for me to take back to La Guaira, which would
relieve me from difficulty.

I then took my letter of introduction to Mr. Anderson's house,
which he had given to me when I left La Guaira. I found them pleasant people and they wondered I had not called on them before. I
found that Mr. Anderson had written to them about my affairs, and
requested them to do what they could for me, and I most seriously regretted I had not called there before I went to the lawyer's. I told them
all that had occurred. They told me that Mr. Ackers' partner had been
up in Caracas, and they had no doubt but he had influenced the
lawyer.

I told them all I could do was to get back to La Guaira as soon as I
could, and wished them to let me have some money, as my expenses,
on account of my sickness, had been more than I had expected, and
that I would return it to Mr. Anderson, when I got to La Guaira. I
had, from my arrival, drawn money from the consignees every opportunity I could, and had over a thousand dollars in gold on board of the
vessel, as I soon after my arrival suspected that something might occur
when I should require it.

When I got back to La Guaira, my charter days had expired, and I received a protest, signed William Ackers & Co., stating that they had waited to the last moment, hoping that the vessel would be ready to receive the cargo of coffee according to the charter party, which they were anxious to ship on board, and which I had not been able to receive, thereby breaking the terms of the charter party, and that they abandoned the charter, and should procure another vessel. I had been on board the vessel, and found everything as I had left. Mr. Bixley said the crew were very discontented and unruly. The soldiers were still on board.

I called on Mr. Anderson, and paid him the amount I had received from his partner in Caracas, and told him what had taken place. He said he would assist me all he could, and was of the opinion that Ackers' partner who had been up to the city was at the bottom of the trouble. He no doubt saw the lawyer there, and was the cause of his changing his mind.

I then went to my boarding house, to dinner, and had but just got seated at the table when one of the *alcalde*'s men came for me to go to the *alcalde*'s court, where I found all the crew had come on shore, having taken the boat whilst Mr. Bixley was down in the cabin to his dinner. They had made a complaint, that I had threatened to poison the water, and kill them and the soldiers. The steward, who was also cook, swore he heard me tell the mate to do it. I ridiculed such an idea, and told the magistrate that it was impossible to do anything of the kind, that I would procure new casks and that the crew could fill them with water and secure the bungs so that no one but themselves should have access to them, and requested him to send them on board, which he refused to do. I had a talk with the men, and tried to persuade them to go on board, but they refused, excepting two of the best sailors, who were foreigners. They went with me to the boat and I went off to the brig.

Mr. Bixley said he was eating his dinner and hearing a noise on deck, went up and found half of the crew in the boat alongside and the rest determined to go, that they wanted to see me and get their discharge, and he could not stop them. We talked the matter over, but could not see how we were to help ourselves. To discharge them, I would not, as the time of their articles of shipment was not up, and there were no seamen to be had on shore. I passed a restless night on board, talking with Mr. Bixley most of the time, contriving various plans, but none seemed to answer. The charter was lost owing to the seizure, and detention. Everything looked against me. The soldiers were on board, and how to get clear of them, I could not see. There was no American consul, and no one to apply to for assistance. The crew were on shore protected by the court, and supported by the sailor landlords, who expected the sailors would be paid their wages, and of course that they would get the best part. My consignee, as he was absent from La Guaira, as it was told me when I called at the counting room, no one there speaking English, I could get no satisfaction.

I went on shore with a Capt. of a Baltimore schooner, in his boat, who kindly offered me his boat when ever I wanted it. I called upon the clerk at the consulate. He did not know what was best to be done, he had no power to act, excepting through the *alcalde*'s court, but he would try to see the *alcalde*, or something to that effect was all the satisfaction I could get. I called upon Mr. Anderson, who was cordial, but very much engaged in his business, and I could not trouble him with mine, but whilst at his counting room, I heard that there had been a disturbance in Caracas, and that the military had been called from La Guaira to go up there at once, which gave me hopes that I should be relieved of the guard on board of my vessel.

I had made enquiries for sailors on shore, but found only one who had run away from a vessel in the harbour. He told me he had been discharged. I found that one of Mrs. Rouilee's waiters was a sailor, and he wanted to ship with me. I then went on board the vessel, and to my relief found the guard boat had been alongside and taken the guard away. I then made up my mind to get away as soon as I could, and planned with Mr. Bixley to cut the vessel out, and leave the port as soon as possible. I found he seconded my plan, and was disposed to do everything in his power to forward my plans.

In the first place we required ballast, which must be got on board in the night, so as not to excite any suspicion of our intention. I was fortunate in procuring two loads of sand from the beach which was to be brought alongside the following night. I also engaged three men from the shore, one besides the two I had seen previously. I then got the sails bent to the yards. I was anxious for two or three more to complete my crew, which had been eight, but we thought we could do with less. We had now only five. The next day I went on shore, and got my papers from the consulate, where I had deposited them when I arrived. I fortunately picked up another sailor, and went on board. It was about noon, and I determined to cut the cable and proceed to sea that afternoon, as the wind was fair out to sea.

I had found out whilst on shore that morning, the colonel had sent in a bill to the consignees for two hundred and forty five dollars, which they had refused to pay, and that they intended to demand damages from me for not fulfilling the charter party, probably the penal sum, and that the crew which were on shore through the assistance of their landlords had brought a suit against the vessel for their discharge and wages, and then there were the port charges and other expenses to be paid. The consignees were responsible for them, but would claim from the vessel. These were trying questions to decide, and I could think of no other way than to cut the Gordian knot by cutting the cable and making sail for sea.

So on the 26th of April 1826, I cut the cable, and hoisted the sails, and sailed out of the harbour of La Guaira. We soon passed the fort, the only thing I had to fear, which would have fired upon us, had they been notified by the custom house officers. I had taken the time between two and three o'clock, when the custom house, and other public offices were closed, to make my attempt to escape the unfortunate position I was in. When I got beyond the reach of a shot from the fort, I hoisted the American flag at the peak, and fired one of our six pound guns, to bid them goodbye. All the American vessels in the harbour hoisted their flags. We had a fine breeze, and I steered up for the Roquillos passage, the one vessels generally take when they leave port.

There was a small armed vessel called the *Caracas* under the Colombian colours, lying at anchor in the harbour. She had no sails bent and was not prepared to go to sea. I had some suspicion that after the soldiers were removed from my vessel, that she might have been notified to guard us. I therefore kept a watch of her with my spy glass, to see if there was any movement on board of her. In about a couple of hours, I observed they were bending their sails. By that, I knew they would be giving me chase as soon as they could get ready.

I had a pretty good start of them, and when it had become dark, I altered my course, and steered off between Curaçao and the main land, as I felt certain they would steer up to the northward, through the Roquillos passage into the Caribbean sea, whilst I was running to the westward. At dark I could see nothing of her, as I was some twelve miles, or more from the harbour, but as she was a sharp vessel and a fast sailer, I knew she would overtake me if I did not alter my course. We had a fine night's run, and at daylight nothing was in sight.

I had made my mind up to proceed to Havana for a cargo of sugar to Europe, and steered to the northwest so as to go round the western end of Jamaica, and pass between that island and the south of Cuba. We had pleasant weather and a good run up to Cuba, and the trade wind being fair we run along the south of Cuba not meeting any vessel.

At noon one day I found by reckoning that I was nearly up to the Isle of Pines, and I went up on the fore top sail yard after dinner to see if it was in sight, and whilst sitting there I got sight of a schooner standing out from the land, and as she became more in sight, I noticed she was a suspicious looking vessel. Although I could not see the hull, I judged by the rake of her masts, that she might be a piratical vessel, as there were many pirates in those waters.

I sent for my spy glass. She was right ahead and standing south, across our course. All at once, I missed her, and with my naked eye could see nothing, but with my glass, I discovered her bare masts. She had lowered all her sails, to lay in wait for us. I came down on deck at once, and took in the studding sails, and hauled the vessel on the wind to the south. I soon saw that the schooner had hoisted her sails and was standing on the wind the same as we were, and as she being a fore and aft vessel could lay two points nearer the wind than we could, she was sure to cut us off at a certain angle, particularly as my vessel was in a very light set of ballast and making leeway.

I could perceive she was drawing up to us quite fast, and soon her hull was in sight, and I could with my glass see she had a great many men on board, and that she was armed, having a long gun forward on a swivel. She neared me quite fast. I hoisted the American flag. They hoisted no flag. I saw that the way she was drawing up to us that in an hour or two she would be up to us.

It was after sun set, and I noticed a heavy cloud rising, which in that latitude generally produced rain and thick weather. Mr. Bixley and some of the crew were anxious I should fire some of our double head shot at her and try to cut away her masts. We had nineteen, what was called double headed shot, that is a round shot cut in two, and the two halves connected by an iron bar about eighteen inches long. This was calculated to cut away small spars and rigging but I thought it more prudent not to. Some of the sailors got large stones up on deck to throw into the boat if she came alongside.

She was less than a mile under our lee when the squall struck us, and we were enveloped in a thick rain and mist. I had anticipated this and had everything prepared to tack ship as soon as the squall struck us, and had given all orders to that effect. The vessel went round on the other tack, without any noise from the men or rigging, and stood to the north. It soon became dark and nothing could be seen of the schooner. The weather remained thick and misty through the night, and we saw no more of the vessel.

The next morning we were close to the Isle of Pines, and shaped our course along the coast of Cuba to the west. At noon we saw a man of war brig ahead, which proved to be the *Douro*, which hoisted English colours. She sent an officer on board, who made particular inquiries about the schooner I had seen the day before. He said by my description of her, it was a piratical vessel that they were in search of. I gave him all particulars of the way she was steering when I last saw her, and the course and distance I had run since. He warned me to give the western end of Cuba a good berth, to avoid the pirates, and went on board of his vessel. They soon made all sail and stood on a course to overtake the schooner. A few weeks after, I saw a Jamaica paper giving the account of the British man of war *Douro* having captured the pirate schooner *Las Adamantis*, which had robbed several vessels, and murdered the crews, one of them being the English brig

Carabobo, [and] that she had sixty men on board. All of them were hung at the yard arm of the brig, and the vessel sunk.

I arrived safely at Havana after a passage of eleven days from La Guaira. I consigned my vessel to the house of Drake and Mitchell, who gave me a freight of £4.10 per ton of sugar to Amsterdam. I learned that there were many pirates about the island of Cuba, and that a number of American vessels had been robbed and the crews murdered, and it was known that some of the piratical vessels were fitted out at Regla, a little town on the opposite side of the bay from Havana. Mr. Mitchell told me that only a short time previous, a Hamburg ship had arrived off the port too late to get in before dark, and whilst lying under short sail outside the harbour until morning, a schooner came out of the harbour with a large number of men, and tried to come alongside. The Captain, who was an old trader to Havana, suspected her to be a pirate, and ordered her off, and as she did not incline to go, he fired into her and sunk her, with all on board.

He came into port the next morning, and was consigned to Messrs. Drake & Mitchell, and related the circumstance to them. They knew at once the schooner was from Regla. They cautioned the Captain and all on board not to say a word about it, that they would load the vessel and get her away as soon as possible, for if it was known, they all would be murdered by the friends of those who were on board of the schooner.

All vessels were obliged to go armed in those days on account of the pirates, and foreign vessels whilst laying at anchor in the harbour kept an armed watch in the night, or all went below, and fastened themselves down in the cabins until morning. There were several robberies of vessels in the harbour during the time I laid there, but my vessel was not troubled.

The city was very badly governed. It was not safe for any one to go about the streets at night, robberies and assassinations were of constant occurrence. The streets were not lighted, and are very narrow. There were placed along the back of the Palace, a row of wooden benches, for the deposit of bodies of those who had been assassinated in the night and picked up in the morning, that their friends might find them. I saw myself one forenoon, eight bodies laying there, mostly young looking persons, and some of them quite well dressed.

Mr. Mitchell told me that hardly a night passed that some one was not murdered, that he never went out after dark. He said that sometime previous, he came out of the Lonja, a public place, and one of the most public streets, and going towards his counting room, there were two men walking before him, and as he came up with them they separated, that he might go between them. They each took hold of him, and holding daggers to his throat, ordered silence, and took from him his watch, a diamond breast pin, which he valued at six hundred dollars, and what money they found in his pocket. People were passing close by, and he dared not to call for help. He recognized one of them, and the next day sent one of his clerks, to purchase [his property] back again.

If a robbery or a murder was committed in the streets in the day time, every one would run and shut their blinds to the windows, or run away, instead of rendering any assistance to the victim, as all those who saw it were held as witnesses, and generally were imprisoned until the trial, which sometimes was for months. Such was the state of affairs in Cuba in 1826, under the rule of Vives as captain general of the island. Soon after General Tacón was sent out to relieve Vives, a change at once came over the order of the city. He divided it into wards, and placed a captain with a certain number of soldiers over each ward, or *partidos,* as they were called, and made them responsible for the good order of their *partidos.*

There was no power over the nobles of the island, no court in which they could be tried, or if there was one, it was a dead letter, and they took the advantage of doing as they had a mind to, with the people. Complaints against them were made to Tacón, and he was determined to put a stop to it.

One of the most prominent, and wealthiest, was Conde Morales. A complaint [was laid] against him, by a carpenter whom the Conde refused to pay for his work. An officer was appointed to enquire into the matter, and finding it as the carpenter had represented, sent word to the Conde to pay him his wages. This was considered a piece of impertinence on the part of Tacón and he [Morales] refused to take any notice of it. Tacón sent him word that the amount due to that man must be paid to him before sundown, and gave orders to the officer if it was not, to levy on the furniture of his house, or any other property to the amount required. The officer with a guard of soldiers went the next morning and began to remove the furniture, which brought the Conde to terms. He paid the man. That was a good lesson to the nobles. He [Tacón] issued a proclamation, calling upon the inhabitants to make immediate complaints to him of every wrong, and not to be afraid to come forward as witnesses, that they should be protected.

Robberies and theft was of constant occurrence. This was soon stopped by prompt punishment. There were many in prison, and had been for long times without trials. A commission was appointed to examine, and report the causes to him [Tacón]. They were at once set free, or punished, according to their crimes. For theft, they were whipped at the corner of each street where the theft had been committed, and for higher crimes, either capital punishment, or put in the chain gang. The prisons were cleared, and in a short time the city of Havana was as safe as any city in the United States, and has been so ever since.

The streets are very narrow. Many of them, it is with difficulty for two carriages to pass one another. They were not paved, and were very muddy when ever it rained, and it was the custom for persons crossing the streets to be carried on the backs of Negroes. It is now paved throughout with the reefs pavement and the streets are kept in fine order. The side walks are very narrow, so that two can with difficulty walk together. The houses are mostly of one story, with a large door for the carriage to pass in, which is left in the entry, and the horse taken through the room and put in the stable, which is at the extreme end of the house.

There are many large three story houses built of stone. The lower story is generally used as store rooms, where the planters deposit their sugars. The second is called the *entresuelo,* [and] is seven to eight feet high. The third is seventeen to twenty feet, and is occupied by the family, and generally has a balcony round the court yard, with the doors of the rooms opening on it. Messrs. Drake and Mitchell's was of this description, and one of the largest in the city. It has been occupied by Messrs. Burnham & Co., for several years past. They had a row of rooms built on the *assoltaire,* or roof, which is flat and covered with a cement impervious to water. The rooms were for the Captains consigned to the house. I had one as soon as I arrived, and lived at the house.

At this time foreign merchants were limited to four, who were allowed to do business at the custom house. Mr. Drake was one, and most of the foreign agents did their business through the house, and had rooms there, and lived with the firm, and it was not uncommon to have forty or more at the table at dinner. There was a mixture of all nations. I remember once at dinner the question of nationalities came up and we found that there were sixteen different languages spoken at the tables.

I was there about three weeks, and taken on board two thirds of the cargo, when I went to Matanzas to finish the cargo. I there met a captain of a Baltimore vessel, who was in La Guaira when I left. He told me there was a good deal of excitement when I left, that the armed schooner *Caracas* was sent out to bring me back. She returned in two days and could not find me. Everyone was glad I had escaped the outrageous persecution. I was consigned in Matanzas to Mr. Howland, an American house, a good merchant and an excellent man. This was the first American that I had done business with. My vessel was soon loaded, and dispatched for Amsterdam.

Whilst I lay in Havana, the part of the crew I picked up in La Guaira left the vessel, and the two of the old crew which had been on board from the time we left Boston wanted their discharge, which they had a right to, according to the shipping papers, and I paid them their wages and let them go, as they would not reship. I arranged with a sailors' land lord to ship me another crew, eight men, who were brought on board the night before we left Havana, a big set of scoundrels. I made Mr. Bixley chief mate, and shipped a young man for second mate. I was warned by the ship chandler that [I had] a bad set of fellows for a crew and to be on my guard.

I went on board at about eight o'clock in the morning and as I got up to the rail of the vessel, I told Mr. Bixley to call the crew to the gang way, and standing one foot on the rail, the other on the side ladder, I looked for a moment on each of the men, and slowly counted them. I then said sternly, "Eight. I am eight more, which makes sixteen of us. Go forward and heave up the anchor," and stepped on board. Mr. Bixley told me that they were inclined to be unruly, and he thought my manner would have a good effect upon them. I told him I had been informed that they were a bad set of fellows, and that we must be constantly on the watch.

At supper time, three or four of them came aft with a kid of beef, and wanted to know if that was the beef they were to have. I asked Mr. Bixley what beef it was. He said it was the last of a barrel, he believed. I told him to open a fresh barrel in the morning, and they should have good beef. They went forward. We could hear them grumbling and I foresaw that there was to be trouble. We therefore armed ourselves, and I laid a boat's tiller on the capstan in case I should want a club. It was not long before they came aft again, wanting to see the beef, evidently for the purpose of a row, as the sailors say, to try the officers. I caught up the tiller, and sprung at them. They started forward, getting two or three pretty good blows from the tiller. I heard no more about their beef, and they proved as good a set of men as I ever had. All they required was to be impressed that they had somebody to govern them. I understood the character of sailors, as I had been brought up amongst them, and I knew that they must be governed as children with the powers of men.

I SAILED FROM MATANZAS for Amsterdam the latter part of the month of May, 1826, and had the usual passage of forty to forty five days. It was in the summer time, and very pleasant weather. Arriving in the Helder, I was remembered by many and greeted as an old acquaintance. I employed the same agents I had when in the *Zephyr.*

I found that nearly all merchant vessels went up to the city through the canal, and that they all had to employ one of the Zuider Zee pilots. One came on board and took charge of taking the vessel up to the city. We went along hauled by four horses, very well, passing through the several draws in the bridges without trouble until we arrived to Alkmaar, when the vessel ran aground and there she stuck, although we carried anchors out and tried to heave her off and as it was near dark, we could do no more until the morning.

We had rather a funny time while we laid abreast of Alkmaar. The *Eight Sons* was probably the first American vessel that ever stopped at this inland town, and caused much excitement among the inhabitants. At about dusk the principal officers of the town came on board, who appeared to be a jolly set of old Dutchmen. They could not speak English, and I could not speak Dutch, so at first we could not understand one another. Soon, however, we found an interpreter, and after satisfying their curiosity by telling them who we were, and where we came from, my name, and of what our cargo consisted of, &c., we soon became friends, and I invited them down in the cabin.

They showed signs that they expected something to drink. I invited them to take some supper with us, they declined, when all at once I recollected that when in Matanzas Mr. Howland sent on board a small barrel of apple brandy which had not been broached. I told the steward to broach it, and bring some to the table, which he did in a pitcher, and my company helped themselves rather freely, and lighted their pipes, with an apparent determination to enjoy themselves.

Now, this apple brandy proved to be the most intoxicating stuff imaginable, and the first thing I knew my company were all drunk, and I was puzzled what to do with them. They began to dispute with one another, and such a terrible row I never in my life witnessed. I expected every minute that they would commence a fight. They finally subsided, Morpheus having overpowered them and brought them to their senses before daylight and they left as they came. Seeing the powerful effects of Mr. Howland's present on my visitors, I ordered the steward to empty the barrel of its contents in the scuppers, as it was against my rules to have any intoxicating liquor on board of the vessel.

In the morning, I hired a launch and took out some of the cargo, which lightened the vessel and we were able to haul her afloat, and take the cargo on board again. This operation took up the whole day.

During the forenoon many of the inhabitants came on board, particularly school boys who seemed delighted to run about the vessel. I gave them each a round ship biscuit, which pleased them, and they soon got hold of the vessel's name "Oct Zoons," the Dutch for *Eight Sons*, and what was my surprise when I took a turn on shore to see the town, to have some twenty or more boys running after me calling out "Oct Zoons," each one having a ship biscuit hanging round his neck. I soon retreated on board, not wishing such a marked reception.

The next morning the horses were hitched on, and we passed up the canal to Amsterdam, leaving Alkmaar without a tear of regret. When we got off the city the first person that came on board was the old boatman I had when I was there in the *Zephyr*. How glad he was to see me. One would have supposed I was his long lost son just returned, but I knew his affectionate meeting was for the few florins he expected to get out of me. He was a good old fellow and did me many a service, besides being boatman to the vessel.

The name of my consignees I have forgotten although I recollect their looks, and that they were very gentlemanly, and courteous to me and did all they could to forward my business, in having the cargo discharged and procuring me a freight back to the States.

I received a letter from Bridge telling me to sign bills of lading for goods coming consigned to him, "freight to be regulated in Boston." I thought this rather strange. I did not suspect anything wrong in Mr. Bridge, and as I had bills of lading from others showing the rates of freight, I received a large portion of the cargo on those conditions. By the advice of the ship brokers I had laid on for New York, and had received a small portion of the cargo for that port. When I found no more offering, and a considerable for Boston, I concluded to go to both places. I got in all about two thirds of a cargo. I closed my accounts with the consignees, and remitted balance of outward freight to Messrs. Baring Bros. & Co. London, and got the vessel ready to proceed to the Helder through the canal.

The crew that came from Havana had left, and another crew of Dutch sailors were shipped in their place. Some understood English and some did not. When we got to the Helder and everything ready for sea, I found that the second mate had run away. I tried to procure another but could not find one, and as Mr. Bixley thought we could get along very well without one, we proceeded to sea.

We encountered a head wind in the North Sea, which was very trying, as the crew proved poor sailors, and as they did not understand English, and Bixley, poor fellow, got fairly worn out by the time we got into the English Channel, and gave up sick, I then had no one to help me, and stood both watches, trusting to a little sleep during the day, besides attending upon Mr. Bixley, who having a high fever was daily growing worse, and in five days died. I did every thing for the poor fellow I could, and watched him through his dying hours.

The following day I had him sewed up in canvas, with some old iron at the feet, laid on a plank with one end on the rail of the vessel, the other on a barrel, called the crew together, read the Episcopal funeral service (no one understanding a word but myself) and when finished, two sailors lifted the end of the plank, and the last of poor Bixley slid into the ocean. I really mourned his loss. He was a good fellow, and a good seaman, and with his mild manner could get along with this Dutch crew much better than I could. There was no help for it, and I saw that I must get my vessel across the ocean the best way I could.

It was rather a pleasant season, being the latter part of summer. I arranged to have my bed spread out on the cabin floor under the skylight, and gave orders to the man at the helm to stamp on the deck, and also to call me if there was any alteration in the wind or weather whilst I was below, which was never more than an hour either day or night, as I never thought of taking my clothes off. We got along very well until about half passage when one afternoon, the vessel running along with a fair wind all sail set, the weather appearing settled, I cautioned the helmsman to look out sharp and give me a call in case of any change, and went below for an hour's rest.

I had been asleep but a short time, before the helmsman stamped on deck. I rushed up on deck and found a violent squall had struck the vessel, and the sails shaking in the wind. I sung out "Hard up your helm" but the sails soon got aback, and the topmast studdingsail boom broke, and the pieces flying aft, I turned round to get out of the way of the pieces. I saw that the man had the helm hard down. I sprung to the wheel to get the helm up as soon as possible to prevent her getting stern way, as she might have gone down stern first. I suppose in doing so I pushed the man away rather roughly, and he thought I struck him, for he struck me a tremendous blow with his fist which knocked me head long into the side of the vessel, where I laid for a few moments senseless.

When I came to my senses, I found that the squall had passed, but had left the vessel almost a wreck about the foremast. The fore topsail and fore top gallant yards were broken in the slings, and the sails badly torn, the studding sail booms broken and the sails nearly destroyed, but as the wind had gone down, I thought it best to first get command of my vessel, by first mastering the big Dutchman that had knocked me down.

I went to my cabin, put my loaded pistols in my pocket, and took my sword in my hand, & came on deck, called another man to the helm, and set the rest in hauling in the wrecked sails & broken booms. I then collared the man that struck me and after some tussling I mastered him. He was a stouter man than I was and spoke no English. I had him down, and was tying him to one of the guns, and had got him almost fast when I observed the crew coming aft. I fortunately finished by the time they got to me.

I sprung up to them with my sword in my right and pistol in the left hand, and treatened to kill the first one that interfered. I did not understand their Dutch spluttering, but knew they were making threats—but my decided manner had brought them to a stand, and I made them understand that this man knocked me down on the quarter deck and that it was a mutiny, and by the laws of the United States I had a perfect right to shoot him, and that I would shoot the first man that made the least resistance to my authority, and started them forward to the work I set them about, and to the fellow I had tied down to the gun, I gave him several blows with my sword, and made him beg for his life, & promise he would behave himself in the future.

I then went forward, had the fore top gallant yard and sail sent down, and the foretopsail yard fished by having the two top gallant studding sail booms run across the break and well lashed, two reefs put in the sail and set. It was now about dark and the weather being squally—I was on deck all night on the watch. I had no more trouble with the men after that. They were pretty well frightened and watched sharp to obey every order.

Shortly after we arrived off the coast I discovered that the foremast was sprung above the eyes of the rigging, which must have occurred when our yards were broken. We fished it as well as we could and favoured it by sending down the topgallant mast, and keeping the fore-topsail reefed. This discovery decided me to proceed at once to Boston. I had intended to have gone into New York first, and delivered the part of the cargo I had for that port, and then returned to Boston and delivered the remainder.

We at last arrived all right after the absence of more than a year. The first thing to be done was to write to each of the consignees of the cargo in New York of the circumstances that had caused the vessel to put into Boston, and that we would pay the extra insurance & freight if they would authorize their agents to receive the goods in Boston, and that we could deliver them at once. This was finally arranged and the cargo discharged. I put in a new foremast, overhauled the hull, sails, and rigging for another voyage. I then was married to Miss Anna S. Arnold, the niece of Judge Wilde of the Superior Court in Massachusetts.

Mr. Bridge proposed that I should go out to Havana and load the vessel with a cargo of molasses on vessel's account, to which I agreed, and leaving my wife at my father's during my absence, on account of the stormy months at sea, I at once got the vessel ready, shipped a crew and sailed for Havana. I will here mention a little mistake I made when I sailed from La Guaira to Havana. I had been told that when I got off the harbour of Havana I could leave the vessel in my boat, and go into the harbour and ascertain what chance there was for a freight, and I undertook to do so. When abreast of the Morro Castle, the sentinel hailed me and said something I did not understand. I answered by telling him I wanted to see the American consul. He said something more, and the sailors rowed on, when the first thing we knew he fired upon us, the bullet whizzing close by our head. That we understood and wheeled about in post haste, and returned to our vessel.

We arrived at Havana, and I at once consigned the vessel to my old friends Messrs. Drake Mitchell & Co., and gave them orders to purchase a cargo of molasses. We laid in port about three weeks before we got loaded. It was slow work. It was quite sickly, & many were dying with the yellow fever. One of my crew died soon after we arrived, and we had to bury him on a little island in the harbour, as none but Roman Catholics were allowed to be buried in the cemetery. This island was small, not over twenty rods across it in any part. It had been buried over and over, three or four deep—and we found difficulty in getting the coffin covered with earth. The end of the island was washing away, and in some places we could see the ends of four coffins, one above another, with the ends broken & the skeletons sticking out, ready to fall on the shore, which was strewed with human bones.

There was a man by the name of Nickols, who had the special privilege granted to him to bury all foreigners who should die there. I think he was an Irishman. He spoke good English and was rather a witty fellow. He introduced himself to me on the wharf one day, informing me of his rights, and handing me his list of prices for coffins, which were as follows, "Common ones for sailors, one Spanish ounce ($17), when buried with the body, but if only used at the funeral and returned half an ounce ($8.50). A nice coffin covered with black cloth two ounces ($36), good for a mate, and a very nice one covered with black cloth and trimmed with brass headed nails and black tape two ounces ($51), a very good kind for captains. Also a very handsome one, covered with fine cloth and ornamentally trimmed, and nicely lined, from four ounces ($68) to six ounces ($102)." He always carried a cane, marked with feet and inches, and would step up to the side of any stranger he saw and take his measure so as to have a coffin ready for him. He died in the midst of the cholera [outbreak of] 1833, regretting he was to lose such flourishing business.

The crew were enticed away by one of the runners from the boarding houses, and I sought in vain for them, until the vessel was near loaded, when a fellow came to me and wanted to ship a crew, or would find me the old crew, at the same rate, which was one month's advance pay. I agreed for the old crew for I knew who they were, and I thought I could let this advance pay go into their accounts. I did not want to run the risk of a new set of pirates, so I arranged with him to bring my crew on board the afternoon before we sailed with the receipts of each one for the money advanced.

The vessel was loaded and cleared, everything ready for sea, and to sail in the morning. She was hauled off from the shore to her anchor, and in the afternoon the crew were brought aboard, and [they] being under the influence of liquor I though it best to let them go below & go to sleep. The mate and I stood watch, as we suspected it was their intention to run away before morning. My watch was until 12 o'clock, which I strictly kept, and before I called the mate, I went forward and listened at the forecastle, and heard them snoring away like good fellows.

I was down in the cabin but a few minutes calling the mate and went on deck again, and in a few minutes the mate came up and whilst we sat talking, we heard some one hailing, telling us our men were swimming on shore, and one of them was struggling as though he could not swim. We ran forward, and to our surprise found they had all gone. We soon had the boat in the water, and gave chase, but as we got sight of them they were climbing up on the shore, and we close after them, following up a narrow street where we lost sight of them. We cruised round the by paths and narrow lanes for some time, and could neither see or hear anything from them, [so] concluded we had better go back to the boat.

When on our way, we saw a number of men standing at one of the corners. We went to them and I asked if they had seen any sailors about there? One rather a tall looking fellow who spoke broken English said "Yes you want sailors?" I said, "Yes." "What vessel?" I said, "American." He said, "We go." It was some time before we understood, that it was not my sailors he was talking about, but himself and ship mates. I found they were the crew of a French vessel laying at the wharf, & wanted to leave, and as I thought a fair exchange no robbery, I agreed with them, and was back to the vessel in less than an hour with a new crew.

The second mate, who was left on board, when he saw the sailors come up the side of the vessel said, "These men are not our crew." I said "No, we have exchanged, show them forward." It was fortunate that the second mate spoke French, and they had quite a talk, and I was glad to lay down and take a little rest before daylight, as I left orders to be called at that time. I found in the morning that [the] second mate had stowed the crew away in with the cargo, as they were afraid that their Capt. would come on board when he saw our vessel hoisting sails, and find them. I went on board of a vessel whose Capt. was a particular friend, and got him to come on board with his crew and help us weigh our anchor and hoist our sails, and see us out of port. I noticed the Frenchman's boat pulling round watching us, but as he saw all our crew were Americans, or not his Frenchmen, he did not come board, and we got outside of the Morro nicely.

WE HAD A PRETTY GOOD RUN up the coast until we came in the vicinity of Nantucket shoals, when there was every appearance of a N.E. gale, which is anything but pleasant on our coast in the winter time, and I made up my mind to make a harbour before night, and stood in for the land. In the forenoon I took on board a Vineyard pilot, just as it shut in thick with a heavy snow storm. We got into Holmes Hole, and came to an anchor under the lee of the high bluffs in a well protected harbour. There were several vessels there at anchor which had run into a safe harbour.

As soon as we had the sails furled and everything snug for the gale, I went on shore and took lodgings at the only tavern in the place. There were several captains there before me, but I got a very good room and had a good comfortable night sleep in a real bed. In the morning what was my astonishment in looking out of my window to find the harbour frozen over and my vessel, as well as the others shut fast in the ice. I had left orders for my boat to come for me in the morning, which now was impossible, and how long I was to be detained there was a problem. All I had now to do was to be contented, and make the best of my situation.

Upon becoming acquainted with my comrades, I found two or three good sort of fellows, particularly a Marblehead Capt. I do not recollect his name, so will call him Marblehead. He had arrived a few hours before me in the ship *Henry Clay*, with a cargo of pepper from Palau Pinang bound to Salem. The vessel belonged to Mr. Peabody. He [Marblehead] was a large man, and as full of fun as he was large, excellent company. We kept together most of the time and amused ourselves as best we could during the gale, which lasted a couple of days, snowing and blowing hard, so that we could not go out of the house.

The next day after our arrival, the landlord received a newspaper, which we were all anxious to see, but an old fellow, captain of the schooner *Dollar*, got hold of it first and it appeared that he was bound to look at every advertisement before he was done with it & so the rest of us had to wait patiently. Finally he got through and was just laying it down when he grabbed hold of it again saying, "I did not look at the deaths." In a minute a change came over his features, striking his fist hard on the table, saying "By G———d the old woman is dead." His manner and the whole thing appeared so ridiculous that we all burst out laughing. The poor old fellow seemed to feel pretty bad at his loss. He was from Demerara with a cargo of molasses bound to Salem.

A religious revival was going on among the Methodists, a business I had never heard of before, and had some curiosity to witness the manner they made converts. The next day being Sunday, Marblehead and I concluded to go to meeting. The meeting house was a large old fashioned wooden building with no fire to warm it, and it was a dreadful cold day—and not many there. The minister mounted the pulpit and made a short prayer, and then said "Fellow brethren, I think it is too cold for the spirit of the Lord to be with us. I would recommend that we adjourn to neighbour Brown's house." We cleared out as fast as we could for our tavern.

In the afternoon Marblehead proposed that we should take a sleigh ride, which I at once assented to, and our landlord procured a horse and sleigh from one of his neighbours. It was rather an antique affair, both horse and sleigh, and the harness was rather the worst of the three. We started out for a ride and took the road pointed out to us by the land lord, and went up the hill to a little town called the Vineyard. We stopped at a small tavern and had some warm drink and then concluded to return back.

We got along very well until we got within about a mile of the tavern, when going down rather a steep hill the breeching broke, and the sleigh took against the horse's hind legs, and the way he let his heels fly was a caution. Marblehead tumbled over the back of the sleigh, saying, "If the horse is going to get in, I will get out." I jumped out in a snow bank, and that was the last I saw of either horse or sleigh. The next day, not an extortionate bill was presented for the damage, which we cheerfully paid, feeling thankful we got off as well as we did. We had something of a walk, a mile through deep snow, back to the tavern.

After supper the land lord told us there was to be a revival meeting at a neighbour's nearby, and recommended us to go, as there was to be a Negro who had been converted, to make a confession. So we went to the house, found a good many there. We stood close to a door which opened into another room, and listened to the greatest nonsense and excitement we ever heard. Finally the Negro was called. He had learned a verse in the Bible, which he repeated several times—and then said, "Suppose you no repent, you will go to hell." He stood pretty close to Marblehead, and said it over two or three times rather pointedly to the old Capt., which the Capt. could not stand, and he said "Go to hell yourself, you bugger," which caused quite an excitement and we were hustled out of the house. I never have been to revival since.

10

A Belated Honeymoon

AFTER BEING DETAINED there for a week, the vessels got thawed out of the ice, and the wind coming out fair, we all weighed anchors, took pilots and went on our way to our destinations. I arrived in Boston, found all right, discharged the crew, and landed the cargo, and Mr. Bridge sold it. We decided that the vessel should go back to Havana and take a freight of sugar to Europe. I wanted the vessel's accounts made up, and [to] have some settlement with Bridge & Co., as we had had no settlement of accounts since we bought the vessel which was about eighteen months. Mr. B. promised that they should be made out at once, but for some reason or other put it off until the vessel was ready for sea, when they were handed to me.

I was no accountant, never having any experience that way, but I saw at once that the account was wrong, or at least very different from what I had calculated. I however determined to proceed on the voyage, as I had the provisions on board and the crew shipped. A young man by the name of Clement Parsons shipped as second mate and a man by the name of Smith as first mate. As there were many piratical vessels about the Cuban waters, the underwriters refused to insure the vessel or freights without we increased the crew, also the armament. Our complement of sailors had been six, and we had two six pound carronades. I now added two to the crew, two howitzers, twelve muskets, and the same number of pistols & boarding pikes, also a copper magazine, well supplied with powder, and musket cartridges.

We had a pretty good run out to the Hole in the Wall. During the passage I had endeavored to exercise the men with the muskets, & boarding pikes, also with the cannon, so that by the time we arrived off Abaco, they were pretty well drilled. When about ten miles from the passage of the Hole in the Wall, which is on the south point of the island of Abaco, we discovered a rakish looking schooner to the southward of us, standing towards us, apparently trying to cut us off. I put on all studding sails and run before the wind which was fresh from the eastward, blowing right into the passage.

I could now see with my glass that she had many more men than necessary for a merchant vessel, and made my mind up that we must have a fight. It was about mid day, and I got all the small arms on deck, muskets & pistols loaded. Mr. Parsons had charge of that part, and Mr. Smith had the charge of the cannon, which were also loaded. The schooner gained upon us, and I saw no chance of escape but to fight to the bitter end. She was now in our wake, about two miles astern. I could with my glass plainly see the large gun mounted forward, and the men moving about her deck.

Every man was now at his station and ready to do our best. Mr. Parsons now informed me that the cook was advising the men not fight, for if they did, they would all be killed, and if they did not probably they would not be hurt. I ordered the cook aft and told him to keep beside me, and if he showed any cowardice, that he would be the first man I would shoot. I then ordered the forecastle scuttle, also the cabin scuttle, to be nailed so that it would be impossible for any one to go below. I tried to persuade my wife to go below in the cabin but she refused, and quite coolly sat on the hen coop making cartridges out of some old flannel for the cannon. We now scaled our cannon and reloaded them so as to have everything in order.

The schooner had now got within one mile of us, everyone watching her. We now began to gain on her, as the wind was dead aft and became lighter so that her sails would not draw well, and as the swell of the sea was on her broadside, she rolled badly and slattered the wind out of her canvas, whilst our sails being square were well filled, and studding sails, and all, drew beautifully, and we were decidedly gaining on her, and before dark we were four to five miles ahead of her, when she hauled her wind and stood in a different direction. Our scare was over and we gratefully relaxed to our normal condition. I now felt certain that our men would fight if necessary.

We crossed the Bahama Banks, and steered for the Cuban shore. These banks are a wonderful curiosity. The bottom is as white as snow, probably of a chalk formation. The water is as clear and transparent as the purest crystal glass, averaging about twelve feet all over their extent, which is from seventy to eighty miles. It is said that no living creature can live in their waters. We saw nothing like life anywhere.

We soon sighted the coast, made the Morro, and passed into the harbour. I called on my former consignees for business. They offered me a freight of sugar to Antwerp, at £4.10 per ton. I at once closed with them, as it would give me about $6,000. I and my wife were invited to make our home at a small farm close to the shore of the bay, where lived a Cuban lady who had lived in Newburyport with her children and knew us very well. This was much pleasanter to my wife than living board of the vessel in port, which I always avoided whenever I could.

For once I had no trouble with my crew. They behaved well and went the voyage to Antwerp. We laid in Havana about thirty days before we got our cargo on board and ready to sail. We had a fair passage of about forty five days, arriving in Antwerp in the month of May 1827. We sailed up the river about forty miles to the docks, which are a large excavation, apparently in the middle of the city of Antwerp. Most splendid stone works surround the basins, which are capable of accommodating several hundred vessels. I took a suite of rooms at the hotel of the Place Verte, Green Park, and arranged with a restaurant to supply us with our meals. Our table was set morning, noon and

evening in the most recherché style, the food was most excellent, and
the charges quite moderate.

We were consigned to Messrs. Delisle Janosin & Co. This was a
branch of the old house Janosin & Co. London. There is another
branch in Paris, Janosin Delisle & Co. In Antwerp there was no one
but Mr. Delisle, a most excellent man. His family consisted of a wife
and several small children, his eldest a daughter of about 15, a very interesting girl, who was very attentive to my wife. We had a pleasant
time of some weeks in Antwerp, which is a very old fashioned city &
very Roman Catholic. On every gate to the houses, every pump in the
streets, of which there are many, and on every fountain, were either a
cross or the figure of some saint. Priests in their long black robes, and
large rimmed hats and monks of the various orders in their religious
costumes were constantly to be seen in the streets.

We went to Brussels, which is about thirty miles from Antwerp, and
passed two days at the Hotel De Swiss—which gave us time to see
every thing we wanted to about the city. At this time it was part of
Holland and King William resided at his palace in Brussels. He was
pointed out to us one day walking alone in the streets dressed like any
other gentleman, which was his practice, as he disliked any forms, or
ceremonies.

The field of Waterloo, where Napoleon's last battle was fought, being within twelve to fifteen miles from Brussels, we hired a carriage
and rode there. I had provided a map of the ground, also a description
of the battle. They were then building an immense mound of earth,
with a stone column running through the centre, which was to be the
base of a granite monument with an immense iron lion on its summit.
This mound was more than one hundred feet high. The base was
about one third of a mile. The earth was all carried up in baskets by
women. They had been over ten years at work upon it and it was not
finished then. It was [made,] however, so that we could walk up on
one side where sort of steps in the earth had been made by people going up. From the top we had a good view of the field, and as it were,
fought the battle all over again. An old soldier who was in the battle
was there and explained the various movements to us. It was a most

interesting day to us. We got back to our quarters in Antwerp, and found all going on right, the vessel most discharged.

We then visited the old and famed St. Domingo church. It is of large dimensions, as we should judge from its inward size, as there was nothing but an immense door to be seen outside, the church building itself being completely buried from view by houses being built on, and apparently over it, of the most antique shape. We therefore could form no opinion of the architecture, but the inside was grand in the extreme. The altar and its surroundings, as well as the several pulpits, are celebrated for their wood carvings, which in the days of its construction were much superior of anything in modern days.

The vessel was advertised for Boston, and after taking on board all the freight that offered, and closing the accounts with Mr. Delisle, I remitted the balance of my freight money to London, took a pilot, and proceeded down the river to sea. Whilst we were in Antwerp, [we found] the brig *Harbinger*, Capt. Charles Savage, who had married Anna Thacher, daughter of Judge Thacher of Newburyport. She was a great friend of my sister Mary, and knew us very well by hearsay. She and my wife formed a strong friendship whilst they were in Antwerp, being together a great deal of the time. The vessels sailed from Antwerp about the same time. We saw nothing of one another sailing through the North Sea, but going through the Straits of Dover, we came together and sailed side by side, with the land of France in sight on one side and England in sight on the other, the vessels so near that the ladies could converse with ease. Night coming on, we bid one another good bye, wishing good voyages, and steered off our courses, and saw no more of one another.

When about half across the ocean, we fell in with an electrical storm, with a great deal of thunder and lightning & heavy rain. I had never met one before although I had heard of them from those that had experienced them. The air was sultry and heavy and had a sulphuric smell. There was very little wind, most of the time it was calm, and at night there were several of those phosphorescent air globes, called *ignis fatuus,* floating about the masts and yards, the largest as big as a hat, and down to the size of an apple. They would hang on the end of the yards, and on top of the masts. They were about the vessel for an hour, or more, and the sailors are very superstitious, and do not like to go up aloft when they are about.

After a fair passage of 40 days we arrived in Boston. The vessel was then freighted with a cargo for Rotterdam, and as Mr. Bridge & Co. had not rendered to me satisfactory accounts I concluded to remain at home, and put a Captain Potter in my place as master for this voyage, which was during the winter months, and as it was more than fifteen years since I had just commenced going to sea, and had never given myself a voluntary vacation, I thought it a good time to improve the opportunity and take a rest for the winter.

II

A Man Overboard!

THE BRIG [*EIGHT SONS*] was gone on the voyage about four months, and when she returned I was determined that Mr. Bridge and I must separate as joint owners, he being determined to get more than his share of the earnings. I therefore proposed that we should sell the vessel at public auction, which he agreed to, as he was under the impression that I was building a vessel at Newburyport. The vessel was advertised for sale, and a few hours before the sale was to take place, I employed a broker to buy her, not giving him any price, but to buy the vessel. I took this course as Mr. B. was largely in my debt, and I knew it was the only way for me to get my money.

We were all on the wharf at the sale. Mr. B. expected to have bought her for a song, but the broker always bid over him. I said nothing to any one, until Bridge suspected the broker was for me, when he bid it once from $10 to $500, when I said to Capt. Uran who stood by me, "Come give us a bid, do not see the vessel sacrificed," and Bridge watching this conversation was thrown off his guard, and the auctioneer's hammer went down on the broker's bid, and the vessel was mine. I immediately told the mate to haul her to the next berth.

Mr. B. was taken by surprise. He asked, "Is that your vessel, Capt. Tyng?" I said "*Yes,* Mr. B., I have taken a lesson from your book." I found that Mr. B.'s half of the vessel did not meet the amount he owed me by some hundreds of dollars, and I bought the amount in linseed oil from his clerk in the store and had it put on board of the vessel. This closed my account, to the disappointment of Mr. B. and I knew him no more.

I put Mr. Parsons in as chief mate, and fitted the vessel out in everything necessary for a year's voyage both in provisions and sails & rigging, had a crew shipped and sailed for Havana in the early part of 1828.

Arriving at Havana, we were invited to stay at the *estancia* (farm) of our friends, where we stayed before. We were in Havana about a month. Nothing particular occurred during the time, excepting the death of Mr. Blanchard the second mate. He had the yellow fever. I sent him to the hospital and he was sent back well, but he chose to sleep up on deck in the dew, and had a relapse, which took him off. Mr. B. was a middle aged man, and a good sailor. He had some funny ways, one of which was, he would whistle in his sleep, and I used to think what a good watchful officer he was, as when I woke up in the night I could hear him whistle, I knew he was awake and looking out.

One night as I went on deck hearing the wind blowing, I called out to him, "Mr. Blanchard, take in the royals, there is rather too much wind for them." He kept on whistling standing up by the helm. I walked a little nearer to him, and said in a louder voice, "Mr. Blanchard, let the men take in the royals." He jumped, saying, "Sir." "Why, Mr. Blanchard," [I said.] "Do you whistle in your sleep? I thought you was very watchful, because I heard you whistle, now if I hear you whistle I shall know you are asleep."

I called on my old consignees Messrs. Drake & Mitchell & Co. and they soon obtained a freight of sugar for me to Antwerp, at £4.10 per ton, which amounted to about six thousand dollars. We had a very good passage to Antwerp. I consigned the vessel to my old friend Mr.

Delisle. The ship brokers do all the business of foreign vessels in Antwerp, so that the consignee had not much to do with the vessel. Still it is necessary to have a consignee, as the ship brokers are not allowed to take a consignment of vessel or cargoes. I decided to go back to Havana, and had the vessel advertised for freight, and this brought me in acquaintance with Mr. Jean Baptist Donnett, a merchant in the place, who besides shipping a portion of the cargo to Havana, offered me a charter back to Antwerp, which I accepted.

Antwerp, as well as other cities in Europe have a regular bourse every week day from one till two. In English it is called Exchange, where the merchants meet & where most of the business is transacted. The Boursenhall, as it is called in Antwerp, is a large square surrounded by a two story building, the lower part around the square being open, forming a piazza of about twenty feet wide, supported by stone pillars beautifully carved, every pillar being different. There are two wide entrances to the square, having iron gates, which are closed and locked at one o'clock precisely as the town clock strikes, and are not opened until the clock strikes two, so that all the business men have to be punctual, for neither love or money can open the gates during the hour, and no talking through the gates is allowed.

This is a very antique building, quite a curiosity in itself and well worth seeing, particularly during change hours when the hundreds assemble, and are all talking at the same time, making a buzzing of human voices, which must be heard, as no description can give one an idea. All the principal merchants have their particular stand, where either they or some of their clerks are always to be found during change hours. I as well as all other Captains went on change every day to meet our merchants or brokers.

The cargo being all discharged in good order, and the vessel being nearly loaded with another cargo for Havana, I closed my accounts with Mr. Delisle, and remitted the balance of my freight money to Messrs. Baring Bros. & Co. London, and sailed for Havana, where I arrived after a pleasant passage of about forty days. We found our friends glad to see us, and as they insisted upon our staying with them, we were [only] too glad to accept their hospitality.

The vessel was consigned to Messrs. Forcade & Co. according to the terms of the charter party with Mr. Donnett. My freight from Antwerp amounting to near five thousand dollars was all rightly delivered, and the vessel loaded with a cargo of coffee, at £4.10 per ton, according with the terms of the charter party. She was again ready to sail for Antwerp.

I generally carried a goat with me on my various voyages, for the sake of the milk, and on my passage from Antwerp I had a very superior one, with two kids of good size, and on our arrival in Havana, I had put them on shore at my friend Patterson, who had a molasses establishment on the bay near where our vessel lay at anchor, so that they could run about and pick up shrubs & grass. After being there a week or more I called to see how they were getting on. I met Mr. Patterson, who was a man of 60, and of rather an irascible disposition, who told me one of my kids was lost. He expected it had been stolen. I told him it was of no consequence as I did not care about them, as it was only the goat that was of any use.

About two days after, it being Sunday, I thought I would go over and see my friend Patterson, who invited me to stop to dinner, which I did. After dinner he wanted to show me his establishment, which was a large stone building divided in three parts. On one end was his molasses tank, built of brick and held twelve hundred hogsheads of molasses, in which he received the molasses from the various plantations he contracted with. It was full, and covered over with planks. The other end of the building was filled with empty hogsheads to put the molasses in when he sold it to the American vessels which hauled to his wharf to load. The centre of the building was used by his workmen & coopers. Over the tank was a second story where he lived. There was a bad smell all through the building, which he thought was caused by dead rats.

He said he would like to show me his molasses, and called some of his men to remove one or two of the planks, when the first thing that came in sight was the "long lost" kid, puffed up tremendously with the hair all off, and producing the most dreadful scent. The sight of Patterson at this discovery would have made a picture for a Hogarth. He threw off his hat, and his gray hair stood on end. He could at first hardly speak, and when he did such a round of curses poured forth that would have frightened all the goats in Cuba, could they have but comprehended it. The amount of it was that he considered his molasses spoilt, and himself ruined. I of course felt very bad, but could say nothing, except to express my sorrow, and take myself and my goat & kid off.

The day before I sailed I called to bid my friend P. good bye. There was a Portland brig loading molasses at the wharf, Capt. Winslow, one of the oldest traders in that article. Patterson, as soon as he saw me, called me one side, and asked me not mention a word about the dead kid, as he wished it kept a secret. He then told me that a few days after I was there last, old Winslow called to enquire about a cargo of molasses, the price &c. "I did not expect to sell, so I put on a high price, half a bit higher than others were selling for. He said he would like to look at it, so I called a hand and ordered him to bring a bucket full from the tank. Old Winslow examined it, and after a little while decided to take a cargo. He said it was the best molasses he had seen. He told other Captains and I have sold every hogshead I had in the tank, and could sell as much more. Your kid instead of doing me harm has put a thousand dollars in my pocket."

The vessel being loaded and ready for sea, our good friends at the farm wished me to send our large long boat and get some coconuts and other fruit for our use on the passage, which I did, and it was filled with all kinds of fruit, besides some large loafs of sugar just from the plantation. We had a pleasant passage to Antwerp. Nothing occurred that I recollect worth recording. The vessel was consigned to the Widow Donnett & Co., to whom the cargo of coffee belonged.

I found that Mr. Jean B. Donnett, who had chartered the vessel, was the son of the widow who carried on the mercantile house. It seems his father who was a wealthy merchant died when his son was too young to attend to the business of so extensive a house. His mother therefore took charge and carried on the business under the name of Widow Donnett & Co. She was one of the most extraordinary women I have ever met. It was then ten years since her husband died, and she had not only kept the mercantile house up, but had extended it largely. The counting room, as is generally the custom, was in the lower rooms of their mansion house. Mrs. Donnett always went with her servant to the market to provide the dinner before she came into the counting room, which was generally about 10 o'clock, when she would take a seat at her large and beautiful desk, and commence opening the pile of letters that had been received from the post office, and as she read them, she would write a note with a pencil on each one, which was the answer, and hand them to the corresponding clerk, who would write the letters in reply.

She seemed to have the immense business which the house did to the East and West Indies at her fingers, and I have been in the counting room to enquire about my own business, and have sat and watched with wonder at her prompt manner in answering all questions, to the brokers, as well as to her Captains. They owned several large ships which traded to Batavia, and other places, and her son Jean, who was a man of thirty and a partner in the house, would always refer to her about any business.

She gave reception dinners twice a week, and we were most always invited. These were indeed grand affairs, never less than twenty, and sometimes over thirty. A long table—she sat in the middle on one side, and her son Jean on the other. Every one of the guests had their name written on a piece of paper, which was placed under the wine glass where they were to sit. Quite a number of courses, and the cloths removed, showing the beautiful black mahogany tables, which were covered with a great variety of fruit and wine.

I decided to go back to Havana for another freight and advertised the vessel for that port. The ship brokers Messrs. William Marsilly & Co. procured nearly a full cargo. I closed my account with the consignees, and remitted the balance of the freight money to Messrs. Baring Bros. & Co. London. Every thing being ready, the pilot came on board and the vessel was taken down the river to Hellevoetsluis, which is a little fishing town and pilot station at the entrance of the Scheldt, and where vessels exchange the river pilot for a sea pilot, which all vessels require to pilot them over the various bars at the entrance of the river.

It was now the middle of winter and very cold, and as the ice began to make I was afraid the vessel might be frozen in. In those days there were no steam boats to tow vessels as there is now, and as no vessel could go to sea except the wind was fair, we had to come to an anchor and wait for a change of wind. Some vessels had been laying there for several weeks windbound.

We had been there about ten days, when in the middle of the night I observed a change in the weather, and expected a change in the wind. I sent my boat on shore for the pilot, who at first was not willing to come on board, but after some persuasion by Mr. Parsons, and an offer of a gratuity, if he would at once go on board, he consented. The reason he declined going on board, was that it was not customary for pilots to go off to vessels before daylight, and he did not believe that the wind would change. As soon as he was on board I had the sails loosed, and the anchor hove up. By the time it was daybreak, and the wind although light was fair, and the tide being the right way for an hour or two more, we got out of the river and over the bars into the North Sea, when the wind hauled back to the old quarter, and our vessel was the only one which got to sea. The others, and there were many, were detained for several weeks. Some of them were shut in with the ice and were detained until spring.

Soon after we got into the North Sea, a heavy gale came on from the S.W. which was direct ahead, with rain & snow, and ice began to form on the rigging. The weather was very thick, and no lights could be seen, so that we had to go by the lead. We stood over to the English shore until our soundings shallowed. I then wore round and stood back to the Belgian shore.

At 12 o'clock, the gale increasing, I close reefed the sails, and kept the lead agoing when all at once the water shoaled from 16 fathom to 4 fathom. That completely puzzled me, as I could find no such soundings on my chart. I therefore wore ship, and when in the act of wearing one of [the] best sailors fell overboard in the lee side of the vessel which at the time was hardly moving through the water. The man floated alongside and I got a coil of rope around him, and as I hauled on it turned him round. In vain I called to him to hold on, but he took no notice of it, and I could not save him, as he was soon sucked under the counter and sunk. The seas were running so high and the night so dark that I dare not lower a boat.

I felt the loss of this man seriously, and together with the doubtful position of my vessel I was almost in a state of despair, for it was a most dreadful night, as it was snowing and blowing a gale of wind. I determined when it was daylight, if possible, to find a pilot to take the vessel into some port for safety. I therefore in the morning stood in towards the Belgian shore, with the hope to fall in with some fisherman, or pilot boat that could at least tell me the position of the vessel.

At about 9 A.M. we saw a small vessel to the leeward. We at once run down to her, and although the sea was running very high I sent by boat on board and brought one of her men on board of our vessel. He could not speak a word of English, but I found out that the craft was a French fisherman. The fellow would not tell me a word how the land bore, or give me any information until I wrote him an order on Antwerp for his money. He kept saying "vant louidor," which I understood very well to be twenty louis d'ors, which was entirely out of the way, so I wrote an order on Mr. Donnett, to pay five louis d'ors. He took the paper and stowed it away in his leather pouch, and made me understand to keep on as I was going, and I should make Ostend.

In the course of an hour we were close into the land of Ostend and the pilot hoy was in sight. I run up close alongside and asked for a pilot. I sent the Frenchman in my boat on board the hoy, and brought a pilot on board. By this time it was noon, and the gale increasing. The pilot spoke a few words of English and his first order was "Go to sea." In vain I tried to get him to take the vessel into Ostend, but he said it was impossible with the wind then blowing, and so we had to stand out to sea again, and passed an awful night as the sea was running very high, and every now and then they [the waves] would break over the vessel, and I expected that she would founder before day light. It being in the middle of winter when the days were very short, and the nights very long, blowing and snowing, with the air piercing cold, it was indeed awful.

At last day light came, and we saw the island of Walcheren under our lee. The pilot knew the land, and said we could make a harbour. I told him to take the vessel in. We passed by a point on which there was a light house, and then up a small bay about 8 or 10 miles, when the water became smooth, and we came to an anchor, and every one on board were glad of a rest.

The following day a boat from the town came alongside to enquire who we were and where we came from, & various other questions. Finding that we were from Antwerp and part of our cargo was gin, they said we should put on board an officer of the customs, who was to watch that none of the cargo was landed, and I was requested to go up to the town and make an entrance of the vessel. This I refused to do, as I had made the harbour only for safety, and should go to sea with the first fair wind. The head officer of the boat gave some orders to the pilot and the custom house officer which was left on board, which I of course could not understand, but supposed them to be orders not to allow the vessel to proceed to sea until she was entered at their custom house.

That night there was a change in the weather, and the wind hauled round to the northward, which was fair to go out, and the cold was increasing so that we should soon be frozen up in the ice, and might be detained for months. I therefore made up my mind that the vessel should go to sea at once. It was about one o'clock in the night. I called the pilot and told him to pilot the vessel out to sea. This he decidedly refused, as he had no boat to take him off from the vessel. I tried to reason with him, promising I would put him on shore at the light house, and pay him double pilotage. It was no use, he would not listen to it.

I then consulted with my mates. They agreed with me, that we should get to sea before the ice made. I then ordered the men to be called to weigh the anchor. The pilot was still obstinate, and as the crew were shipped in Antwerp I presumed they could speak [to], or understand the pilot. I called him to me, and forbid him to speak a word to the men, and stand by my side at the helm, and to steer the vessel out of the bay, and that if he run her aground that I would shoot him, showing him my pistols, which I held rather near his head. This frightened him, and he became subservient to my will.

The anchor was taken up, sail was set, and the vessel taken safely out of the bay. We run close into the light house, and the boat with four men and the second mate were alongside ready to take the pilot and officer on shore. I gave the pilot double pilotage, and provisions for him and the officer, and made him get into the boat. I then called the officer, who was rather a large man of about sixty. He was asleep below. When he came on deck and saw that the vessel was at sea, he became quite enraged, and would not get into the boat, but began to blow me, the pilot, and everybody else up sky high in Dutch. I tried to make him understand that he must get into the boat and go on shore at the light house, or go to Havana. He became rather violent, and I called Mr. Parsons and the steward, and we forced him over the side into the boat, and they were landed without further trouble. The northerly wind held on and we had a fine run through the English Channel, into the Atlantic Ocean, and arrived in Havana, having a pleasant & quick passage.

I called upon my old friends Drake Mitchell & Co., who offered me a freight back to Antwerp at £4.10 per ton for a cargo of sugar, which I at once accepted. The family of Gomez, with whom we stayed during our former visits to Havana, had moved from their farm to the city. We called on them, and they very cordially invited us to stay with them, which we declined as they would not allow us to pay our board. They could not think of such a thing, but insisted upon our staying with them. We had brought from Antwerp a handsome marble clock, which we gave them.

The vessel was soon loaded with a cargo of sugar, and we sailed for Antwerp, with a new crew, the one which had come from Antwerp having run away, as is the usual custom in Havana. They were a rough looking set, and I expected trouble with them.

The steward was a large Negro, who as I was told, took the command of the schooner [that] he came in to Havana, and I was warned to look out for him. He came on board very much dressed up with a black suit, and a ruffle shirt of some extension. He marched aft in rather pompous a manner, said he was the steward. I asked him if he could make hot cakes for breakfast, and some other questions respecting his business as steward. He answered in his pompous style "Yas Sir," and took from his pocket a book of recipes, which he handed to me. I looked over it and saw that most of the recipes required milk. I asked him what he did in such cases, as there was no milk on board.

He said "I find um substitute, Massa Captin." I sent him about his work, thinking I had a pretty good steward, and told him to make some hot cakes for breakfast. They proved to be the worst mixture of flour I ever saw.

For dinner a roast chicken was brought to the table, not cleaned. I told him not to let me see anything of the kind again. The following day the same thing occurred. As I carved the chicken, the crop filled with corn burst out. He became very impudent. I ordered him up on deck, and followed him up. He turned around and showed fight, using abusive language. I sprang upon him, and with the assistance of the mate soon overpowered him, and had him tied to a bolt in the deck. He was in a perfect frenzy, foamed at the mouth, & roaring out "True blue never die." I returned to the cabin to finish my dinner, after putting him in irons, and left him to cool down.

In the course of an hour I went to him & finding him still in a very excited state, he was put below for the night, with the irons on. In the morning he was brought up the most humble Negro ever seen, and I had him set to his work again. He behaved himself during the passage, but he was the worst steward I ever had, and I turned him ashore as soon as we arrived in Antwerp. The crew were disposed to be unruly at first, but finding they had someone who knew how to handle them, they did very well, and there was no serious trouble with them on the passage, which was rather a stormy one of about forty days.

We were in Antwerp but a short time discharging the cargo from Havana, and taking on board what freight offered for Boston, to which port we sailed after taking leave of our good friends. We arrived after a pleasant passage of about six weeks, nothing particular occurring worth mentioning. It was now early in the summer of 1829. My wife having made three voyages from the West Indies to Europe, and being in poor health, we thought it would be better for her to remain on shore whilst I went to Havana again in the brig. She had become so attached to the sea life, and to our cozy quarters on board of the *Eight Sons*, that she at first was disinclined to remain on shore.

———

I REMAINED AT HOME but a short time, when I again sailed for Havana, arriving in the middle of summer. Business was very dull, as is usual during the summer months, but I had not to wait long before my friends Messrs. Drake & Mitchell procured me a freight for Cádiz, to be taken on board at Trinidad de Cuba, a port on the south side of the island. This was a charter from Don Joaquin Arieta, a Spanish merchant in Havana who had a contract with the government to furnish all the salt required, no other person permitted to import any to the island. My charter was for a cargo of sugar to Cádiz, at £4.10 per ton, and a return cargo of salt to Havana at six reals per *fanega*, which was about $1800.

I sailed round the western end of Cuba (Cape Saint Antonio) and had rather a long passage, as I had the Gulf Stream against me to the cape, and then had to beat up, over two hundred miles against the trade winds, to Casilda, which is the seaport to Trinidad. I was told that I was fortunate in not having a longer passage, as few vessels came from Havana in a shorter time at that season of the year when there was so much calm weather, that the last vessel had sixty days, and I had but fourteen. That vessel, after leaving Havana, fell in with a calm, and the current of the Gulf Stream carried her away up the Gulf, so that she was obliged to go round the island of Abaco, and cross over the Bahama Banks, to get back again from where she started from, so that I considered myself lucky in coming a distance I could easily have run in four days, in fourteen.

The town of Trinidad is situated on the side of a mountain about five miles from Casilda, which is the port of entry to Trinidad, and is quite a little village, being the place of deposit for all the sugar and molasses which is shipped from Trinidad. I at once on my landing procured a horse and rode up to the city, and presented my letter of introduction to Mr. John Young, an English gentleman who was to ship the cargo. I found Trinidad to be a neat Spanish built city. The streets were narrow, and the houses mostly of one story. It contains between ten and twenty thousand inhabitants, the larger portion being Blacks and mulattoës. I was very agreeably entertained there, and returned to Casilda to make arrangements for discharging the ballast & preparing the vessel to take on board the cargo of sugar.

About ten days after my arrival, the Captain of a Philadelphia ship, which was at anchor near our vessel, loading a cargo of molasses, proposed that we should go up to the city, as the mail arrived from Havana that day, and we both expected letters. In the afternoon we hired horses and rode up to the city, where we had to pass the night, as it was after dark before the mail was sorted. We both got interesting letters, and early in the morning mounted our horses to return to our vessels. On our way down we met a person who told us that two American vessels had been struck with lightning. It at once occurred that they might be our vessels, and we hurried on to Casilda, to learn that a heavy squall with thunder and lightning passed over between seven & eight in the evening, and struck both of our vessels, setting them on fire, but as it rained very hard, the fire was soon put out. We of course hurried on board.

I found the lightning had struck the main top gallant mast, and run down the main mast to the deck, doing much damage to the pumps and the decks, starting the planks. It then followed the chain cable through the hawse hole, and staving the long boat which was lashed to the cable, I found that it had set fire to the main top sail, which was badly burnt, and went down through the main mast, splitting out a piece twenty feet long, and to the depth of ten inches, thus ruining the mast.

It was fortunate that neither the Captain of the ship [from Philadelphia] nor myself were on board, as it is probable we both would have been killed, as I was in the habit at that hour of walking the deck just where it was torn up, and no doubt would have felt the shock. The [Philadelphia] ship was struck on the mizzen mast, the lightning passing down through the deck and, entering the Captain's room, tore his berth to pieces, and setting the bed clothes on fire, passed through the cabin over board.

I went on board to examine the damage done the ship, and the mate told me that the Captain usually went in his berth about the time the vessel was struck, and of course would have been killed. It was a god send that we went up to Trinidad that afternoon, and were detained there through the night.

In the course of three weeks, we had the cargo of sugar on board, and sailed for Havana to get a new main mast, in the place of the one that was ruined by the lightning. This detained the vessel for a week or more. I made up my mind that I would return to Boston, and put Mr. Parsons in command of the vessel, which I did and dispatched her for Cádiz. This was my last trip in the brig *Eight Sons*. She was a very lucky vessel during the time I owned her, which was about five years.

12

The Brig Creole

WE ARRIVED IN BOSTON in the fall of 1829. I remained at home for a couple of months, and finding my wife's health failing, I thought it would be beneficial for her to avoid the winter at the north, and we took passage in the brig *Newton*, Captain Luce, to Havana. We found him a very unpleasant man to be with. Instead of trying to please us, he did everything to make us uncomfortable, and we were very glad when we reached Havana, and got clear of a disagreeable man and his vessel.

Mr. Shaler had been appointed consul general of Cuba. He had been consul general of Algiers, and was the first officer of this kind in Cuba. His friend Richard Cleveland was the vice consul, who with his wife were keeping house, and Mr. Shaler, who was unmarried, was living with them. Mr. Cleveland & his wife were both cousins of my mother, and were glad to have us join them in the expenses of living, and which we were very glad to do, as they had a large house and we had fine rooms, and found a very pleasant home, as Mr. & Mrs. Cleveland were not only relations, but exceedingly pleasant people.

We were invited to visit a sugar estate belonging to a brother of Mrs. Cowan, the lady with whom we had stayed on our various visits to Havana. It was about twenty miles from Havana, and we rode there in volants. We stayed there three days and enjoyed our visit very much. It was the first time we had been in the country, and everything looked strange, and interesting.

It was grinding time, as they called it. In the fields were gangs of Negroes, cutting the sugar cane, and loading the ox carts with it, which brought it to the mills, consisting of three large iron cylinders, which were kept turning by machinery, worked by oxen (now they use a steam engine for that purpose). The cylinders pressing close together would squeeze the juice from the cane, which ran down to large copper tanks, in which lime was put to clarify it, when it was ready to go into the large sugar boilers, three set in a row, called the train.

These iron boilers held about seventy gallons of juice, which were kept boiling. A sugar master watched when the juice had boiled enough in the first boiler, when the hands bailed them to the next, and when it boiled to a certain consistency, it was bailed into the next, and after a certain time, when the sugar master thought it had boiled enough, it was bailed out into large wooden vats to cool.

During all the time of this operation, two Negroes at each boiler, with skimmers, full of holes fastened to long handles were constantly skimming off the boiling foam. The skimmers were like the covers of the old fashioned warming pans, and the bailers were like the bottoms. It is said that Lord Timothy Dexter of Newburyport once sent a cargo of warming pans to the West Indies, and they being well adapted for this purpose have been in constant use ever since.

After the liquid had partly cooled in the wooden vats, it was put into the forms, made of baked clay, open wide at the top, running down to a point, in which was a hole, stopped by a wooden plug and when quite cool, these forms were taken to the sugar house, and placed in holes made in the floor, for the molasses to drain out into large brick vaults underneath. A mixture of clay & other earths were then put on each form, and the wooden plugs taken out, and the molasses drained out, which required about thirty days, when the loaves already done were taken out of the forms, and placed in the dryers which were large drawers, about eight inches deep, which were kept in the sun during the day and run under cover during the night.

The loaf when taken from the form, presents three kinds of sugar. The upper part is white, the middle light brown, and the lower part quite dark. These different kinds were put into different drawers, and when thoroughly dry were packed in boxes, and sent to the city for sale, and shipped to the United States and Europe. There were then on this estate one hundred and twenty slaves, men, women, & children. All worked excepting women with infants, and small children. We should judge they were well treated and well fed.

On the morning that we were to return to the city, we were called at four o'clock, so as to arrive before the heat of the day. One of the servants brought into our room a lighted candle, which gave but little light, but enough for us to dress, and to discover something moving in one corner of the room, which I thought was a land crab. I threw my shoe at it, and knocked it over. It proved to be a large tarantula, an immense spider whose bite is very poisonous. Its body was as large as my fist, and its legs when spread out covered a space of more than eighteen inches in diameter. They were covered with long red hairs, from half to an inch long. I secured it and put it into a box to preserve it. The family said that they often saw them, but never saw so large a one.

Speaking of land crabs, I should speak of my experience of them the night I slept in Trinidad. I was awakened in the middle of the night by what I supposed was some one in my room, but it proved to be land crabs which had entered through a hole from the outside. The floor of the room was of boards, on joists laid on the ground. They made a tremendous racket with their big claws as they moved about the room, which was very dark, and I could not for the life of me think what was knocking about in the room. Once or twice I felt the sheet being pulled, which hung down near the floor, and they would seize it by their claws.

When it came daylight nothing was to be seen, as they had gone out the way they came in. The ground in some places were covered with them. At certain seasons of the year they came down from the high lands to the sea side, by thousands, and that was the season when I was there. They are ugly looking things. They do not look like the common sea crab. They have a large round body, like a ball, the largest about as big as a man's two fists put together, and one immense claw like a lobster's. They are not eatable.

We arrived in Havana at noon, having had a delightful visit. A few days after, I met on the mole a Captain Hall, belonging in Gardiner, Maine. He owned the brig *Creole*, which had lately arrived from Europe. The captain, my friend John Barnett, had left her and gone to New Orleans, to take charge of his half brother's sugar estate.

Capt. Hall wished to sell his vessel, and wanted me to go on board and see her, which I at first declined, as I did not want to buy a vessel, but finally by his persuasion went off with him to see her. I found she was partly loaded with sugar for Marseilles at $4 a box which was a good freight. I examined her and was much pleased with her. He named a price higher than I felt inclined to give. Going on shore in the boat, he wished me to make him an offer. I offered him five thousand dollars, one half cash, the other half [in] six months, and to my surprise he accepted it, and the vessel was mine.

I then made a charter with a Spanish house for a cargo of wine back to Havana from Barcelona. The brig was soon loaded with her cargo of sugar, & dispatched from the custom house, and the papers with orders given to the Captain who was recommended by Mr. Hall, and was to sail the next morning. I forget the Captain's name.

In the evening I went to the Lonja to see the news of the day, and to my astonishment, I found the Captain quite intoxicated, sitting in a chair at one of the small tables. I spoke to him. He did not seem to know me. I noticed the papers I had given him, but an hour or two before, sticking out of his coat pocket. I took them and went home, told my wife what had happened, and that I must go in the vessel to Marseilles, giving her the choice to remain with our friends, or go to Marseilles with me. She preferred to go in the vessel, and we got all our things ready to go on board in the morning.

The wind was not favorable to go out in the morning, but in the middle of the day, it became a little more fair and I made the attempt, but owing to the heavy seas at the entrance to the port, she was thrown against the rocks of the Morro Castle, and the planks on the starboard side stove in. The under current, and the little head way she had, carried her clear of the rocks before another sea struck her.

It was now late in the afternoon, and I thought I should have to go back into port again to repair damages. I had a stage rigged over the side and went over to examine the extent of the damage. [I] found two of the waist planks broken. I repaired it as well as I could by caulking oakum into the cracks and tacking several thicknesses of tarred canvas over the broken place, and securing the whole by nailing boards over all, and made up my mind to proceed on the voyage, and if she leaked bad, to put into Charleston for repairs, which I had no occasion to do.

It was the season for light winds and calms, of which we experienced a good share. After being out some twenty days we made the island of St. Marys, one of the Western Islands. I wanted to pass to the south of it, but owing to calms was not able to. There was a strong current setting to the north, and on the following day we found ourselves drifting on the Formigas, a reef of rocks some six or eight miles to the north of St. Marys. It was noon, and the vessel was drifting towards the rocks quite fast, and it was entirely calm.

The boat was manned to tow her off. The men rowed for dear life, as the rocks were less than a quarter of a mile from us, and the swell of the sea was breaking over them with crushing force. We got some few things together, and prepared to leave the vessel before she was cast on the rocks. We had all our light sails set, and made a smoke to show us if there was any air moving aloft, so that we could trim our sails to catch the least breeze. It was now a very anxious moment with us, as we were nearing the danger every minute. Most fortunately, a little air filled our light sails at this moment, which with the exertions of our men, carried us by the outer point of the rocks, within half the length of the vessel, a most wonderful escape, for had she touched the rocks she would have gone to pieces in a short time.

We had a pretty fair run to Gibraltar, which we passed one Sunday forenoon, so near that we could see the people on the beach, under

the immense rock and fortress of Gibraltar. We sailed up the Mediterranean with very light winds, making our passage very long from Havana, and we were short of everything in the way of provisions
excepting salt beef. About this time I discovered a brig coming towards us, and thinking she must be out from some port near by [and]
that she possibly might have something to spare in the shape of fresh
vegetables, I determined to speak her, and stood towards her for that
purpose, and what was my delight and surprise to find it was my own
brig, the *Eight Sons*, Capt. Parsons.

He of course was as much surprised to meet me, as he knew nothing of my buying the *Creole*. He supplied us with all we wanted. It was
really a very happy meeting, and when I arrived in Marseilles, I had
both vessels painted in the act of speaking as it was something beyond
my anticipations to meet my own vessel on the ocean, and being supplied with provisions, when I was captain of the other. I keep the
painting hanging in my room at Newburyport, in commemoration of
an event which seldom occurs to any one struggling through life.

After an hour's chat, we parted, he on his course toward Cádiz, and
I on my course toward Marseilles, where we arrived in a few days,
took a pilot, and was nicely moored, in one of the finest harbours I
had ever seen. After calling on my consignees, and delivering my letters and papers, the first thing was to seek out good lodgings for me
and my wife, is which we were very fortunate.

Marseilles is finely situated at the head of the Gulf of Lyons, on a
rising ground. The old part of the city contains many quite ancient
and curious old buildings. The new or modern part is covered with
most splendid stone buildings, in blocks along broad boulevards, with
wide side walks, many of them lined with beautiful trees. I have found
that all the old cities in Europe which I have visited have their old and
new parts, so that Marseilles is like the rest.

We had been there but a few days, when one morning we were
awakened by the guns firing and the bells ringing, and looking out of
our windows we saw white flags flying in every direction. The white
flag is the old French Bourbon colours, and as Charles 10th was the
monarch, of course that was the French flag at that time. It was about
the middle of July 1830. Upon enquiry we learned that all this "hub

bub" was the rejoicing of the populace over the news of the taking of Algiers, by the French army, which had besieged the place for a length of time.

We had a very pleasant time during our stay in Marseilles, as it was in the summer time, and charming weather all the time. We made several excursions in the country which we highly enjoyed. The cargo was discharged in good order, and we made preparations to proceed to the port of Barcelona for the cargo of wine, according to charter party made in Havana. All being ready on the 30th of July, the pilot came on board and hauled the vessel out of the harbour and anchored her outside.

There was a tremendous confusion in the city. The roar of guns, both artillery and small arms, convinced us that serious fighting was going on. We saw that the tricoloured flag was hoisted, taking the place of the white, and we supposed a revolution was going on. Some time after, we heard that a revolution had taken place throughout France, and that Charles the 10th had fled to Hamburg and the duke of Orleans had been chosen as [Louis] Philippe the king of France.

We had a short run over to Barcelona, the capital of Catalonia in Spain, which is situated on the west side of the Gulf of Lyons, on low level land, with high mountains in the back. It is a place of many centuries in existence, and like other old cities, has its old and new parts. The old part, which is still surrounded with its ancient walls & bastions, is very disagreeable to the modern eye. The streets are very narrow, from 12 to 15 feet in width. Some of them are less. The houses are five and six stories high, each story projecting over the next one below, so that the upper stories are but a few feet apart, and the tenants often place boards from one window to the other opposite, making a sort of garden with their flower pots. This causes the streets below to be dark and gloomy. The sun never shines upon them, and as they have no sewers the mud and filth are a permanent institution, and sickness prevails to an alarming extent.

The new city, which is by far the largest, has wide streets well paved with stone, and brick side walks, the houses handsome, and built after the French style, inhabited by the wealthy and well to do citizens. In the old part, there are no side walks, and when a team or carriage passes, those passing on foot are obliged to step in to the court yard, which every house has as the grand entrance to houses, a door on each side, with wide stair cases to each story, each a separate tenement having a large door for entrance on a wide landing in the stair way. And what strikes a stranger as curious is that every door has a small opening covered with an iron grating, and a slide on the inside, so that when one knocks, the party inside can draw the slide and see the visitor before the door is opened.

The harbour, or dock, in Barcelona is a large excavation capable of holding some hundreds of vessels, opening to the sea by double gates about three hundred and fifty feet apart, so that when a vessel enters first, the outside gate is opened, the vessel is hauled in, and the gate closed, before the other is opened, so that there is always one gate closed. We arrived on a Saturday, and went immediately on shore, and took lodgings at the principal hotel in the city, called the *Tres Reyes*, Three Kings, which is on a small open square fronting the gates in the wall, which opens upon the wharf surrounding the docks. The captain general's palace, and several other government buildings are on this square, so that it is quite a noted place, and a band of music plays every evening. We had quite a nice room, and after a good supper retired for the night.

A little after day light, a loud knock at our door aroused me, and I was told I must go at once to the captain general, as he had sent a *guardia civil*, police officer to take me there. I could not conceive for what purpose I was wanted, as I was not aware that I had done anything wrong. I found there the captain of the port, the American consul (who was a Spaniard), and several other officers. I was taken into the presence of the Conde de España, who was then the captain general of the province of Catalonia. He was a fine looking man, but I heard afterwards, that he was a great tyrant, and much disliked by the inhabitants.

An interpreter was called, and I was questioned about a flag flying at the mast head of my vessel, which as I had not seen, I knew nothing about. I was shown from the window of the palace, the vessel, with a long line of signals hoisted to the main mast head, the upper one being a tricoloured flag. I told them that I knew nothing about the flags, but presumed they were the vessel's signals hung up to air, a very common thing with vessels. That was what the Captain of the port told him, but he was not satisfied, and ascertaining it was an American vessel, he sent for the American consul, who knew nothing about it, then ordered the Captain to be brought to him, and I was sent for.

I found out afterwards, that evening previous the captain general had received the news of the revolution in France, and when he rose in the morning, looking out of his window and seeing the tricoloured flagging flying in the harbour, he became alarmed, fearing that a revolution had commenced in Spain. He ordered me to have it hauled down at once and never hoist it again. So ended this tempest in a tea pot.

We had some pleasant walks around the city on top of the walls, on which there is quite a nice road way. The extent of the walls is about two miles, built many centuries ago, of very large square stones. Every few rods there are bastions mounted with cannon, and a guard of soldiers to each. At the entrance to the harbour there is an immense artificial mound, about one hundred feet high, with an extensive fortification on top, which commands the harbour, as well as the city.

From our windows, which opened out on the square, it was amusing to watch the various people moving about. By far the greatest proportion were monks, priests, and others connected with the church, all with dresses according to their order, the St. Franciscans, with long blue gowns, tied round the waists with a white cord, the tops of their heads shaven, the St. Dominicans with white flannel gowns tied round the waist, with heads shaven and cowls hanging behind. The monks generally go bareheaded. The priests have long black gowns, and hats with large rims turned up on each side. The soldiers were the next in numbers to be seen, also a few Catalans with their red caps hanging down behind a foot or more. These are the workers, about one third of the Spanish nation, who do the work to support the other two thirds of idlers.

———

THE VESSEL WAS fully loaded with wine, and other small packages to make good stowage. The wine was brought up in lighters from Tarragona, a port lower down on the coast. I had an invitation to go down and witness the operation of treading out the juice from the grapes, by men with their feet, which I was obliged to refuse. I settled up my business with the consignees and employed a pilot to take the vessel to sea. The capt. general, Conde de España, was assassinated about six months after I left. He was a splendid looking officer, and a most splendid horseman.

We had a pretty fair run down to Gibraltar, when the wind hauled dead ahead. We beat about for some days, and finding it impossible to get out of the straits until a change of wind, I run in and came to an anchor in the western shore near in to the beaches and went on shore with my boat to get a couple casks filled with water, as I feared we might get short before we arrived at Havana. I went up on the hill, whilst the men were filling the casks, and came upon an extensive vintage, a glorious sight, the grapes perfectly ripe and hanging in large clusters. I gathered a quantity and took them on board.

The place where we anchored was about four miles from the town of Gibraltar, and in the morning we found that the vessel had drifted into the middle of the bay. The anchor had slid off into 60 fathoms of water, the chain hanging straight down from the bow, and the anchor several fathom from the bottom. The water was only five fathom deep where we anchored. It was quite a job to heave up the anchor, with such a length of chain, which we did as soon as we could, and sailed up among the shipping in the harbour, and came to an anchor, as the wind was blowing strong right ahead out in the straits.

I was afraid we should be put in quarantine, coming from Barcelona, was the reason I did not run to the anchorage instead of coming to anchor outside as I did. It was fortunate that we had not drifted on shore some where in the bay, as the night was very dark, and the shore could not be seen. I afterwards learned that the bottom where I anchored shelved off quite steep to the middle of the bay. Soon after we anchored, the government boat came alongside to enquire who we were, and where from, and we were delighted to know that there was no quarantine, and that we could go on shore as soon as we pleased, a favour we soon improved, and got nice rooms at the hotel, which was near the Government House.

Soon after dark the Scotch band began to play on their bagpipes in the square fronting the hotel. It was new music to us, and not very inviting to listen to. We remained there several days, until the wind changed so that we could go to sea. We had that music every evening at eight o'clock for an hour, as the Highland Regiment were stationed there, and their band honoured the governor with their presence.

We were glad to get among people that spoke our language, as we had not been since we left home. We enjoyed ourselves whilst we remained in Gibraltar, made the acquaintance of an officer in the army who was extremely polite. He went with us to the fortress, which is in the rock of Gibraltar, and showed us through the various galleries excavated in the solid rock, with the immense iron guns pointing out the port holes in every direction. The rock is of immense size, and has always been a fortress. The excavation was made by the Moors who formerly held Spain for eight hundred years, and the English government have done a considerable since it has been in their possession.

We were detained there about a week, when the [wind] changed round fair, and we made sail for Havana. We arrived there in October, having had a passage of sixty days from Barcelona. We found our friends all well and glad to see us. The cargo of wine was landed all in good order, and the freight paid. The vessel had paid her cost and something over in the six months I had owned her. I soon chartered her for another cargo of sugar to Hamburg, at £4.10 per ton, and put in Captain Farwell as commander, as he was highly recommended by Mr. John Moreland, a merchant in Havana. He proved a worthless fellow, got the vessel ashore on the Jutland coast in the North Sea, by which I lost much money. I sent Captain Clarkson from Newburyport to take charge of her. He made a very good voyage in her to Demerara and back to Amsterdam.

I should have mentioned before that whilst [we were] absent on our voyage to Antwerp in the summer [of] 1829, my good old father died, having suffered for two years previous, excruciating pains from the Bright's disease.

13

The Wreck of the Munroe

I BEGAN TO BE TIRED of doing nothing, and I chartered a Spanish brig to go to Baltimore for a cargo of flour as the duties by a Spanish vessel was only two dollars the barrel. According to the charter party the vessel was to have twenty days in Baltimore to repair and be new coppered before she was to be at my disposal. I at the same time chartered the American schooner *Munroe*, which had previously been a revenue cutter, to take a cargo of coffee to Philadelphia, as that was the best market. The vessel was coppered & looked in fine order.

The Captain was an old man, and rather sickly looking, and I had some doubts about his being the right man to navigate on a winter's coast. The vessel was loaded with a full cargo of coffee on my account, and after making the necessary arrangements for my wife to remain in Havana, I bid my friends goodbye and sailed away in the schooner for Philadelphia.

On the 14th day of December, we had got in the latitude of the Chesapeake Bay, and there was every appearance of a heavy gale from the N.E. and I said everything I could to the obstinate old Captain, to get him to make a safe harbour until the storm passed over, but in vain, he chose to keep on. It was of a Sunday, and in the afternoon it came on to blow and snow from the N.E. a tremendous gale. We had to take in all sail and lay the vessel to under a little canvas, by hoisting the throat of the mainsail a few feet, whilst the rest of the sail was lashed down. It was dark long before we got the vessel snug, and I was cold and wet. I went below and took off my wet clothes and put on dry flannels, and got into my berth, and wrapped myself up in the blankets to get warm, as there was no fire, and it was very cold.

About 12 o'clock as near as we could judge, a heavy sea struck the vessel, and Mr. Ducatel the mate who was on deck called to the Captain that the pintles of the rudder were broken, and the rudder was loose. I found that the Captain did not know what to do. He pretended to be sick in his berth. I called to the mate to pull out the tiller and let the rudder go, before another sea struck her, as it would tear off the stern plank. The Captain forbid it, and in a few minutes a sea struck her, and two of the lower planks on the stern were torn off, and the water began to pour in between the timbers of the stern frame.

I jumped out of my berth, having no time to put on my clothes, and run up on deck, got the tiller clear of the rudder, and let it go before it could do any more damage, and with the assistance of Mr. Ducatel and some of the men, got a sail over the stern, which kept some of the water from pouring in through the cabin. We then got the after hatch off, and commenced throwing coffee overboard to lighten the vessel by the stern. We all but the Captain worked for our lives, for two hours or more at the pumps and throwing cargo overboard, all of no use, as the vessel was filling fast.

Our only chance now was to lighten the vessel all we could, by cutting away the anchors, and letting the chain cables run overboard and throwing everything of weight from the vessel with the hope that she would float when full of water. As she sunk down, the seas began to break over, washing the boat, cambose, and every thing from the deck, and we all had to lash ourselves to the sides of the vessel, to keep from being washed overboard. Soon the foremast and bowsprit were carried away, and the seas breaking over the vessel with the greatest fury. We all expected she would soon sink, and that would be the last of us.

We were in the Gulf Stream, and the water was much warmer than the air, so that it was more comfortable under the water than above. Every once in a while a heavy sea would keep us under the water longer than at other times, when I would think she was going down. During these times strange thoughts would come over my mind. I recollected when I was a boy at Bridgewater drowning some kittens, which I had tied to a stone & thrown in a brook, and watched them kick and squirm. I thought how much better off I should be, naked as I was, on top of the highest pyramid in Egypt. I thought I should never see the sun again. At last the day began to break, and it became light, still snowing and blowing a gale. During the night a large piece of wood had been washed by the sea, and had struck me on my left leg, splintering the shin bone just below the knee, which gave me a good deal of pain.

Not long after daylight, we saw a schooner standing towards us, and our hopes of relief were raised. She passed very near us, to the windward. We hailed her, and made all the signs to attract their attention, but in vain, she passed on without noticing us. The wind had moderated and it ceased snowing by twelve o'clock. My plaid cloak had washed up through the skylight, and I was able to get it. I wrapped it round me, and tied it with a rope yarn. The sea was high during the day, and continually washed over the vessel, and we could get nothing to eat or drink, and could see no sign of a vessel, or prospect of relief, and had to pass another dismal night lashed to the wreck. The following day about noon, we saw a sloop standing towards us, and fortunately we made her see our signals, and she run close to us, and we were able to get on board of her, after several attempts to run alongside of us near enough for us to jump on board.

She proved to be a wood coaster belonging to Little Egg Harbour, a small port on the Jersey Shore. She had delivered a cargo of wood at New York, and had sailed from there Sunday morning, and was overtaken by the gale, which had disabled her, by breaking one of the pintles of her rudder, and the end of her main boom and other serious damages. She had two men besides the Captain. Their compass was broken, and the Captain had no idea where he was. When they left New York they had a small cask, with a large square hole on the bilge, filled with water, and a piece of fresh beef which was the usual allowance, as they never before had more than one day passage. During the night the sea had come over the vessel and filled the cask with salt water, and there was nothing to quench our thirst. There was a barrel of biscuits, which we eat, or tried to eat. We could chew the ship biscuits to powder, but could not moisten it enough to swallow.

The Captain was a very good fellow. He let me have a pair of socks and trousers and some other clothes, to cover my nakedness, and with my cloak, and a handkerchief to tie round my head I did very well. Our Captain was sick and useless and I and Mr. Ducatel assisted the Captain, with our men, and got the boom repaired and the sails set, and stood in to the westward, or what I judged to be west, for we had no compass, and the weather was very thick and not a star was to be seen. It was after dark before we got everything ready, and the night was cold and freezing. I kept up on deck & helped navigate the vessel.

At daylight in the morning, we were close in to a reef of rocks, and now land could be seen in the distance. I did not know exactly where we were and no one on board seemed to know the coast. I thought we must be somewhere abreast the north cape of the Chesapeake. We therefore beat against a headwind to the southward, and by noon we made Cape Henry. We stood in past Fortress Munroe, when we saw a small steamer that had come out of Hampton Roads, standing towards Norfolk. We hoisted our flag half mast, union down, a signal of distress, and she came towards us, and learning our trouble, sent a boat and brought us on board. This was about five o'clock in the afternoon.

We had had nothing to eat but dry biscuits and not a drop of fresh water to drink for three days. I cautioned the men to be careful, and not to drink too much at first, as it would be likely to make them sick, and I was the first one that did it, as I stepped on board and went into the cabin, whilst the Captain & passengers were questioning the men about the wreck, and on the cabin table was a pitcher of water, and I thought I would just take one swallow, but when I put it to my mouth I could not take it away until I had nearly emptied it of its contents. The result was that I suffered excruciating pain and was very sick afterwards.

I discovered among the passengers Mr. John Roberts, with whom I had done business in Norfolk. He of course could not have known me in the dress I was in, which was an old plaid cloak tied with a rope yarn round the waist, no shoes & no hat, and an old patched pair of pants, turned up at the bottom, as they were too long for me, and belonged to the Capt. of the sloop. Roberts was surprised, and made me change for a suit of his, shirt and all complete.

On arrival in Norfolk I took lodgings at the hotel, and eat too much supper. The consequence was that I was obliged to send for a physician in the night and was detained in Norfolk for more than a week with sickness. My leg, which was injured the first night I was lashed to the wreck, had become much swollen and was very painful, owing to the wet and cold it had been exposed to.

As soon as I could I went up to Baltimore and called on Mr. Lambert Gittings, to whom I had a letter of introduction from my friends Drake & Mitchell, whom I engaged to purchase a cargo of flour for the Spanish brig I had chartered in Havana. I found letters from Messrs. Reynolds & Bros. of Philadelphia when I arrived in Baltimore, telling me the cargo of coffee by the schooner *Munroe* was fully covered by insurance, according to my order from Havana. I concluded to stop in Baltimore, where I had good quarters at the best hotel in the city, until the Spanish brig arrived, as well as to give a chance for my leg to get better of the inflammation and swelling, which was extremely painful. There were many vessels wrecked on our coast in the gale of the 14th, among the rest a new brig in which my old friend Mr. Patterson of Havana was a passenger (I have alluded to him previously), with many others who were all lost on the night of the 14th December 1830.

In the course of a fortnight the brig arrived, and was consigned to Colonel Tennant, an old merchant of Baltimore and father to Gittings's wife. The vessel according to charter party was to have twenty days to be repaired and coppered, before she was to be at my disposal to receive the cargo of flour. I gave orders to Mr. Gittings to purchase one thousand barrels of flour for her cargo, and went on to Philadelphia in the stage coach, as there were no rail roads in those days. I went to my brother Stephen's house for the few days I was to remain there to settle up the insurance for the lost cargo of coffee. I found Mr. Reynolds a perfect gentleman in all my transactions with him. We had no difficulty with the insurance offices in collecting, and placing the money at my disposition.

I returned to Baltimore, and in a few days, the Spanish brig arrived, bringing some sugar & consigned to Colonel Tennant. After waiting a sufficient time as I thought for her to be ready to receive cargo, I called on the consignee to ascertain, who told me that upon taking the old copper off, they found the planks rotten, and he had decided not to do anything to her until he could hear again from the owners in Havana, for it would take more money than was sent for her repairs to put her in good order. I therefore had to protest, and abandon the charter, and ordered Mr. Gittings to sell the flour, which had declined in price since he bought it, which with expense, made a loss of about six hundred dollars which I had to claim on the owners for the nonfulfillment of the charter party.

My object now was to get out to Havana as soon as I could, as both of my adventures had failed, which would have proved very profitable had there been no misfortune. I saw by the papers that there was a schooner to sail in a day or two from Philadelphia for Havana, so I closed up my accounts with Mr. Gittings and proceeded on to take my passage. But when I got there Mr. Reynolds informed me that the schooner was an old vessel, and advised me not to go in her, and as I had experienced enough in an old schooner, I took his advice and decided to go to New York, and take passage in a new brig which was advertised to sail on the following day. I therefore wrote a few lines to my folks in Havana by the schooner, and took passage for New York, by the mail stage which proved to be a light uncovered wagon with four horses, which was to start at 3 o'clock in the afternoon.

It was Saturday, early in January 1831. It was very cold, and blowing a gale. There was no other passenger, and the driver seemed to express

himself as if he wished I was not there, which I [also] did most sin-
cerely long before daylight. A long dreary night was before me to ride
a distance between 90 and 100 miles, over a rough frozen road, in an
open wagon, with two or three large mail bags, as my only compan-
ions, jolting about in the bottom of the wagon. Sometimes I would be
on top, and sometimes they would be on top of me.

Early in the night it began to snow. I almost began to despair, and
told the driver I would stop at the next tavern, when for the first time
he seemed to show some sympathy for me, and told me that at the
next stopping place, we should have the mail coach, and he thought I
would be more comfortable. That consoled me a little and as I was so
anxious to take my passage in the vessel which was to sail on the following day, I decided to keep on. When we stopped, sure enough,
there was a mail coach, but it was only for the mail bags, being a small
carriage body shaped like a coach, with a door on the side to put the
bags in, and as there was no room for me, and the seat for the driver
was only large enough for one, I had to set jammed in on a place behind, which I thought was so much better than to be tumbled about
with the mail bags in the wagon, I did not complain.

The snow continued through the night, and at last, near daylight,
we arrived at the post office to deliver the mail bags. I was so jammed
in between the small railing on the back stand, and the coach body,
and stiff and cramped with the cold, and wet with the snow, that I required a considerable [amount] of help to get out of my confinement.
Everybody wondered that I should come on from Philadelphia such a
stormy night, and under such circumstances. I thought they must suspect that I was some criminal running away from justice. I suppose if
there had been detectives watching round for a job as there are now a
days, I should have been taken up on suspicion and lodged in the station house. I finally reached a hotel in New York by 8 o'clock and got
a comfortable breakfast, and then hurried down to the vessel.

It being Sunday morning, there was no one on board, and no one
moving about. After waiting some time the ship keeper came on
board, and told me the vessel had been detained by bad weather and
would not sail for some days. I was disappointed, but there was no

help, I must go back to the hotel and patiently wait until the vessel was ready. I went to my room, and as I had no sleep during the night, was glad to go to bed and rest, as well as to forget my troubles for a time.

The following day I went to the office of the consignee, and paid my passage. He said the vessel would be ready Wednesday morning, so on that day I went to the vessel, [and] saw the Captain, who told me she would not be ready for a day or two as all the cargo was not yet on board. I saw some of the passengers. They did not impress me favourably, and they proved to be a dreadful set.

The brig did not sail until Sunday. She seemed to be overloaded, setting very deep in the water. I asked the Captain what was his cargo. He said there were one hundred marble well curbs, weighing about a ton each, besides other heavy goods, and he told his consignees that the vessel was too deep, for winter weather. I was so displeased with the vessel, and passengers, that I hesitated to go in her, although I had paid my passage. I would not have gone in her, if there had been any other vessel going soon. When we got to sea, I found it was even worse than I had anticipated. The passengers were four dissolute women, and two miserable Spaniards who were accompanying them out. I refused to eat with them, and demanded from the Captain a separate table.

Soon after we left the pilot, a heavy gale came on and the vessel pitched about in a dreadful manner, the seas constantly coming on board of her. In the night a heavy sea struck her bows on the starboard side and started the cut water and stem from the bow planks, and the vessel began to leak so that both pumps could scarcely keep her free. The Capt. was about my age, but not of much experience. He was glad of my advice, which was to keep her off more before the seas, for if another sea struck her in the same place, she would go down. We put her under short sail just enough to keep her steady until day light, when we found the ends of the bow plank had started from the stem, leaving the seam open half of an inch for some six feet. It was a wonder that the leak was not greater.

The mate, who was as inefficient as the Capt., did not know what to do, and consulted me. I at once not only saw the danger we were in, but advised the remedy, which was to take a board six feet long and six inches wide, secure oakum on one side, and with a plenty of stout nails fasten it the whole length of the open seam, which with some difficulty was finally accomplished. The oakum was sucked in by the force of the water running in & the leak was stopped so that she was easily kept free.

We had a long passage of about 25 days, and one of the most disagreeable ones I ever made. I was thankful enough to get back to Havana again and find them all well, after an absence of more than two months. I called upon the owners of the Spanish brig and made a demand for the penal sum in the charter party for the nonfulfillment of the charter. They refused payment of a single cent, and the result was (by the advice of my friends) a law suit, which proved a losing business.

I REMAINED A FEW WEEKS in Havana, when we heard of some wrecks in Key West, and I thought I would go over and see what was for sale. I took passage in a fishing smack, after arranging with Drake & Mitchell for a credit to purchase. It is only about ninety miles from Havana across the Gulf of Florida to Key West, and instead of half of a day as I expected, it took us two days to get there. I was just in time for the auction of a cargo of sundries. I bought a lot of whale oil in casks, which I shipped over to Havana, which paid a handsome profit. I also bought a lot of dry goods, in which there was some profit.

Soon after, there was a vessel with a large cargo of cotton wrecked on the reef near Key West, in a ship from New Orleans bound to Europe. The cargo which was saved, being about a thousand bales, was brought into Key West, and after a while was advertised for sale at auction. This I thought a pretty good chance, and I went over to attend to the sale. I bought about seven hundred bales, and chartered a brig which was laying there, to take it to Boston at two dollars per bale. I was detained in Key West for a month or more in getting this cargo off, as every bale had to be weighed and marked.

I employed a young man who had been a midshipman in the U.S.

Navy. I forget his name. He was afterwards a commodore in the Texan navy. He was then under indictment for the murder of a young man who he thought was too intimate with his wife. It was impossible to get an impartial jury to try him. During the time he was at work for me, he was twice called up to the court room, where they tried to impanel a jury. I went up to hear the result, and to witness the manner of the proceedings. Every man had formed an opinion, and of course could not be impartial. It was finally decided to abandon the trial.

At last the cargo was all on board, and the vessel dispatched for Boston. The cargo was consigned to my uncle James P. Higginson, and I returned to Havana in a fishing smack, which was laden with live fish. The centre of the vessel, called the well, had holes bored through from the outside so that the salt water could pass in and out, giving the fish a chance to live whilst crossing the gulf.

I sometimes amused myself sitting beside the hatch way on deck, putting my arm down and trying to catch hold of the fish, and in doing so, I lost the ring, which was rather loose on my finger. I saw a fish catch it, and swallow it. I extremely regretted it, as it was a mourning ring left me by my father's will. I was a good mind to buy all the fish and open each one until I found the ring, but the Captain told me he could not sell them, and when he told me that there were several hundred fish, and were worth more than a dollar each in Havana, I entertained the idea no longer. But when we arrived, I told Pancho Marti, the owner of the fish market, and to whom the cargo was consigned, that I had lost my ring, and one of the fish had swallowed it, and that I would give a Spanish ounce of gold ($17) to anyone who would find it, but I never saw the ring again.

I had previously lost this ring several times, and it always come back to me. The last time was when I was lashed to the wreck of the schooner *Munroe*, and of course did not expect to see it again, but to my surprise one of the sailors saw it hanging on a crooked nail on the outside of the schooner, where the boards had been broken off from the stanchions, and when we got on board of the sloop asked me if I had lost a ring, and told me where he found it.

Key West is a small island not more than a mile and a half or two miles across in the widest part, and at this time was owned by four Americans, one quarter each. Capt. Green, one of the owners, was the only one who resided, and whom I employed to assist me in my business. He was a piratical looking fellow and I was in fear every day of having my throat cut. There were about two hundred inhabitants on the island, mostly fishermen who had come from the Bahama islands. They had little huts built close together, forming a little colony by themselves, where they had their families.

The island came in possession of the U.S. government as part of Florida when the Spaniards sold that country to the States. As there were many wrecks along the coast of Florida, it was necessary that a United States court should be established at Key West to adjudicate on wrecked property, and Judge Webb was appointed. He in fact was the ruler of the island, as every one had the greatest confidence in him. There had been a murder committed, in a drunken brawl, a short time before I was there, and the murderer was tried by Judge Webb, was convicted and sentenced to be hung, which took place whilst I was there. A gallows was rigged up on the beach for the purpose.

The criminal was a middle sized man of about thirty years, a foreigner of what nation I do not know, but he looked like a Spaniard. There was no jail, or place to confine a prisoner on the island. He was placed in charge of the sheriff, who kept him locked up in his house, until the time came for his execution, when they walked arm in arm down towards the gallows. On the way they passed a barber's shop, and the prisoner expressed a wish to be shaved, which the kind sheriff could not refuse, and into the shop they went.

The prisoner requested to take the razor and shave himself. This the sheriff refused, as he feared he was agoing to commit suicide, but the prisoner told him he had no idea of depriving him of the pleasure he anticipated. After shaving and brushing himself up so as to look decent, they walked together to the gallows, and ascended the steps arm in arm to the scaffold, which was about four feet square.

In the centre was a square hole, covered by a hatch secured by a spring underneath, on which the prisoner stood, who began to make an address to the crowd below, during which the sheriff was fixing the rope around his neck. He said that the people in Key West wanted to hang some one, and they had picked him out as a sample. He had got thus far in his speech when the sheriff, unperceived by him, touched the spring and the trap fell, dropping the prisoner about ten feet, which broke his neck. This was the first and last hanging that has taken place on that island.

There is quite a large pond in the centre of the island with an opening to the sea, through which the salt water pours in, and in the summer months, owing to the heat from the sun, large quantities of salt form, which is raked from the surface in large piles along the margin of the pond, and is shipped to the various ports along the coast.

The cargo of cotton which I shipped to Boston arrived in good order & sold well, giving a profit of about ten dollars a bale.

14

A Painful Loss

WE REMAINED IN HAVANA until the month of May, enjoying ourselves as well as we could, and then went to Matanzas, and made a visit of some weeks to our friends Mr. Stephen Gomez & family. We then took passage in the ship *Majestic*, Capt. Woodbury Langdon, an old acquaintance of our family. We arrived in New York on the first of June 1831, landed at the Battery in a boat from the ship, and walked up Broadway, where we met my brother Dudley opposite the Bowling Green, who recommended the Hotel of the U.S. to us. We took up our quarters there for a couple of days, whilst we had to wait for our baggage to pass the custom house. We then went on to Providence and passed a day with Dr. Arnold, my wife's brother, and then to Newburyport. We had been absent from home over a year, and my wife's health had not improved. As soon as I could arrange my business in Boston, I purchased a carriage and span of horses, with the intention of traveling through the States, with the hopes of improving my wife's health. We stopped at my good old Aunt Becka's, who was more like a mother to me than an aunt, where we had every comfort and attention that could be had, but my wife seemed to become daily more sick, and on the fifth of July she passed off to higher spheres, and the first time I used my carriage was to her funeral. My days became extremely sad, and I did not know what to do with myself. I deeply felt my loss, and could see nothing worth living for.

I felt the necessity of doing something to arouse me from the gloomy state I had fallen into, and the only thing was to go to sea again. I had no vessel, as I had sold the *Eight Sons* and the *Creole* was on a voyage from Demerara, so the only thing was to purchase a vessel, and fortunately about this time there were two fine ships advertised for sale at auction in Boston, the *Margaret Forbes*, and the *Bashaw*. These were two fine East Indies ships, both nearly new, and sold to close Mr. John Cushing's interest in them, as he had returned from Canton, and retired from the house of Perkins & Co. Messrs. Bryant & Sturgis had the selling of the ships. I examined them both, and preferred the *Bashaw*. She was a superior Medford built ship of 376 tons, [that had] brought from China one thousand tons measurement goods, which proved she was a good carrier. There was a good deal of competition at the auction and I was run up by Mr. Abraham Williams of New-buryport to twenty five thousand five hundred dollars, when she was knocked down to me. I might have bought him off, and got the ship two thousand dollars less.

This was amusing, and showed the man whom I had some experience of afterwards. The terms of the sale were satisfactory notes at six months or six per cent off for cash. I saw Mr. Sturgis, who was present at the sale, and proposed notes for half and cash for the other half. Although I offered the best names on my notes, they were refused by Sturgis in a way which offended me. Then I asked him when the bill of sale would be ready. He replied in a very abrupt manner, "Tomorrow at half past one, and I must have the cash."

So the next day at the appointed time, I was prepared, after some difficulty, with $24,785, being the amount of the purchase with 3% ($765.00) off for cash. I had this amount in as small bills as I could get, not one over $10. I mixed them all up together, and tied them up in a bundle handkerchief and took them into their office. [I] called for the bill of sale, which was not quite ready. I had to wait a little while, and when they handed me the document, I handed them the bundle handkerchief of dollar bills.

Mr. Bryant asked me why I did not deposit the money in the bank and bring them a check. I told him, that Mr. Sturgis had refused to take any paper I had offered him, and must have cash. I therefore have brought the cash, please to count it. I enjoyed seeing them count over the many bills, every now and then making some mistake, and when Mr. Bryant would scold a little, I would say "Mr. Sturgis was very decided, that I must bring the cash, and I had some trouble in picking up the cash here and there." The head clerk, whom I knew very well, who was helping Mr. Bryant count the money, saw the joke and could hardly contain himself from laughing. It caused some amusement on change the next day, to those that knew Mr. Sturgis's dogmatic manner in business transactions.

It was on Wednesday when I bought the ship, Thursday paid for her, and by Sunday she was ready for sea, having had her overhauled, papers & register changed at the custom house, crew and officers shipped, provisions, water &c. put on board, and at ten o'clock Sunday the pilot came on board to take her to sea, but when we got down as far as the light house, he advised me to come to an anchor, as he thought the crew too much intoxicated to proceed to sea. I told him to take the ship out, that I would regulate the crew. After the ship was well out, I told the mates to examine the forecastle and the sailors' chests, and throw overboard all the rum they could find. They came aft and told me the sailors would not permit them to go down the fore castle.

I now saw that I had a poor set of mates. I went forward to the fore castle, and called the crew on deck. They all came up. I then went down myself, and told the first mate to send down one sailor, and to keep the rest on deck. One who seemed the bully came down. I asked him which was his chest. He pointed to one. I told him to open it. He was insolent and refused. I called to the mate to hand me the cook's axe, which he did. I then told him again to open his chest, and upon his refusing, I struck the chest with the axe, and he struck me. I then knocked him down, and opened his chest, and took out a keg of rum, handed it to the mate, who threw it overboard, then called another sailor down, and told him to open his chest. He hesitated at first, but seeing his shipmate humbled, and my determined manner, he opened his chest, & I took another keg of rum, and served it the same as the other. In that way I went through with the whole crew, and took seven kegs of rum from them, about twenty gallons, which was enough to keep them drunk for a week.

The ship was cleared from the custom house for Hampton Roads. I was going for a freight, but I did not know where I should get it, whether at Baltimore, Petersburg, or Richmond, so that at Hampton Roads, I was ready to go up James River, or the Chesapeake Bay. After the crew got sober they did very well, and in about a week we were off the Chesapeake Bay. Two pilot boats run towards us at the same time, one on each side, and hailed us to know where I bound. I answered the one which I thought was the first one to speak, and took from her a pilot for Hampton Roads. I noticed that there was a strong competition between them.

When we anchored, I went up to Norfolk & called on my friend Roberts. He thought I could get the best freight at Richmond, and gave me a letter to Mr. Richard Anderson. I went back to the ship, and sent on shore for the pilot who had bought the ship into the roads. His name was Cunningham. He and another came off on board, which was the other pilot who spoke the ship at the same time that Mr. Cunningham did. Both were head pilots, and both insisted upon taking the ship up James River.

I told them I did not want two pilots, and drew up a paper stating the facts in the case, and that the one that signed this paper held himself responsible for any claim that the other might bring against the ship for pilotage. Mr. Cunningham at once signed the paper and I put the ship in his charge as the pilot up to City Point, which is as high up the river as a ship of the *Bashaw*'s size could go. When we arrived there, I took passage in the steamboat up to Richmond, and called upon Mr. Anderson, who was one of the first merchants there. He offered me two freights, one to London at 70 shillings a hogshead for tobacco, and one to Rotterdam at 72/6. I gave the preference to the latter, as it was the best. The ship took 660 hogsheads, which gave me a freight of about $13,000, more than half what I paid for the ship.

I took lodgings at Mrs. Wood's, the same place that I boarded when I was at City Point in the brig *Eight Sons*. We took on board 500 hogsheads, and then dropped down the river below Harrison's Bar, as there would not be water enough to cross the bar when entirely loaded. This was about 20 miles below City Point, and named after the English gentleman whose large estate and mansion house was on the banks of the river opposite the bar. This was a large brick edifice, built one hundred and twenty years previous, and some fifty years before the revolution. The bricks were brought from England.

THE SHIP REMAINED THERE for about ten days, during which time I was daily on shore & visiting the mansion house. The balance of the cargo being on board, I went up to Richmond, settled my accounts with Mr. Anderson, & cleared the ship for Rotterdam, took a pilot, and dropped down the river. I had ordered a new hemp cable to be made in Norfolk, and when the ship anchored in Hampton Roads, I went up to Norfolk, to arrange for it to be sent on board. I went to the same hotel that I did when I was brought in from the wreck of the *Munroe*. They all seemed to know me.

I had no sooner got there, than I was arrested by an officer on the demand of the pilot who had wished to pilot the ship up James River. This man made his appearance, and proposed a compromise for one half, which I at once refused. The officer, thinking to frighten me, said he would be obliged to put me in jail, without I settled with the pilot, or gave bonds to appear at court. I took him round to my friend Roberts' office. He signed the bond, and then went with me to one of the first lawyers in the place, to whom I explained the case, and gave him the paper, which was signed by Cunningham, the pilot who took the ship to City Point. He understood the whole matter, knew that Cunningham was a responsible man, and told me to give myself no trouble about the business. I heard afterwards, that these two pilots carried on this law suit until they were both nearly ruined.

I went down to the ship with my cable and went to sea. Nothing particular occurred during the passage of about forty days, when we arrived at Hellevoetsluis, which is a small fishing town on the north side of the entrance to the river Meuse, and is considered the sea port of Rotterdam, which is situated on one of the mouths of the Rhine, about 15 or 20 miles to the north. A ship canal has been cut through from Hellevoetsluis, as vessels drawing over ten feet cannot enter the river to Rotterdam. We took a pilot at sea, who piloted the vessel up to the city through the canal. We had twelve horses, six on each side, which took the ship up to the city in fine style. The river in front of the city is about half a mile wide, and shipping lay moored at the bompeys, which are a number of large spars driven into the bottom of the river, leaving about twelve feet above the water, secured together by large iron chains.

Rotterdam, like most of the cities in Holland, is on quite low ground, with a high dyke running along the river side to protect it from the overflow of the river, and makes but little show from the ship. There are many wide streets with fine modern buildings in the French style of architecture, as well as some of the oldest looking Dutch houses to be found in Holland, with their high steep roofs, standing end to the street, covered with the old fashioned varnished black tiles, with three stories above the eaves of the building. There are many canals passing through the city, in which are conveyed the cargoes from the shipping in long barges to the warehouse.

I consigned the vessel to Cramer & Wilkins, the consignees of the cargo. I was extremely pleased with their management of my business. I took rooms at the Hotel des Pays Bas and enjoyed myself during my stay in Rotterdam. The duchess Polignac, the daughter of Charles the tenth of France, who was driven out of France the year previous, was staying there with the younger children of the duchess of Berry, whose father the son of Louis 18th was assassinated in front of the opera house in Paris, the year previous, and whose mother was still in France striving to get her son, the count of Chambord, acknowledged as the king of France, as he was the legitimate heir to the French throne.

The duchess had rooms on the same floor with mine, and the

children amused themselves by running through the hall, and we soon made acquaintance. There were two little girls, the eldest, Princess Elisabeth, about five, and the other three. We became very good friends. I used occasionally to give them some little "bon bons" and they would pay me with a kiss. The duchess, finding I was an American, had no objection. She disliked the English. She had her meals in her parlour, not wishing to come to the table. Her husband was in exile with his father in the vicinity of Hamburg. I never knew what became of that family. The comte de Chambord, I saw in Hamburg some years afterwards, a handsome looking lad of about fourteen years old.

At the *table d'hôte* I used to meet many strange people, and made some pleasant acquaintances. A Captain Hunt sat next to me at the table, and we became quite intimate. He was a tall fine looking gentleman, and I used to call him Duke, and a good many thought he was the duc de Polignac. One day there was a new arrival, of an old German, his wife & sister. They had just arrived from England in the steamer, & were going up the Rhine to visit their old friends. The old man sat next to me on my right, & his wife & sister next to him. We soon got into a conversation. He said that he understood that the duc de Polignac was at this hotel. I jogged him with my elbow, giving him a hint by my look that the duke sat on my other side. The old fellow whispered something in German to his wife, and they bent forward to get a good sight of the duke. In a low tone I asked him if he would like to be introduced to him. He expressed great delight at the idea.

I said "You had better call for a couple bottles of champagne," which he did, and glasses were placed before the duke, myself, and one or two of my friends. I had given the Captain a nudge, which prepared him for the joke. The glasses were filled, when I said "Duke, allow me to introduce to you my friend 'Bumkins,' just arrived from England, going up the Rhine to visit his old friends," and we emptied the glasses. It was as much as I could do to keep from laughing to see Hunt smile & put on the dignity of a duke as he bowed to my (quondam) friends, who could hardly contain themselves from expressing their delight at being introduced to a live duke. It is needless to say we emptied the bottles and gave our new friends a hint that a little more champagne would be agreeable to the duke, which the old fellow immediately ordered.

I remained in Rotterdam three weeks, delivering the cargo, and taken on board ballast. When I settled my accounts with the consignees, and remitted the balance of my freight money to Baring Bros. & Co. London, and went with the ship down to the Hellevoetsluis, I found the ship required new copper, and I decided to stop in England and have the ship coppered. The wind was ahead to leave the river, and the pilot could give me no encouragement of a change of wind. I concluded to put the chief mate in charge, and go over to London myself in the steamer that was to sail in a few days from Rotterdam. I therefore ordered Mr. Sands, my first officer, who had previously commanded a vessel, as soon as the pilot could take the ship to sea, to get underway and go to Portsmouth in England, and I would meet him there as soon as he arrived.

15

~*~

Rough Passages

I WENT TO ROTTERDAM and took passage in the steamer *Jaliff* for London. It was in the early days of steam navigation, and vessels were not built then for steamers, but machinery was put into sailing vessels, which were poorly calculated for such purposes. The *Jaliff* was formerly a brig of about 200 tons, and rather old. There seemed to have been but little alteration in the hull, besides taking out the masts, & putting in a small schooner's masts, and two large wheels, one on each side. The cabin was small, with narrow state rooms on each side, with two berths in each. There were four on a side, which accommodated sixteen passengers, most miserably.

There were a commission of about a dozen Hanoverians, all men of title going over to assist in the coronation of William the 4th, to be crowned the king of England. The Captain was a jolly old fellow, a real John Bull, of about sixty, who had been sailing in the North Sea for fifty years of his life, and the exposure to the winter storms had made his face look as if it was all tied up in hard knots, and like all Englishmen in his line of business, liked his glass of whiskey at sea, and his mug of brown stout on shore.

We sailed in the morning. It was a cold winter day, and before the night a heavy gale of wind came on, and the vessel began to pitch and tumble about in the sea ways, and the passengers became sea sick, and sought their berths. I had a very nice young man with me in my state room. He was a Hanoverian count, one of the commissioners, and was quite sea sick. I helped him to undress and to get into his berth, for which he seemed very grateful.

The night was very tempestuous, and I went on deck, to keep the Captain company. I found he felt anxious about the position of the vessel, as we were close to the Jutland shore, and the gale blowing directly on, the vessel was head to the wind, with all steam on, pitching heavily into the seas which were breaking over her with great fury. He was holding the lead line, with the heavy lead on the bottom, and told me that she did not go ahead. I saw at once the dangerous position of the vessel, that if the gale increased, she would not hold her own, and must go on shore, and as the frame of the vessel was working badly, she would soon spring a leak and go down, if kept head to the wind much longer. We consulted together and finally concluded if the gale did not moderate soon, as it was now twelve o'clock, and the Capt. said it was sure to moderate, that we must alter our course, bringing the sea more on the side of the vessel.

I had been holding the lead line for the last hour, anxiously watching which way she moved for some time. I found she was drifting towards the shore. It was very dark and raining, and I saw no hope, if the gale continued, but most fortunately, at this moment the wind lulled, and she went ahead, slowly dragging the leads & we knew the gale had got to its height, and that we could now expect it would soon moderate, and as there is not much depth of water in the North Sea, the seas would soon go down.

I then went down to my room, to get some cigars. The passengers were in a sad state, groaning and taking on, expecting every moment the vessel would go to the bottom. The stewards were sick and stowed away in their berths, so that they could pay no attention to the wants of the passengers, and the cabin was in a dreadful mess, the floor covered with the filth from the sick passengers, the chambers upset and rolling from one side to the other, also the chairs, and other furniture which was not secured were tumbling about, making a dreadful racket. The cabin was dark, having only one small hanging lamp which gave hardly light enough to show where it was, and take it altogether, it was dreadful. It seemed some relief to the passengers to have some one come down to tell them that the gale was subsiding, and the danger was most over.

I went to my state room, and found the count in a quite excited state. I tried to brighten him up by telling him the danger was all over, but it was no use, he would have it that they would all be lost, and he kept moaning in broken English, "My vife, my kildren &c." I then asked him if he had made his will. "Vy do you ask that?" "Because if you have not, I want you to will me your gold snuff box," which he had handed to me half a dozen times during the afternoon to take a pinch of snuff, which I had always refused. Evidently this struck him rather comically, as he looked at me with surprise, saying "How can you joke in the hour of death?"

I then went on deck, and was satisfied that the gale had subsided, although the seas were running high & were sweeping the decks fore and aft. There were six horses (most beautiful animals) on deck, when we left Rotterdam, on freight to London. These poor creatures had been washed overboard during the night, and in fact every movable thing was washed away, and the covering of the wheels were torn off, and as they turned round, threw the water over us, which in that cold night was anything but pleasant.

At last daylight came, and the engineer reported to the Captain that the coal was getting short, that we had not enough to steam the vessel into port. We then changed our course to the nearest land on the English coast, which was Yarmouth. We first saw the land, about eleven o'clock, and although the engineer had burned everything he could get hold of, including a portion of butter from the cargo, the steam gave out by two o'clock and the wheels stopped going round. We then came to an anchor. We were between six and eight miles from the land. The boat was manned with four stout sailors, and the mail master was sent on shore with the mails, and to order coal to be sent off. I went in the boat with him. We were but little over an hour, when we landed in Yarmouth, the wind having moderated, and the seas gone down.

We were fortunate in finding a small vessel laden with coal, which was at once sent off to the steamer, and we went up to the hotel and got a good dinner. The boat was sent on board with the coal vessel, and I and the mail master remained onshore, as we knew that the steamer would come into the harbour as soon as she had got coal enough on board to bring her in, as it was too rough for the coal vessel to lay alongside to discharge more than was absolutely necessary. It being in the middle of December, the days were very short, and it was dark by four o'clock and I had no opportunity of seeing much of Yarmouth.

Between 9 & 10 o'clock the steamer came into the harbour with the coal vessel, and took on board all the coal she required, and by 12, was ready to proceed to London. I went on board, and found that all the passengers had left the steamer to go by land from Yarmouth. I remained in the steamer, and had a very pleasant sail up the Thames River, and arrived early in the afternoon. I took rooms at the North & South American Hotel, the general resort of Americans in those days. I called round to see Mr. Joshua Bates, then a partner of the Barings, my bankers, and arranged with him to let me know when the *Bashaw* had arrived at Portsmouth. He invited me to dinner the following day, which I accepted, and had a very pleasant time.

Mrs. Bates was a Miss Sturgis, and when young lived opposite my father's in Federal St., Boston, and knew our family, particularly my eldest sister who was about her age. She was very sociable, and liked to talk about those times. She told me various anecdotes which were interesting, one in particular. The chamber windows in both houses were exactly opposite, and she and my sister had certain signs to communicate with one another, and were in the habit of showing anything new, or pretty, up to the windows, each trying to out do the other. One day she had shown something which she considered beautiful, when my sister brought to her window one of those red tubs with gilt rims, which had just been introduced as wash bowls from China. They were made of wood, and Mrs. Bates said she thought it was the most beautiful thing she ever saw, and she considered herself completely beat.

They had one child, a daughter, who was just married to the Belgian minister, Mr. Van de Wyer. They were both at the table, a family dinner, how beautiful and quiet, no ostentation, two courses, a roast and boiled, no wine drinking, a bottle of hock, in a silver stand set in the middle of the table, which was drank in water with the dinner, only one servant to wait on the table, dressed in black with white gloves. After the table cloth was removed from the beautiful polished black mahogany table, some fruit such as nuts & raisins, and one decanter of madeira were placed on the table. Each took but one glass. They were all extremely sociable, and I never enjoyed myself more at a dinner in my life.

I remained in London for some weeks waiting for the arrival of the *Bashaw* at Portsmouth, and amused myself as best I could to pass the tedious time. One night I was at the Covent Garden theatre, and between the acts I sauntered out in the saloon, and there met several of the passengers that were on board of the *Jaliff*, and among them the count, my room mate. He seemed delighted to see me, hugged me, and I do not know but he kissed me, as was the custom with the Hanoverians and pulled out his gold snuff box, and insisted upon my accepting it, and it was as much as I could do to make him keep it, by telling him that as I did not take snuff, I had no use for it, that my proposition on board the steamer was only a joke to change his thoughts at the time, and I begged him to keep it in remembrance of me, and the narrow escape we had that night from being wrecked in which case we all would have been lost. He, nor the rest of them had any idea of the dangerous position the steamer was in during that night.

We sat round a small table, and had a sociable chat, smoke, &c. I made the acquaintance of the clerks & secretary of Mr. Martin Van Buren, who was the American minister to England. I had called on him, but as he was not in I did not see him, but was introduced to him afterwards at the North & South American. A young man by the name of Bartlett, belonging to Plymouth in Massachusetts was his private secretary, and I became intimate with him, and he wanted me to join him in a trip round to Southampton, in a new London packet, Capt. Champlain, who had invited him and me to go.

I rather objected as I knew at that season of the year, the month of December, we might expect bad weather. The ship was to stop at Southampton, as was customary with the packets from London to

New York, for the passengers from London to join the ship by land. I however consented, and we went on board the ship as she was hauling out of the London dock. She was a beautiful ship, with a superb cabin, and Capt. Champlain was more of a lady's Capt. than a sailor Capt., but was a very gentlemanly person, and we had a very pleasant run down the river Thames, and at night the tide and wind being against us, we came to anchor.

The next morning we started again, and got as far as South Fore-land [near Dover], when it commenced blowing a gale from the S.W. We beat against it all that day, and at night it was very violent, and I kept up on deck with the pilot. Bartlett was dreadfully sea sick and he and the Captain kept below in the cabin. The mate seemed inefficient, and the crew had not yet got over the effect of their carousing on shore, and during the middle of the night one of the anchors got loose from the lashings and was thumping against the bow, and would probably have made a hole through the vessel very soon if it was not secured.

I went forward and found that the mate did not know what to do, as the ship was pitching bows under every few minutes, and there was no one of the crew who would go over the side to put on the anchor hook to hoist the anchor up in its place. I told him that I would go, and having had the purchase tackle fixed, and every thing ready to raise the anchor as soon as hooked, I took a rope and made a good bowline round me, & watching my chance when she was a little still went over the side with the hook and put it on the anchor. I got safely on deck again, somewhat wet, and assisted in getting the anchor on the bows & properly secured.

It was now between 12 or 1 o'clock, and the gale was at its height, and the ship making bad weather of it, and with difficulty getting clear of Dungeness Point. I advised the pilot to put back, and get some snug anchorage until a change in the weather, which after some hesitancy he concluded to do, and we run back, and came to anchor in the Downs. I was not a little surprised that Captain Champlain did not come on deck during the night, but trusting his ship entirely to a pilot, to say the least, was a piece of unseamanlike conduct. It was about noon when we got safe anchorage in the Downs, and several boats came alongside.

Bartlett, who had been sick all night, was glad to go on shore, as well as myself, and we engaged a boat to take us on shore at Dover, about three miles from where the ship laid. Capt. Champlain seemed to feel as if he would be glad to go with us. There was a heavy surf on the beach where we had to land, and we got pretty wet in the operation, and we were glad to get up to the hotel, to warm & dry ourselves. We got a good dinner, which we highly enjoyed, as we were very hungry.

It was Saturday, and as we did not wish to pass the Sunday in such a desolate looking place as Dover, we took the coach to Canterbury, and spent a very pleasant Sunday in this old city, visiting some of the old buildings, particularly the cathedral, which was built in the twelfth century, and to me was a wonderful piece of architecture. We attended service in the forenoon. I was not well impressed with the imposing performance, as there was more show than religion, and I thought more performers than listeners. When they got through, we took a good look round, examined the tomb of Cardinal Wolsey which is a large sarcophagus made of marble, which originally was white, but now was almost my colour. It is raised on three elevations of a foot each from the floor, formed by large stone slabs, which appear like steps, and is surrounded by a bronze ornamented railing, open on one side where the pious disposed ascended to kiss the covering of the holy relics. The steps were well worn, showing that many thousand had passed up & the dirty places of the marks of the kissing were still quite visible.

The next day, Monday, we took the coach for London, having to ride on the outside, as nearly all the passengers have to, as there are but four seats in the inside. It is about forty miles from Canterbury to London, and as it was a miserable foggy day we had a forlorn ride. I was not well prepared for such a cold wet ride, having only a light overcoat, and the result was I took a bad cold, and by the time I got to the hotel, I was well used up, and soon retired to my bed. In the night I suffered dreadfully from a pain in one of my ears, and sent for a physician. He found me in a high fever, & the pain in my ear caused by an imposthume.

I was now in for a fit of sickness, how long or what the result would be I could not even guess. I did not think much of the doctor. He came too often, and I made up my mind his object was to make as huge a bill out of me as he could. I suffered excruciating pains in my head for several days, and without sleep, until the abscess broke. I was confined to my room for about four weeks, and a more uncomfortable time no poor mortal could have. The weather was thick and foggy, as it generally is in London in the winter time. As I lay in my bed I could see the grasshopper vane on the Exchange, always pointing the same way, a head wind for my ship to get to sea from the Rotterdam river. How very lonesome it is to be sick at a hotel in a foreign country. How long were the days and nights, I might say nights, for it was so dark during the so-called day, that the gas had to be kept burning to see across the room.

At last I received notice from Mr. Bates that the *Bashaw* had arrived in Portsmouth, and I at once decided I would take the mail coach that night, which left at six o'clock. Mr. Bates called round to see me in the forenoon. [He] had not heard that I had been sick until he received my note that morning. He was very kind, thought it not prudent for me to go at present. I told him I would stand anything rather than stay in that room any longer. He sent one of his clerks round to help me get ready, for which I was very thankful. He went at once to the stage office, and secured a seat in the inside of the coach. He bought me a large thick traveling wrapper, furs for my feet and neck, so that I had everything to make me comfortable. He paid the doctor's bill, and settled my account at the hotel, did everything I wanted him to do, so that when the coach came I could go direct from my sick room to the carriage.

I must say that I dreaded the undertaking when the time came for me to go. I was a little nervous as I thought of riding seventy two miles, in a stage coach that cold stormy night, sick as I was, but I said "In for a penny, in for a pound." I bundled myself up, bidding the young clerk (I cannot remember his name) good bye. I got into the coach and took my seat, No. 1 as my ticket directed, which was the right hand back seat. The other three seats were occupied, according to their numbers, how many on the outside I never knew. I wrapped myself up snug in the corner of the carriage, and the last I could recollect was the rattling of the coach wheels on the London pavement.

All of a sudden, as it seemed to me, the coach was stopping in front of a large door, and a man pulling my wrapper, saying "Mr., are you not a going to get out?" "No," I said, "I am going to Portsmouth." "Well, you are in Portsmouth." I found that the passengers had got out, and so I got out and went into the hotel. Still confused and doubting, I asked the first person I met, "Is this Portsmouth?" and was told it was. I went in the back room, where some of the others had gone, and sat with them at a small table and took a cup of coffee. I could not conceive that I rode 72 miles, the coach stopping several times to change horses, and once at midnight all the passengers got out and took their suppers, and I not waking or knew anything about it. It was to me an instantaneous change.

I looked at my watch and found it was between four & five. I was very much refreshed, and felt like a new man, from the effect of this night's ride. I took a hearty breakfast, a good beefsteak, and the "et ceteras," which I enjoyed exceedingly, as I had fasted pretty well for the last four weeks, and I went out to find my ship, and went on board. Everything was in confusion. Mr. Sands seemed to have lost the command of his men. They were mostly Dutchmen which I had shipped in Rotterdam, and I found I must get clear of some of them, and take command of the ship again, which I did not intend to have done, if Mr. Sands had shown himself fit to command.

THE REASON I HAD ORDERED the ship to Portsmouth instead of Cowes, was that when I was there in the *Eight Sons* I had been badly swindled by Mr. Hunter the American consul, and by Mr. White the owner of the dry dock, and I was determined not to go to Cowes again if I could help it.

Of course, there was a strong feeling with the Cowes people against any American vessel going into Portsmouth for repairs, and when White heard the *Bashaw* had gone there to be coppered, he was in a tremendous passion. He came up to Portsmouth and tried to persuade me to let the ship come down to his dock, that the work could not be done at Portsmouth, but I would have nothing to do with him, as I had agreed to use the dock in Portsmouth, which was a floating dock, and was guaranteed to be long enough to take the ship in, of which I had my doubts. I therefore, when all was ready to haul her into the dock, had a strong hawser out from the stern fast to good moorings, and taken round the windlass to heave her out of the dock if found too short, which proved to be the case, and the moment she was in, I gave the order to heave her out, before any trick was played on me to keep her there.

The passage boat was just then ready to go Cowes, and I got on board and went down to see Mr. White. I walked over to his dock in a careless sort of manner, and met Mr. White. He asked me how I got on with the ship. I told him, not very well, they were so slow I did not know when they would get done, that they had done hardly anything for the last few days but put the ship in the dock, that they had not the facilities there that he had here, and that I most wish I had brought the ship there to be coppered. He at once took the bait & said if you will bring the ship here I will dock her and copper her for a certain sum, which was about half of what I had agreed to pay in Portsmouth. I said, "I had a good mind to have the ship brought down, but it was no use to talk about it, as you have a vessel now in the dock." He said that vessel should be hauled out tomorrow, and my ship should come in, and he offered every inducement to have her come, and finally I agreed.

He proposed that a written agreement should be drawn up and signed at once, which I agreed to, and we went up to his house, and two contracts were drawn up, one for him and one for me, both signed by us and witnessed by two men who he called in to sign their names as witnesses. He looked pleased that he had got the business from "those Portsmouth fellows" as [he] called them, and he locked his contract up in his desk, handing me the other, which contained everything I wanted, in the most binding manner. I put the document in my inside pocket, and we walked together down to the dock. We had been there but a moment, before a stranger stepped up and observed to Mr. White, "What a trick they played on that Yankee ship at Portsmouth, their dock was not long enough." White turned to me, and asked if that was so? I said, "The dock was not quite long enough." He turned white with rage, and said "If I had known that, I never would have made that contract with you," &c., &c. I bid him good afternoon, and took the boat back to Portsmouth.

I had some trouble with the dockmaster, who claimed the business & was disposed to stop the vessel from going to Cowes. I however employed a steamer and had her towed down to Cowes, and made fast at the entrance of White's dock, and the next day she was docked, and as far as I recollect Mr. White did everything he agreed to, and did it well. I had to deposit the ship's papers at the American consulate. Mr. Hunter was absent and his clerk acted as vice consul.

I had to ship a new crew at Portsmouth, which proved a miserable set of English man of war's men. I decided to go to Cádiz for a cargo of salt to Havana, and arranged with Capt. W. Clark of the Boston ship *Arnold Wells*, then laying in London, to meet me in Havana, and take command of the *Bashaw*. All being ready, and my bills all paid, I ordered a pilot to take the ship to sea.

We had no sooner got into the Channel, when a gale came on from the southwest, which was directly a head, and began to blow heavy. I reduced sail accordingly. I regretted that I had not remained at anchor in Cowes roads a little longer to have avoided this gale, but there was no help for it now that I was out in mid channel, and I must beat the ship out. During the night the sea increased, as well as the wind, and at 2 o'clock Mr. Sands called me saying the ship was labouring hard in the head beat sea, and thought we better close reef the main top sail.

I went on deck & found as he said that the wind and sea had increased, and told him to call all hands, and reef the main top sail. I walked the deck some time, and the watch below not coming up, I told Mr. S. to give them another call, and after waiting some time I asked Mr. S., why the watch did not come up. He replied that he had called them three times, and they wouldn't come up. I then went forward to the forecastle companion way, and called them my self. Soon the bully of the crew came part way up on deck, using the most insulting language. I asked him if he knew who he was speaking to. He said "Yes," and commenced cursing me, and at once sprung upon me, and with all his force pushed me to the lee rail forward of the fore rigging.

The ship was laying over, and the sea breaking over the bow. I had him with my left hand hold of his neck handkerchief, and my right arm round the forward shroud, struggling to prevent him from pushing me into the sea, which he was using all his force to do. I screamed as loud as I could for the mates to come to my assistance, but they probably did not hear me. Fortunately at this moment the ship fetched a lurch to the windward, and the fellow slipped. I came in upon him with a belaying pin in my hand, and being on top of him, had given him two or three cracks with it on his head, and would soon have mastered him, had not Mr. S. come forward and took hold of me, & pulled me off. It being dark, he thought it was the sailor on top of me.

The fellow immediately sprung to his feet, and with his fist knocked Sands over, and then quick as a wink, gave me a blow in my right temple, which sent me headlong in the lee scuppers. For a few moments I lay there insensible. I then picked myself up, and started for my cabin, and got my pistols and came on deck, and enquired for the man, but to my surprise the hands were up on the main top sail yard reefing the sails, and as I was about to start forward for the chase, a man fell from the yard to the deck, striking within a foot from where I was standing. It was so dark I could not at first see whether it was a coil of rigging that some of the crew had thrown from the main top, or one of the crew from the yard. I called the mates, and we carried him to the house on deck and laid him on one of the settees. He proved to be an Italian sailor, and was armed with a long sheath knife, which proved he was in for a mutiny. I found he was a good deal injured, and his right thigh bone broken. We had to leave him to attend to the vessel, & I thought it better to defer settling with the bully until the next day.

We hoisted the sail & let the watch go below. The wind had begun to moderate & I noticed it had changed more to the westward, which was more favourable for us to run into the Bay of Biscay. I then gave my attention to the Italian, put splinters and bandages on the thigh bone, and bound up the other bruised parts, and fixed him as comfortable as I could.

The next day the weather was more moderate, and arming myself, I went on deck and ordered Jim (which I found to be the name of the fellow who within an ace threw me into the sea the night before) to be sent for, as I could not let such a mutinous act pass without further notice. My intention was to put him in irons. He came strutting aft in the most defiant manner. I saw that I could not put much confidence in my mates, and if possible, I wanted to avoid shooting him, so I commenced talking to him, showing him the great offense he had been guilty of &c., and to my surprise I found that he felt sorry & would not be guilty again. I then after a severe admonition sent him forward again to his duty.

Ten days from the day we left Cowes we arrived at Cádiz, and were placed in quarantine. The passage had been boisterous, and the ship's company mutinous, and I determined to get clear of both crew and mates as soon as I could. We were kept but 24 hours in quarantine, the reason given, was that I had not brought a bill of health from England. The first thing I did was to call on the American consul, I forget his name. I found him a very kind and gentlemanly old man. I told him of my trouble with the crew & mates, and I wished to get clear of them, and ship another set, which he thought the best thing I could do, and he would assist me.

He at once recommended a Mr. Tay of Salem for the first mate, and sent for him to meet me the next day at the consulate, which he did, and liking the appearance of the man, I arranged with him to ship as the first mate. I then discharged and paid off the mates and crew, and soon had another set in their place. I employed the consul to purchase a cargo of salt for the ship, as he was a commission merchant, as well as consul, and was then the only American consul holding office that had been appointed by General Washington.

Cádiz is a small & pretty city built on the isle of León, which is connected by a cause way to the main land at Jerez, which is famous for its wine, called "sherry wine" by the English. This causeway forms the southern part to Cádiz harbour, which is protected from the Atlantic by a massive break water, built of stone, a mile or more in length, ending with a fortification, the light house being placed on the fort. The city is laid out in streets of good width crossing one another at right angles. There are some fine buildings, the largest being the cathedral, which is not yet finished, and probably never will be. It was built from a duty laid on all the silver & gold that was brought to Spain from the Spanish American colonies, amounting to many millions. Cádiz was the harbour where all the Spanish galleons landed the immense wealth from the Indies, and was so well fortified that it was impregnable in old times.

The great peculiarity of Cádiz is its cleanliness, neither carriages or horses in carts are seen in the streets, and ladies & children are seen at all times, promenading the streets without fear. There is a stand for carriages just outside of the gates on the causeway, where vehicles of all kinds can be obtained at moderate prices to pass into the country, but are not allowed to come into the city. The houses are large, and families live on flats, similar to most of the large cities in Spain. I took very comfortable lodgings at a boarding house kept by a widow and three daughters. They gave us breakfast, but nothing else. We dined at the restaurants, and I enjoyed the Spanish cooking.

The houses have no chimneys, and of course no way of making a fire to keep themselves warm, in such cold weather as it was when I was there. It was amusing to see the ladies huddling round an iron pot of ignited charcoal to keep themselves warm. I suffered from the cold nights, as the bed clothes were for a mild climate, and rather limited at that. I was there a little over a fortnight, when my ship was fully loaded, and settling my accounts with the consul, I sailed for Havana.

The ship was deeper laden than I intended to have her, and sailed slower than was agreeable. We had, however, a pretty fair run across the ocean. I was steering for St. Domingo, intending to run through the Bahama Channel to the north of St. Domingo and Cuba, when a most violent hurricane came on from the northward, and I was obliged to flee before it under bare poles until I was driven over one hundred miles out of my course, and had to go through a new passage, between the islands of Antigua and Barbados, leaving St. Kitts to the north. The hurricane lasted about 48 hours, and raised a tremendous sea, which caused the ship to labour badly, and to make water, so as to keep the pumps going most of the time. She was a noble ship, and well managed, or she would have swamped, and taken us all to Davy Jones's locker.

We finally arrived in Havana after a passage of about fifty days. I called upon my friends Messrs. Charles Drake & Co. to talk about business. They thought the ship was too large to find a freight to fill her. They could give me two thousand boxes of sugar for Antwerp at £4.10 the ton. I considered she would take about five hundred more, which I was willing to ship on my own account. I told them I would decide the following day, as I wanted to see what price I could get for the cargo of salt. I understood there was but little salt in the place, and I hoped to obtain a good price. It turned out well, giving about eight thousand dollars for freight.

Having made all necessary arrangements for loading the ship to Antwerp, and having nothing to detain me in Havana, I took passage for New York. I, soon after my arrival, received from Messrs. Drake & Co. the accounts of the ship, and my invoices for six hundred and eighty boxes of sugar, a rather larger interest in the cargo than I expected. I found that the *Creole*, Capt. Clarkson, had sailed from Amsterdam to Curaçao, on a very good charter for a cargo of sugar and molasses, back to Amsterdam, and having nothing to detain me in the States, I decided to go to Europe and meet the *Bashaw*, to attend personally to my interest in the cargo.

16

Dining Out in London and Paris

O<small>N THE FIRST OF JULY</small>, 1832, I sailed in the New York packet ship _____, Capt. Hebbert, for London. There were about thirty passengers, all very pleasant people. My companion in the state room was a Mr. Destout, a merchant established in business in Philadelphia. He was on his way to Bordeaux, his native place. I found him a very pleasant person of about my age, and we agreed very well together. We had a passage of about forty days, to Southampton, and took the coach to London, a distance of about 70 miles.

Destout and I went to the Adelphi Hotel on the Strand, near Temple Bar on Ludgate Hill. I did not like this hotel, or the plan on which it was kept. We went to the Adelphi Theater, and witnessed the play of _Macbeth_, which I had never seen before. The theater was well filled, and the play was perfect. I returned to the hotel at eleven o'clock, and it was still twilight, it being the height of summer [mid-August] and the days amongst the longest. I woke up at six in the morning, the sun shining in my room, and as I could sleep no more, I rose, dressed, and went down stairs between 7 and 8, not a soul up. I returned to my room and waited until I heard somebody moving, which was near 10. I then went down to the parlours, and had to wait until 11, before I could get any breakfast. I was out of all patience.

I sauntered out to see the sights, and to call on my friends the Barings. Mr. Bates invited me to dinner on the following Wednesday, which I had to refuse, as I had arranged with Destout to go to Paris on that day. I met my friend Bartlett, whose acquaintance I made when I was in London before, and I invited him to dine with me at the Adelphi. We went there at half past six, the hour they told me dinner would be ready, and found many people sitting eating their dinners at small tables, which set round the room.

The waiter showed us to one that was not occupied, which we set down to, and I asked the waiter to bring us some dinner. We sat talking for some time and I began to get a little impatient, when I asked another waiter to bring us some dinner. He wished to know what we would have. We ordered roast beef and vegetables. After waiting some time, I called for the head waiter, and asked why we were not served. He coolly asked, "Did you order dinner?" I said, "Yes, we have ordered it twice, and are tired of waiting." He turned away and was gone some time. When I got sight of him, and called to him, he came, and said, "I believe you did not order dinner?"

This rather disturbed me. I told him I had ordered dinner three times, and wished some to be brought at once. Soon the lady of the house came, and said "I believe you did not order dinner." It was in vain I told her I had. She then said, "Our gentlemen always are expected to order their dinner at the office before they go out in the morning, and you did not order any." Here was a fix. I had invited a friend home to dine with me, and there was no dinner for us. The only thing for us to do was to seek some restaurant, and get what we could to eat, as we were both hungry.

The next day we were to leave for France and in the forenoon Mr. Destout and I took the coach for Portsmouth and there took passage in the steam packet for Havre, leaving there at dusk. The packet was similar to the one I had crossed the North Sea from Rotterdam to London the year previous, a poor concern, being the hull of a sailing vessel with wheels attached to the sides, a small miserable cabin with about a dozen state rooms opening out from the cabin. Destout had engaged one when he paid our passages in London.

It was about nine in the morning when we started. There were a number of passengers, more than there was any kind of accommodation for. There was an Irish gentleman by the name of FitzGerald, and his family, consisting of a wife and three daughters, most lovely young ladies. We made the acquaintance of this family, and enjoyed their society very much. Soon after we sailed, the old gentleman and his wife retired to their state room, leaving the young ladies on deck, in our company. They were very well informed, and lady like in their manners.

It was a beautiful moonlight night & the water in the Channel was quite smooth and we passed our time in conversation very pleasantly. The ladies did not seem disposed to retire, which rather surprised me, as it was past midnight, when by accident we found they had no state room to retire to, their father not being particular enough to secure two state rooms, instead of one. We at once gave up our state room to them, which pleased them exceedingly.

We arrived at Havre in the morning and were soon boarded by the custom house officers who are very watchful to see that nothing is smuggled. Our trunks were overhauled from top to bottom, to find something English upon which they could claim a duty. Destout, who knew how very particular they were, had bought some lace for his sister and had placed it between the lining and outside of his cloak, and carrying it on his arm, as he passed along through the custom house at the landing, feeling quite secure, when he was rudely stopped and his cloak seized by one of the vigilants, who had discovered a small hole in the cloak through which the lace was exposed. Destout had to pay a round sum, more that the duties would have amounted to.

Mr. FitzGerald & his family and ourselves went to the same hotel, which was exceedingly agreeable to us. They were to remain two or three days in Havre. Their home was in Cannep, a town on the coast about twenty miles from Havre, where they had a splendid estate. He was a wealthy gentleman, had his traveling carriage with him, which was the custom in those days, both in England and on the continent. When we parted, they for home and we for Paris, they gave us a pressing invitation to visit them. During our stay in Havre we were together a great deal, used to take long walks about the city, and visit the places of amusements together, and had a nice time generally.

Mr. Destout & I took the steamer up the river Seine to Rouen, one of the oldest cities in France. Here we landed, as we had to change for a smaller steamer of lighter draft to take us to Paris. We remained in Rouen two days, enjoying ourselves by visiting the various places of interest, of which there are many in this old city. The cathedral is a perfect curiosity, said to be eight hundred years old. It is built of stone. The front is almost covered with statues of various sizes, and carvings most exquisite, for so coarse a material. The interior has a grand appearance, with the hundreds of stone pillars and arches, and the grand dome, of great height from the floor, covered with paintings, highly coloured, representing the various scenes of Jesus, as given in the New Testament.

The picture gallery is magnificent. We spent hours in examining the pictures & statuary. The buildings are unique, particularly some of the oldest houses which attracted my attention, with their curious constructed roofs and ornamental gables. There is a bridge of boats from the city across the river to the opposite side, moored stem and stern to resist the tide, which I observed run with great force. There seemed to be no opening for vessels to pass through, and I do not remember to have seen a sailing craft on the river.

From Rouen to Paris, which is about thirty miles, we took the *diligence*, a funny old sort of vehicle with three compartments, drawn by four horses, three abreast connected with the carriage, and one ahead. The driver was a blowsy looking fellow, more like a country bumpkin than a stage driver. How very different from the English coach, with the jolly looking John Bull in white top boots, and his big coat with half a dozen capes, and his four in hand, which spring & prance at the crack of his whip.

We arrived in the evening at Paris, and went to the Hotel de Bourse, each taking a suite of rooms which consisted of a parlour & chamber. It was very convenient for me to be with Destout, as I spoke no French. He did all the talking, and as he had been in Paris frequently before, was well acquainted with the city. Before leaving England, I had written to Messrs. Delisle & Co. that I was going to Paris, and should remain there until the arrival of the *Bashaw*, and requested them to write me when when she made her appearance & I would come on to Antwerp at once. Destout had some business in Paris that would detain him for a day or two and then he would hurry on to Bordeaux, to see his family.

As I was determined to see all I could of Paris, I engaged a Swiss valet, who spoke good English and French, also a cabriolet by the day. I procured me a small book at Galignani's called *Paris to Be Seen in a Fortnight*. I also read the New York papers, which are kept on file at their office, and got the first notice that the Asiatic cholera had broke out in that city the day we left for London, the first of July, and was rapidly spreading.

How different the French hotels are kept from the English. Here one can enjoy himself. I rise in the morning, ring my bell, and the waiter at once in attendance, I order my breakfast, toast, omelettes, coffee, or what ever I like. The table is at once set in my parlour, and in a very short time my breakfast is ready. That is the only meal given at the hotel. For dinner we go to the restaurants, which are superb places, particularly in the Palais Royale, where I used to dine daily. The rooms are very large. Small tables are set all over the room. At one end of the room, on a raised platform, sits a lady who watches over the various tables and waiters to see the guests are properly attended to, and also as cashier to receive the money according to the tickets presented. These tickets are given by the waiters to the guests showing the cost of each dish called for.

The French cooking is superior to either the English or American, and a good dinner at a French restaurant, with a bottle of common Bordeaux claret, at dinner, and a half bottle of Château Margaux with your dessert, is something worth remembering, as the dinner at the London Adelphi is for forgetting. It is a common thing to see the most of the tables filled by families, who to avoid the trouble of cooking at home, go to the restaurants with their children for their dinners.

The Palais Royale is an immense building, built round a square laid out in walks, with fountains playing, and seats placed for the accommodation of all. Here I used to while away an hour quite pleasantly, smoking my cuba, and watching the playful gambols of the children. In the evening, I went to the grand opera, or some of the theaters, which I enjoyed highly, and then to my hotel. In the morning I would plan out my day's excursion, guided by my book, and my cabriolet being in waiting with my valet, we would start out to see the sights.

The Père-Lachaise, the famous cemetery of Paris, I first visited. I was not particularly interested in it, as I expected to [see] something more grand, having heard it often spoken of as something wonderful. The tombs of Abelard & Louise at the entrance were interesting as something new to me, although they had the appearance of age. Some of the mausoleums were magnificent, other wise it appeared rather a common affair. One thing I was struck with, that almost every grave had a fresh memorial, made of peculiar black and yellow leaves, formed in round wreaths. I then went to the Jardin des Plantes. This was well worth seeing, the beautiful and extensive flower garden, the various animals, and the extensive museum, containing so many cases of curiosities that it would take a week, instead of a few hours I had to devote to it, to see it all.

The following day was the Louvre. I spent the whole fore noon in looking at paintings and statuary. The Louvre appears more like a gallery of immense length, some twenty feet in height and thirty or more in width, with windows on each side. This was the lower story. I did not visit the second story. Some of the pictures are truly grand. One in particular made a deep impression on my mind. It was one of the first, at the entrance, representing the flood. It was a very large picture, and the scene was so life like, that to me it was a living picture, the struggling of a young man up the side of a cliff with an old man (his father) clinging to his back. He had reached out and got hold of a small tree to help him climb up the declivity. The tree is breaking from the weight & the two are about to be precipitated in the raging waters below. It is so vivid, that you can almost hear the tree cracking, and their faces are so expressive that one cannot help being in sympathy with their feelings. Hundreds of others are struggling in the billows below.

Another large picture is truly wonderful, called *The Wreck of the Medusa*. In the fore ground is a raft made of logs lashed together with ropes, and on it are the crew and passengers. They seem to be life size, and in all states of suffering, some laying stretched out, dying & dead, the waves breaking against and over the raft, the long hair from their heads washing about by the waves. The expression of their faces is almost speaking. It is truly a wonderful painting. I stood before it for a long time, and felt as if I could not move from it. The walls on both sides are covered with paintings by the first masters, as Napoleon was particular in gathering from all the picture galleries of the cities he conquered their most precious paintings and depositing them in the Louvre, which was mostly built by him, and it was one of his greatest hobbies to have it contain the finest pictures in the world.

I passed my time for three weeks in Paris, visiting all the principal wonders of the city that I could in that time, keeping my valet & cabriolet constantly on the move. I received a letter from Messrs. Delisle & Co., informing me of the arrival of the *Bashaw* at Antwerp, and I at once made my preparation to leave Paris for Brussels in the *diligence,* which was to start at six in the afternoon. The *diligence*, which was similar to the one which brought me from Rouen to Paris, only more clumsy, does not go round for the passengers. They have to assemble at the starting place, and take their seats in the different apartments according to the tickets they hold. Mine was in the coupe, which is considered the first class.

After a great deal of bustle, and getting the passengers in their right places, and their baggage packed away, the clumsy carriage was put in motion by the five horses, three abreast next to the [front of the] carriage, and two ahead, the driver plying the whip, and the horses on the jump. We rattled over the pavements in great style. As we had some two hundred miles or more to go, which would take all of that night, the next day, and the best part of the following night, I thought I would take a look at my fellow passengers. On the seat with me was a portly looking gentleman who spoke no English, or French, or at least he would not. On the seat in front was a French lady and her two young daughters, who were disposed to be quite sociable and pleasant.

Soon after we got out of the city, the gentleman at my side began to make himself comfortable for the night. He placed his hat in the beckets under the top of the carriage, and from a bag he took out a black silk cap, which he hauled nicely over his head, then a rubber cushion which he regulated for his seat, and another which he secured on the side of the coach with steel hooks, to rest his head. He evidently was accustomed to night travel. The young ladies asked him some questions, which he declined to notice, whether he understood or not I could not tell. It was not long before they made some remark to me which I did not understand, and told them I did not speak French. That seemed to excite their curiosity.

The younger one had learned a little English at school. She was about 12 or 14, a very interesting child, the other, a year or two older, and when they found out that I was an American, they and their mother were disposed to be extremely pleasant to me, they having relations in America. We kept up a chattering together the greater part of the journey, they in broken English and I in broken French. I learned more French on that journey, than I did all the time I was in Paris. They left us at Mons, where we arrived in about 24 hours after we left Paris. There had been a grand royal wedding there a few weeks before, and the decorations, and royal arches still remained. King Leopold of Belgium had married the daughter of Louis Philippe, king of France, and there had been great rejoicing.

We arrived in the night at Brussels. It was a most fatiguing journey, and I was glad to get into comfortable quarters at the hotel De Swiss, and get rested. I did intend to have gone on at once to Antwerp, but finding that the city of Brussels were to give a grand reception the following evening to the royal couple, I determined to remain and attend. The botanical garden, a place of some acres, had been fitted up in splendid style for the purpose. It was a glorious affair, and I had a good view of Leopold and his queen.

The following [day] I arrived in Antwerp, found the *Bashaw* and Capt. Clark all right. He had had a long passage of about sixty days. I called on Messrs. Delisle, who were very cordial, and told me the market was very good for sugar, and that my six hundred boxes would pay a handsome profit, which was the case, as the profit on them, together with the freight on the two thousand boxes amounted something over fifteen thousand dollars. The ship was well fitted out, and sailed for a freight of cotton from Savannah to Liverpool.

After closing up the business in Antwerp, and remitting to Baring & Bates in London between $12,000 and $13,000, I concluded to take a little tour through the north of Europe, but was prevented from carrying out my plan as I intended, on account of the war between Holland and Belgium. Louis Philippe had sent an army to drive the Dutch from the fort on the Scheldt, about three miles above Antwerp, which was a very strong fortification built by the duke of Alba when the country was held by Spain under Philip the Second. I could not pass in the interior by the way of Aix-la-Chapelle, and had to go to Ostend on the North Sea, and take the steamer to Rotterdam, where I remained a few days, visiting some of my former friends and making arrangements for future business, & then I took the *diligence* to The Hague, which is about half way between Rotterdam and Amsterdam. Here I remained two days, and not finding much of interest, I left for Amsterdam, where I met my former acquaintances & friends, had a very pleasant visit of three or four days, and then proceeded to Bremen & Hamburg, and after making some excursions in the surrounding country I took passage in a new steamship for London.

I met my cousin Thomas Searle, who had lately formed a banking house with Mr. Pickersgill, a wealthy man from Yorkshire, and George Wildes, also a person of capital, under the firm of Geo. Wildes & Co. They were anxious I should do my business with them, which I finally agreed to do upon their offering me large credits for future business. I had made arrangements with merchants of the various cities I had visited, to draw on them for two thirds the cost of any shipments I should make in produce from the United States or the West Indies to their consignment, which I intended to use when opportunity offered.

The credits which I now received from George Wildes & Co. gave me the privilege to draw on them at 60 days sight, for twenty thousand pounds sterling on shipments to Cowes & a market to their order, [and] twenty thousand pounds on shipments direct to the various parties named at each of the European ports. This opened to my view a most magnificent opening for grand speculations in cotton and rice from the U.S. and sugar and coffee from Havana. I had power to draw for over a million of dollars, to be used in shipments of produce to Europe.

I spent a week in London enjoying myself, in visiting the various places of amusements. I dined at Mr. Pickersgill, had a pleasant time. Mrs. P. was very particular in requesting me to look after her son William, who was about to embark for the U.S. I then took the coach for Manchester, and from there to Liverpool, which is about forty miles, I took passage in the cars on the first rail road opened in England. The cars had been running but a short time, and affairs were not well managed at first. But a short time previous, the opening of the road was celebrated, and the duke of Wellington and Mr. Hutchinson were invited to attend. When about halfway from Liverpool to Manchester, the train met another train coming down, and stopped. Mr. Hutchinson and some other passengers got out of the cars to see the train pass, and in the confusion to get out of the way, Mr. H. was run over and lost his life. He was a member of the Parliament from Liverpool, and his death caused much excitement in the country.

When we got to this part of the road, the boiler of the engine burst, killing the engineer and scalding some of the workmen. There fortunately were two engines attached to the train, and after some detention we proceeded with one locomotive, and arrived at Liverpool after dark. I took rooms at the St. George Hotel, which was considered the first hotel in the city. On the following day I saw the duchess of Kent and her daughter the princess Victoria, now queen of England. I engaged passage to New York in the new packet ship *Roscoe*, Capt. York, one of the most experienced of New York captains.

It was now the winter of 1832 and 33, and we expected a rough passage across the ocean, but it proved quite to the contrary. There were about a dozen passengers in the cabin, mostly gentlemen, and we had a pleasant time, amusing ourselves by playing whist, reading, &c. When about two thirds passage, one forenoon, the weather appearing fine, Capt. York commenced taking in sail, furled all the lighter sails, clued down the topsails and hauled up the courses, and as there was but a light breeze, and clear weather, we all wondered what was the matter. I stepped up to Capt. York and asked him if he apprehended a blow, as there was no indications of any in the sky. He said his weather glass had suddenly gone down several degrees, and he expected something as it never had deceived him, and after waiting some time, he said, "I believe it has this time," and ordered the fore sail to be set.

The crew had not got the tack down, before the ship was struck with a white squall, that nearly threw her on her beam ends before she could be got before the wind, when she flew before the wind, trembling in every joint, and in an instant it seemed the ocean was white with foam. A bark which was 3 to 4 miles astern, with all sail set, had her masts swept over the side, and had we not taken in sail as we did we certainly would have lost our masts, or thrown on the beam ends. I had often heard sailors tell of white squalls, but as in all my sailing on the ocean I had never witnessed one, I never [gave] much credit to their stories. They are called white squalls as there is no cloud to indicate their coming as there is to the common squalls.

I then felt much interest in Capt. York's weather glass. If it could give warning in time of such great and sudden changes in the weather, it would be invaluable. It is called a simpiesometer, and was the invention of a Scotchman. He had a patent for ten years. He died without divulging the secret of its construction. I procured one for the *Bashaw*.

17

Out of the Frying Pan
and into the Fire

WE ARRIVED IN NEW YORK after forty days passage. I remained there but a few days, and then took passage in the bark *Woodstock* for Charleston, where I intended to ship a cargo of rice to Rotterdam to Messrs. Cramer & Co., and a cargo of cotton to Liverpool. On my arrival at Charleston, I took lodging at Mrs. Church's boarding house, and then called on Mr. John Stoney, one of the most prominent merchants of the city, and made my arrangements to do my business through him. I then chartered the American brig *Eurotus*, for a cargo of rice to Rotterdam, and commenced buying the cargo.

At this time Charleston was in a great state of excitement on account of the Nullification Act, passed by the South Carolina legislature, which was to refuse to pay duties on goods imported from foreign countries. The people were very much divided on the subject. Those in favour of the act called themselves Nullifiers, and wore blue cockades in their hats. The other party called themselves Unionists and wore black cockades. Both parties were arming themselves and the feeling between them was very bitter, and we did not know what moment might bring an encounter between them. The Governor, a very violent politician, was the leader of the Nullifiers. He wore a large blue cockade, and a wide blue sash, and made himself conspicuous, mounted on his horse, military caparisoned as he rode through the streets.

The Union party were privately drilling in all parts of the city. Our landlord, who was a strong Unionist, was the Captain of a company which met for drill almost every evening in the upper part of the house. General Jackson, who was then president of the United States, had placed a frigate at the entrance of the harbour to detain all vessels with cargoes from foreign countries until bonds had been given at the custom house for the duties. This annoyed the Governor exceedingly, and he called a meeting at the Circus building for the people to express their indignation against the government.

Great pains were taken to fit this building for the purpose, and the most fiery orators amongst the Nullifiers were appointed to address the people. I, with two of our boarders who were English agents sent from Liverpool to purchase cotton, and who like myself had no interest in either party, attended this meeting, and a more rebellious set against the government never met together. Around the inside of the building was hung with flags and hand bills, expressing their feelings to the government, and denouncing the tyranny of General Jackson. The most violent speeches were made, one of the most violent by Governor Pinckney, who stated that he had shipped an invoice of rice to Cuba, and ordered the proceeds to be invested in sugar, and trusted to his friends to help him test the question when the vessel arrived. The meeting ended without bloodshed, which was expected.

At last the vessel arrived that had the Governor's sugar on board, and was detained, as other vessels had been until a signal from the custom house was given that the duties were bonded. The Governor expected when he made his shipment of rice, that the vessel with the returns in sugar would come up to the city, and the mob would overpower the government officers and land his sugar free of duties. He vowed he would not give bonds, and the vessel was detained.

The other consignees, which had a great deal more sugar on board than the Governor, had given bonds, and were anxious to have their consignments brought to the city, and finally worked upon the Governor [so] that he went down to the custom house, and in the most lordly style entered the building, and addressing the collector, who was rather an old man, asked why the brig was not allowed to come up to the city. Without noticing the Governor, he turned to one of the deputies as if he was ignorant of the subject, and put the question to him, who looked over several of the books, apparently to ascertain the cause, keeping the Governor standing, and the clerks smiling. He finally said, "There is one small invoice of sugar, that has not been bonded, consigned to a Mr. Pinckney."

The Governor could stand it no longer, and striking his fist on the table said in a loud voice, "Mr. Collector, it is not the money I contest, it is the principle, by G——, sir." The collector, who had been sitting at his desk with his back toward the Governor, turned round, pushing his spectacles up on his forehead, and in a loud voice, said, "Sir, it is not the principle I contest" (striking his fist on the table) "but the money, by G——, sir." This created a roar of laughter among the employees of the custom house, and the Governor made his exit, about the most offended man in the city of Charleston.

The president sent General Scott to Charleston, and in the course of a few months, quietness was restored. Governor P. was a rather young man, very proud and aristocratic in his feelings, and was constantly annoyed by squibs and caricatures stuck up about the city. One was a large cock painted blue, with the Governor astride, and his aide behind him, with the words hanging from the bill "It is the principle I contest."

It was between three & four weeks before I got the brig *Eurotus* (which was a large vessel) loaded. I abandoned the idea of sending a cargo of cotton to Liverpool, as the cost prices in Charleston and the quotations in Liverpool gave no margin for a profit. After dispatching the cargo of rice and settling up with Mr. Stoney, whom I found to be one of the most upright and pleasant men to deal with that I had met, I made arrangements with him to ship on my account occasionally a small invoice of rice to the Cramers in Rotterdam, and the proceeds to be invested in linseed oil, and consigned to him, they charging their commission, and I standing the profit or loss in the operation.

I then decided to go to Havana and operate in the coffee market, until the *Bashaw* arrived, as I had ordered Capt. Clark to come there from Liverpool, without he could find better employment for her there. At this time, the Spanish government had placed such high duties on produce in American bottoms and tonnage duties that the trade with Cuba was carried on entirely under the Spanish flag. I therefore took passage in a Spanish brig for Havana, taking with me a horse I purchased soon after I arrived in Charleston, a very fine animal, which I used to ride almost every morning.

We arrived in Havana after a disagreeable passage of twelve days. I called at once on my friends Charles Drake & Co. and found them ready to do business on the terms I proposed. Mr. & Mrs. Cleveland wished me to stay with them. I found them and Mr. Shaler very glad to see me. A few days after my arrival, the Asiatic cholera broke out in the city and created a great panic. Every one seemed much frightened. I commenced at once to buy coffee, as the price was low and there was quite a margin for a profit to the United States. I loaded two small vessels, one for Baltimore, and one for Philadelphia. The cholera was increasing, twelve hundred cases a day reported. Common carts, with a black cloth to haul over, were employed to go through the streets, picking up all that died, and many that did not.

There was one case of a Frenchman, which made some stir. He was thought to be dead, and was thrown into one of the dead carts, and carried to the burying ground. A gentleman happening to be passing at the time heard a screaming, went into the burying place, and there saw the Negroes, forcing this body into the hole, where some dozen others had been thrown on. [He] expostulated with the Negroes. They replied that he had the cholera, and if he was not dead, he would be very soon. The gentleman, with much difficulty, stopped them from burying a live man. There were no doubt other similar cases.

The inhabitants were crazy with fright, going about with quills filled with camphor in their mouths, which was thought a preventative. The bells tolling for prayers in the churches, cannon firing, and incense burning in the streets, business had come to a perfect stand, and those that could had gone to the country.

I used frequently to go to the Lonja, a sort of exchange, where merchants & others congregated to hear the news of the day. One Saturday evening I met my friend Mitchell and we sat down to one of the small tables to have a glass of lemonade, and our conversation was mostly on the subject of the day, the cholera. We thought people were more alarmed than necessary, and that we knew no one who had died with the epidemic, and did not believe there was any danger if one took proper care of themselves &c. The fact was, that we both had serious fears, and talked this way to bolster up one another's courage.

We parted at about eight, he for his boarding house & I for Mr. Cleveland's. I rose early the following morning, and walking down to the wharf as was my custom, I met my friend Bruce, who asked me if I knew that Mitchell was dead. I ridiculed the idea, telling him that I parted with him perfectly well the evening before. There were frequently reports of the deaths of persons which proved false, and I thought this one. I afterwards met Peter Hogan, a clerk at Mr. Knight's, who repeated that Mitchell died in the night of cholera, that he was told so by one who boarded at Mrs. Lyon's with Mitchell.

I thought I would walk round there and see for myself. As I turned the corner of the street, I saw a dead cart (as they were called) leave Mrs. Lyon's house. The doctors were under a heavy penalty to give information at once of every case of cholera to the Commissary (the police office), who at once sent a cart to take away the corpse. I saw Mrs. Lyon who told me that Mr. Mitchell was taken sick soon after he got home & died between three & four, and that cart which had just left the house took his corpse. It was then about six in the morning and [I] at once decided to leave the city on anything I could [to] get away from such horrors. I ran home to the house and commenced to pack my trunk in all haste, feeling like one who was escaping from a fire.

Whilst I was packing up my trunk, Mr. Shaler came into my room, and expressed surprise, as he thought I would be the last one to be frightened. He said if he could possibly leave, he would go also. That night this good old man was taken off by the cholera, & within twenty four [hours] from the time he had this conversation with me, his body was thrown into a deadcart, and buried like a dog. I rushed out of the house with my trunk and got the first Negro I saw to take my trunk to the wharf, and embarked in the first boat, and after rowing off into the harbour, the thought came to me "Where shall I go?"

When I noticed a small American schooner hoisting up their sails, I at once went to her, jumped on deck, [and] asked them where they were bound. To Savannah, was the reply. I saw the Captain aft, busy in getting the ropes clear of the sail they were hoisting, [and] told him I wanted to take passage with him. He said he could not take me. I went to the boatman, paid him his fare, took my trunk on board and told him to shove off. The vessel was under way and I was determined to go. The Capt. insisted I could not go, as there was no accommodation for a passenger. I told him I must go, I did not want any accommodation, that I was a Captain like himself and could put up with anything.

The schooner was called the *Sally*, and was laden with fruit, having the decks filled with crates of pine apples, oranges &c. When we got outside of the Morro Castle into the blue water of the ocean, I thought all was safe, and began to feel quite easy, having time to look round the vessel and to see who my comrades were. The Captain seemed to be a clever sort of fellow. The mate and the two sailors were most ordinary, and the vessel was the smallest and the dirtiest that I had ever been on board, but the old saying of "any port in a storm" made me quite contented.

During the day a bark which had left the day before ran down to us, and hailing, asked if we could spare a sailor or two, that the cholera had broken out, and two of his crew had died, and two men were sick with it. He was bound to Antwerp. We of course could not spare a hand and I advised him to make the nearest port and get assistance. Our Captain, who was rather a young man, seemed a good deal affected by the idea that the cholera could break out on board of a vessel after she had left port. He thought there was no danger when once on deep blue water. He talked a good deal about it during the afternoon, and towards night he was taken sick with the symptoms of the cholera.

I had some cholera medicine in my trunk, and gave it to him. I also spread mustard plasters for his chest, and the bottom of his feet, gave him hot tea and made him as comfortable as I could. He was soon out of his mind, talked incoherently most of the night. It was now near midnight and I went on deck. I found it blowing a gale and raining violently from the south, the waves breaking over the little craft, and with the decks filled with crates of fruit, the appearances were dismal enough. I talked with the mate, found he knew nothing of navigation, or of the present position of the vessel, and as the Florida reef was near, and the night was pitch dark & the vessel flying through the water with lightning speed might at any moment be dashed to pieces on the rocks which surrounded us, I began to think my running away from the cholera in Havana was something like jumping out of the frying pan into the fire.

I found I should have to take charge of the navigation of the vessel, and asked the mate if he would look and see what latitude the Capt. made the vessel in by his observation at noon. He went down the cabin, and soon came up saying the Capt. had rubbed out the figures on the slate, and he could not tell, that the Capt. was as crazy as a loon. I thought to myself, here is a mess. All I could do was to find out by guess work the course and distance we had run since leaving Havana, and make my calculations accordingly, and keep a good watch until daylight to avoid the reefs. I passed a miserable night, now & then altering the course as I thought she was too near one side or the other of the Florida channel.

No one ever felt more thankful for daylight than I did when it came. At noon I ascertained the position of the vessel and I felt relieved. The Capt. remained in a delirious state, not seeming to know anything connected with the vessel, but I was satisfied that the disease had been checked by the course I had pursued and that he would probably get well. We had light winds & pleasant weather and on the morning of the sixth day out, came in sight of Tybee light at the entrance to the Savannah River. In the afternoon, we were hailed by a pilot boat, and a Black boy was sent on board as a pilot in a canoe which remained alongside. I asked him what news there was in Savannah. He handed me a late newspaper, which had the governor of Georgia's proclamation ordering the strictest quarantine on all vessels from Havana.

I was in a dilemma what to do. I did not know, as I could not think of being detained under such circumstances on board of such a craft, perhaps for months. I was determined to get out of [it] if possible in any way. I soon saw a sloop coming down the river, which the pilot told me was the Charleston packet, bound to Charleston. I told him, "That is just where I want to go," and to steer so as to speak her. I went into the cabin to get my trunk on deck, found the Captain still out of his mind, but otherwise much better.

We came up with the packet. I hailed "Where bound?" "To Charleston." "Can you take a passenger?" "Yes" was the reply, and I soon got my trunk into the canoe, and the boy pilot to paddle along-side of the Charleston packet, and thus got clear of the schooner *Sally*, and the certainty of a long quarantine. I gave the pilot boy a dollar, which pleased him, and paid the Capt. for my passage to Charleston which satisfied him without asking any questions. I considered I had earned my passage in the *Sally*, and as the Capt. could not tell me how much it was, I thought no more about it.

Early Sunday morning, just a week from the time I left Havana, I was eating my breakfast at Mrs. Church's. I avoided being quarantined all I could, but of course had to answer the boarders, who I knew, as well as I could, for they knew I went to Havana six weeks before. I felt guilty, and wanted to get clear from Charleston as soon as I could, as I saw by the papers there was a good deal of excitement about the cholera. I kept pretty close in the house during Sunday. Monday morning I engaged my passage in the packet ship *Calhoun*, which was to sail the next morning for New York.

We had a pleasant passage of six days, and in a fortnight from the day I left Havana, I was nicely located in the New York Hotel, consid-ered the crack resort, before the Astor House was built, which was not then finished. I remained there about a week, and then went to Balti-more to attend to some business, and there chartered a schooner be-longing in Mystic to take a cargo of corn out to Havana, and return with a cargo of coffee, and made my mind up to take passage in her. She was soon loaded, and we sailed with a fair wind from the city, which lasted us until we entered the harbour of Havana, making the run in five days and a half, a very extraordinary passage.

I found that the excitement from the cholera was over, there being but few cases now and then. I at once bought the cargo of coffee for the schooner and landed the corn, which was in bags and sold at a good price. The schooner sailed within a week from her arrival, had a wonderful short passage back to Baltimore, and the coffee was sold at a handsome profit. I stayed at my friend Mrs. Cowan's. She had a home in the city and wished me to make it my home as long as I was in Havana. My good friend Mr. Shaler, the consul general, died of the cholera the night I left Havana. I also found that several of my acquaintances had passed off with the epidemic. I had been absent a little more than four weeks, and the deaths had numbered some thousands, many were slaves & mulattoes.

I was daily expecting the *Bashaw*, as I had ordered Capt. Clark to come to Havana from Liverpool. I concluded not to operate in the sugar market as I had intended. The prices were high, and the prospects in Europe were not encouraging. In about ten days after I arrived, the *Bashaw* made her appearance. I was not satisfied with Captain Clark's accounts, and as there were no freights offering, decided to send her to Boston, with what coffee I had in store, and sugar enough for ballast.

Business called me in Matanzas, and I took the steamer in the morning arriving there at 11 o'clock. I went to Mrs. Almy's boarding house, which was well filled with lodgers, but to accommodate me, she had a cot put up on the lower floor, even with the street, in a large hall with the windows looking out on the street, and being quite low, any one passing on the side walk could look in, and without much difficulty could get in. The servant, with a little rush light that made darkness visible, showed me to my cot, in one corner of this great space of darkness, at the same time relating the account of a man being assassinated close under one of the windows the night previous.

I had not been well for two or three days, and was feeling quite poorly at the time I retired, and this story, with the gloomy appearance around me, was dismal enough. I however soon fell asleep, but had a poor night, with vivid dreams, one of which was that I was stabbed in my side, and the pain was severe. In the early morning I was called to go in the steamer back to Havana, and I was surprised to find my night shirt soaking with perspiration, and one side of my person covered

red with brick dust, and looking on the brick floor, near my cot, I saw the form of my person, wet, showing where I had laid some part of the night, struggling with pain.

I had a friend who was to go in the steamer with me to Havana. He persuaded me to go, and I walked with him to the boat which was to take the passengers to the steamer, which was at anchor a mile from the wharf. Soon after we left the shore, I began to feel dizzy, large drops of perspiration falling from my forehead, and I became unconscious, and when the boat came alongside, I was hauled up by a rope. I presume some of the passengers thought I was intoxicated. I was laid out on a settee in the cabin, where I laid until a short distance from Havana, when all at once I came to myself, and thought I felt quite well, landed with the other passengers on the wharf, and went direct to Mrs. Cowan's house, and sent for Doctor Clark, who was considered the best physician in the place, and a personal friend of mine.

He saw at once that I had an attack of the Asiatic cholera. It was now about two o'clock in the afternoon, the Doctor was with me the most of the time until 12 o'clock midnight, when he gave me up, as I had all the symptoms of the last stage of the disease. He had given me all the medicine he dared to, and there was no hope. Mrs. Cowan told me afterwards that she never saw a person who suffered so much, that I would go into convulsions so violent that it required four stout Negroes to hold me on the cot.

[The narrative breaks off at this point. Charles Tyng survived the cholera attack to live another forty-six years. He wrote this memoir in 1878, about a year before his death.]

AFTERWORD

❧

B EFORE THE WIND is a memoir of a nearly forgotten frontier. Charles Tyng wrote it in his old age in the latter half of the nineteenth century, at a time when the national imagination had become engrossed by the drama of westward expansion across the continent. Thanks first to a flood of popular fiction and then to an endless succession of motion pictures, that imaginative obsession has been prolonged into our own day as the primary American fantasy, something any Marlboro man will tell us. But Charles Tyng returns us to an era when the locus of opportunity and adventure for most Americans was not the back country that extended to the west of what was still essentially a seaboard civilization, but rather the great oceanic arena that extended to the eastward and around the globe. During the first three decades of the nineteenth century—the span of Tyng's narrative—the path to personal fulfillment and distinction, as well as to national power and prosperity, lay along the trade routes that American vessels were following across the Atlantic and into the Pacific.

In the first half of the nineteenth century the United States came to challenge and to surpass Great Britain in sector after sector of maritime activity, from the transatlantic packet service to the whale fishery. American shipbuilders perfected the wooden sailing vessel as a vehicle of commerce in the extraordinary clipper ship. Even in the imaginative depiction of maritime life, as British critics freely admitted, the American writers of the sea—Fenimore Cooper, Richard Henry Dana Jr., and Herman Melville—overshadowed their own Captain Marryat and the armada of naval scribblers who followed in his wake. It was truly a golden age of possibility for a boy from coastal Massachusetts, particularly for one with the right connections.

The Boston of the young Charles Tyng was at the center of all this buzz of excitement, rivaled only in commercial activity by the port of New York, whose own merchants and shipowners were chiefly transplanted New Englanders. And at the center of Boston's commerce was Thomas Handasyd Perkins, the great merchant prince, who with his brother James as partner and with his cadre of nephews as lieutenants dominated the lucrative China trade. Chief among those nephews was John Perkins Cushing, who ran the family's business affairs at Canton and who was generally regarded as the most influential of all foreigners in China; Tyng meets him in the Far East and shares a wedding cake with him on board ship. Another heavyweight in the clan was William Sturgis, who after retiring from the sea formed the powerful mercantile firm of Bryant and Sturgis as an ally of Perkins & Company; Tyng encounters him as an obdurate businessman who insists on payment in cash. And then there was the spectacular Robert Bennet Forbes—Black Ben Forbes—who, with his brother John Murray Forbes, took over Cushing's operation in China before moving on to speculation in railroads; two years Tyng's junior, he shows up in the memoir as the second mate of a Perkins vessel while Tyng is peddling opium in the *Cadet* at the Lintin station. Last and distinctly least was Charles Tyng himself, whose claim to membership in this circle of nepotism rested on the fact that his aunt Barbara was married to Samuel G. Perkins, brother of the mighty T. H. Perkins.

Tyng began his career as seaman and merchant safely tucked under the Perkins wing. Although his wonderful account of his first voyage in the *Cordelia* invites comparison with Melville's *Redburn* as a narrative of the misery of the young green hand, Tyng was not quite the Oliver Twist that he pictures himself to be. The ship was owned by Perkins & Company, his uncle John Higginson was on board as supercargo, and even his relentless persecutor Charles Magee, the first mate, was a relation by way of the Perkins connection. Tyng's ordeal was thus very much a family affair, an initiatory rite like that which the other Perkins nephews endured and the first step toward proving oneself fit to be a participant in the family enterprises.

Though Tyng left the *Cordelia* wishing never to go to sea again, his father's insistence that he persevere in a maritime career was less an exercise of arbitrary power than a shrewd estimate of the best interests of a gentleman's son who showed no capacity for any of the professions. And, sure enough, the boy made good. After flirting with a permanent descent into the proletarian life of a common seaman by having himself tattooed, the young Tyng pulled himself together, practiced his navigation, and, establishing himself as the best sailor in the ship on his fourth voyage, earned his promotion to mate. From that point on, advancement came quickly, culminating in his appointment to the command of the Perkins brig *Cadet* in his early twenties.

The career that seemed destined to place the young Tyng in a secure and lucrative position within the Perkins empire took a sharp turn upon his return from the Pacific in December 1824. Denied command of a second Perkins vessel, he impulsively cut himself loose from the firm and set out as an independent entrepreneur. First chartering and then purchasing a succession of vessels, he conducted one trading voyage after another to Europe and the West Indies, applying all the nautical and commercial skills that his Perkins training had given him. By the time the narrative breaks off in 1833, Tyng has become a miniature Perkins himself, no longer a sailor but a merchant and shipowner with a line of credit exceeding a million dollars.

In all of this Tyng's memoir is broadly representative of the genre to which it belongs, what one might call the master's narrative. The surge of American maritime activity in the first half of the nineteenth century gave rise to an extensive body of more or less factual accounts of life at sea. Some, like David Porter's *Journal of a Cruise* (1822), detail the conduct of naval campaigns or expeditions. Others, like Dana's famous *Two Years Before the Mast* (1840) or Ross Browne's *Etchings of a Whaling Cruise* (1846), record the experience of common sailors, often exposing the systematic abuse and exploitation to which seamen were subjected. But the master's narrative—the personal history of a merchant captain's career—probably exceeds in number all other categories.

Usually composed in old age (and sometimes with the aid of a ghostwriter), these narratives extend from Amasa Delano's *A Narrative of Voyages and Travels* (1817) throughout the nineteenth century, as one old shipmaster after another sought to give the younger generation the benefit of his experience or, as the century progressed and the age of sail faded, the knowledge of a vanishing way of life. By 1844, the genre had become so firmly defined that Cooper could structure his novel *Afloat and Ashore* as a fictive master's narrative, an old man's recollection of his maritime career from his first voyage before the mast to his rise to command and ownership. Charles Tyng was surely acquainted with at least two major examples of the genre, *A Narrative of Voyages and Commercial Enterprises* (1842) by Richard J. Cleveland, with whom Tyng and his wife had been friendly in Cuba, and *Personal Reminiscences* (1878) by Robert Bennet Forbes, his old rival for the blessing of T. H. Perkins. Indeed, the publication of Forbes's memoir may well have prompted Tyng to write his own.

One can never know whether Tyng intended his memoir for publication or merely for the information of his family. The care with which it is written, its explanation of nautical technicalities, and its avoidance of personal reference to his first wife suggest that he had a wider audience in mind than the family circle. At any rate, he produced a manuscript full of interest to both the general reader and the maritime historian. At the center of that interest is the character of Tyng himself, a feisty little man, ever ready to wade into a gang of mutinous seamen with any available weapon—sword, pistols, capstan bar, belaying pin, or fists alone. The number of rebellions that he must put down is remarkable, all of them occurring in a period when American ships were manned mainly by native-born crews who were supposedly better educated and disciplined than the seamen of any other nation.

The violence that threatens Tyng comes not only from within his own vessel but from the world at large. Added to the terrors of nature—the storm and the shark—are those generated by human predators, the Malay pirates of the East Indies and the resurgent buccaneers of the West Indies, the flotsam of the wreck of the Spanish empire in the New World. The new governments established by the wars of liberation in Latin America offer little security to commercial enterprise, for Tyng finds his vessel endangered by port authorities as much as by pirates. The man who as a young sailor had nearly lost his life in a fall from aloft now as master and owner runs the constant risk of financial destruction.

Through it all, however, Tyng is anything but a passive victim. He twists and turns, improvises and bluffs, ever ready to cut and run if need be. As a boy he pacifies the older sailors with gifts of rum and tobacco; as a man he administers a Mickey Finn to an unsuspecting customs officer. Always there are the extraordinary energy and resourcefulness that save him from one jam after another. Always there is the eye to the main chance, whether it be a promising personal adventure or a potentially profitable cargo. Surely in the annals of American commerce there is no entry more telling of Yankee initiative at its outer limits than Tyng's dry notation, "I had been trying to dispose of the mermaid." Mummified Japanese mermaids, Turkish opium, Cuban sugar—all are his stock in trade.

But there is more to Tyng than the master and merchant. He was one of the first American merchant captains to take his wife with him to sea; his reticent and yet admiring references to the young woman who in spite of her delicate health persists in risking the dangers of storm and mutiny with him speak as well of him as of her. His curiosity about people—not just the great celebrities like Lord Byron and Admiral Cochrane but the wonderful widow of Antwerp, who presides as grandly over her dinner table as over her vast business enterprise, and the gross Mr. Paine of Batavia, who each night must be carried by his servants dead drunk to his bed—is one of his most engaging characteristics. He has an openness to impressions that is striking; one wonders how many of Tyng's fellow merchant captains would find themselves as he does fixed in fascination before Géricault's *Raft of the Medusa* in the Louvre. Unlike most master's narratives, Tyng's memoir admits us into the interior spaces of its writer, giving us not only an account of what was done but a sense of what was felt. Only Tyng would reveal his terror on the deck of the foundering schooner *Monroe* by telling us of the flashback that fills his mind, the image of the kittens he had drowned as a boy, kicking and squirming in their death agony.

But *Before the Wind* is as much the memorial of an age as the memoir of a man. Whole chapters of Samuel Eliot Morison's magisterial *Maritime History of Massachusetts* and its successors are embodied in Tyng's experience. His voyage in the *Cordelia* is not only a personal initiation but the triumphant reopening of the China trade after the years of inactivity during the War of 1812 that had left some 250 Boston vessels rotting at their wharves. His account of his several voyages to the Far East in Perkins vessels provides extraordinary details of the conduct of the trade with China, particularly of the search for a commodity that would replace the shrinking supply of sea otter skins and sandalwood as an object of value in Chinese eyes. That search led Perkins & Company to follow the British example of smuggling opium into Canton, but, denied access to the opium of India, the Americans had to develop a new source of the drug in Turkey. It would seem that the voyage to Leghorn of the ship *Heroine*, in which Tyng served as second mate, was to put in place there the Perkins buying agent for Turkish opium. Significantly, his next voyage, in the brig *Cadet*, was to establish that vessel as a depot to receive the new supply as it was brought to China from the Mediterranean.

Similarly, Tyng's later voyages on his own account provide fresh details about the American trade with Germany and the Low Countries in the period, a sector of commerce that, lacking the glamour of the China trade, has received far less attention from historians. And through Tyng's eyes we briefly glimpse sights that bring a variety of other aspects of the maritime past to life, such as the vast fleet of mothballed line-of-battle ships lying at Chelsea, the wooden walls that had defended Great Britain throughout the Napoleonic wars. To the modern reader the long-gone world in which Tyng lived and moved is full of marvels, here summoned up with an authenticity that no Forester or O'Brian, however skillful, can simulate.

—THOMAS PHILBRICK
University of Pittsburgh

EXPLANATORY NOTES

꘏꘏

CHAPTER I—*A Boston Boyhood*

4   *My father . . . married again:* His second wife was Elizabeth Higginson, younger sister of his first wife, Sarah.

8   *Trinity church yard:* In New York City.

9   *Captain Dacres:* James R. Dacres captained H.M.S. *Guerrière* in her 1812 battle with the U.S.S. *Constitution*; the *Shannon*'s captain was Philip B. V. Broke.

9   *grandfather Higginson:* Stephen Higginson (1743–1828) was a sea captain and merchant, politically active during the American Revolution.

10   *Goldsborough:* Louis Malesherbes Goldsborough (1805–1877); he became an admiral in the U.S. Navy.

10   *Ralph Emerson:* Ralph Waldo Emerson (1803–1882), poet and essayist, known as "The Sage of Concord."

11   *driving hoop was a common amusement:* A child would roll a large, thin, circular wooden hoop, running alongside and propelling it with a stick. To press someone else's hoop meant to capture or confiscate it.

11   *the army which was forming:* In 1812.

12   *He was at one time Mayor of Boston:* Josiah Quincy (1802–1882) was mayor in the 1840s; his father (1772–1864), of the same name, held that office from 1823 to 1829, then served as president of Harvard (1829–45).

13   *the former residence of Judge Dana:* Francis Dana (1743–1811), grandfather of

257

Richard Henry Dana Jr. (1815–1882), the author of *Two Years Before the Mast* (1840). The house, which burned in 1839, stood in the Dana Hill neighborhood of Cambridge, at what is now number 5 Dana Street.

13 *Uncle Perkins:* Samuel G. Perkins, married to Charles's aunt Barbara Higginson.

14 *My uncle . . . was to go supercargo:* As cargo superintendent, the cargo owner's business representative.

15 *the discoverer of ether for the unconsciousness of pain:* William T. G. Morton (1819–1868), of Massachusetts General Hospital.

CHAPTER 2—*First Voyage*

16 *specie:* Coined money.

17 *steerage:* Crew's quarters, just forward of the cabin that housed the captain and mates.

17 *I thought the shrouds was the rigging:* Shrouds are ropes that provide lateral support for masts.

17 *belaying pins:* Removable bars of wood or iron, placed in holes on a rail around the mast; ropes of the running rigging can be made fast to them.

19 *Mother Carey's chickens:* Small black seabirds; storm petrels.

20 *each having one gill:* Half a cup, liquid measure.

20 *we picked oakum:* Oakum is tarred shreds of rope, used to caulk the ship.

22 *guernsey frock:* A heavy knitted wool pullover.

22 *the mizzen:* Mizzenmast; the rearmost mast of a three-masted ship.

24 *Sandwich Islands:* Now known as the Hawaiian Islands, or Hawaii.

25 *stropping the blocks:* Reinforcing the wooden or metal cases of pulleys (for ropes), called blocks, using short, spliced loops of rope, called straps (or strops).

25 *Owhyhee:* Hawaii, the largest of the Sandwich Islands.

25 *where Capt. Cook was killed, and eaten:* Hawaiians maintained that Captain Cook had not been eaten, and resented this story as a fabrication and a racial slur.

26 *King Tamehameha:* Kamehameha I (c. 1758–1819).

28 *lateen sail:* A triangular sail extended by a long spar slung to a low mast.

30 *a peculiar wood:* Balsa.

32 *Houqua was at the head of the hong:* Wu Ping-Ch'ien (1769–1843), known as Houqua, was reputed to be the richest man in the world at the time of his death.

37 *Gaspar Straits:* Selat Gaspar, between the Indonesian islands of Bangka and Belitung, off the east coast of Sumatra.

38 *They had plenty for the cabin:* For the captain and mates.

38 *reefing again became the order of the day:* Reefing is reducing the amount of sail exposed to the wind; when reefed, sails are partly rolled or folded and tied up, to reduce strain on the canvas and masts from strong winds.

38 *bom boats:* Small trading or service vessels, also called bumboats.

39 *Hanseatic cities:* Members of a trading league dating from medieval times.

42   *taking their kids aft:* Kids were wooden tubs used as food dishes.

43   *Colonel Perkins:* Thomas Handasyd Perkins (1764–1854), partner with his brother James in J. & T. H. Perkins, was renowned for his success in business, and his civic contributions to Boston. The title of "Colonel" came from his service in the Massachusetts militia.

44   *Alden Bradford . . . secretary of state:* Bradford was secretary of state for Massachusetts from 1812 to 1821.

44   *I returned from India:* The East Indies and China.

CHAPTER 3—*Return to China*

45   *This ship was much better found:* Supplied.

46   *There was to be no allowance of water:* No rationing.

47   *on the quarterdeck:* The part of the ship's deck toward the rear of the vessel, where the captain or officer of the watch stands to give orders to the crew; it is normally off-limits to the crew.

49   *a fancy double heart with C.T. . . . and S.H.:* Initials for Charles Tyng and Sarah Hickling.

50   *aqua fortis:* Nitric acid.

50   *a becket on the pole:* In this case, a becket is a loop.

52   *I never had been in a brig, and thought I should like the change from a ship:* A brig is a two-masted square-rigged vessel; a ship is a square-rigged vessel with three masts.

CHAPTER 4—*A Leaky Trip to Havana*

56   *letter of marque:* Permission for the captain of a privately owned ship to capture enemy vessels.

56   *St. Marys, one of the Canary Islands:* St. Marys (Santa Maria) is in the Azores.

59   *expecting the schooner to sail:* A schooner is a fore-and-aft rigged vessel with two or more masts. A fore-and-aft rigged vessel has her sails rigged in line with the vessel's length, as opposed to square-rigged (sails at right angles to the length).

CHAPTER 5—*Pirates and Promotions*

65   *I had made up my mind to get out of the forecastle:* The crew's quarters were in the forecastle. Tyng wanted to earn promotion from the crew and become an officer.

65   *grafting all the block strops:* Weaving coverings out of rope yarn for the rope loops (strops) that reinforced the pulley cases (blocks).

66   *Mr. Nash asked me if I could not send down the fore top gallant yard . . . :*
       fore top gallant yard: A spar supporting the third sail above the deck on the forward mast.
       tie: A rope by which a yard is hoisted.
       stopped: Secured.
       hoisted up a cock bill: Tied up at an angle to the deck.
       parrel: A rope holding the spar to the mast.

    lifts: Ropes from the mastheads to the ends of the yardarm.

    braces: Ropes used to pivot a yard.

    gasket: A small rope used to secure the furled sail.

66   *the main top gallant studding sails were ordered to be set . . . :*

    main top gallant: The third sail above the deck on the center mast.

    studding sails: Extra sails set during a fair wind.

    halliards: Ropes used to raise or lower sail.

    rove: Passed a rope through.

    bending it: Fastening the sail to the yard.

    slings: Ropes or chains supporting a yard.

68   *the island of Crocetoe:* Krakatau, or Krakatoa.

68   *small brass swivel:* A gun on a pivoting mount.

68   *nankin:* Durable handwoven cotton cloth, more commonly spelled "nankeen."

71   *four lascars hanging:* East Indian sailors.

71   *Queen Elizabeth's palace:* The building Tyng saw, on the site of Queen Elizabeth I's birthplace, was a late-seventeenth-century structure, now the Royal Naval College.

73   *the green bag:* A mail pouch.

75   *China ware:* Porcelain.

77   *Aunt Elliot:* Catherine Atkins (1758–1829), sister of Dudley Atkins Tyng, married to Samuel Elliot (also spelled "Eliot").

77   *laudanum:* A tincture of opium.

CHAPTER 6—*Sharks, Monkeys, and Lord Byron*

78   *Doctor Physick:* Probably Philip Syng Physick (1768–1837), the "Father of American Surgery."

81   *These I took for my adventure:* Goods bought to be resold on Tyng's own account, rather than for the owner or shipper.

82   *forward thwart:* A seat for a rower, at the front of the boat.

82   *becket:* In this case, a bracket made of hooks or rope loops.

83   *it is tried out in the large kettles carried by all whalers:* "Tried" is the term for rendering blubber into oil.

84   *tumblers:* Straight-sided drinking glasses.

85   *Leghorn hats:* Made of finely braided wheat straw.

85   *Lord Byron:* George Gordon Byron (1778–1824), British poet, satirist, and adventurer.

85   *stocks:* Neckties wrapped high under the shirt collar.

85   *lost his life fighting:* Byron died of a fever, rather than in combat.

85   *George Ticknor:* Harvard professor and linguist (1791–1871), author of the landmark *History of Spanish Literature* (1840).

CHAPTER 7—*Mutinies and the Mermaid*

87   *four six pound carronades:* Short, light iron cannons.

88   *A kedge with the hawser:* Smallest of a ship's anchors, with its cable.

89 *one of the capstan bars:* A movable bar used to turn the capstan, a cranking device for winding up the anchor cable.

89 *Batavia:* modern-day Djakarta, Indonesia.

90 *put in stays:* The bow turned into the wind as the ship changed tacks. A tack is a direction, or angle in relation to the wind.

92 *windlass:* A crank used to raise the anchor, hoist, or haul.

98 *to rattle down the rigging:* Make ratlines, or rungs for footholds.

98 *taffrail:* The upper part of the after rail, at the stern.

99 *quizzed:* Teased.

100 *Patna opium:* From Patna, in India.

100 *draft:* The depth of water required to float the ship.

100 *had a very pleasant intercourse:* Visits, acquaintanceship.

102 *Thomas [Forbes] . . . was lost overboard:* Actually, Forbes's death occurred in August 1829 (not 1823), when his yacht *Haidee* was sailing from Macao to Lintin.

103 *cheroots:* Cigars open at both ends.

103 *waiters:* Trays.

106 *Van Diemen's Land:* Tasmania, Australia.

106 *trusting that I might lay her to:* Head her into the wind.

106 *cambose:* A small kitchen on the deck of the ship.

106 *Antipodes Islands:* Uninhabited islands south of New Zealand.

107 *handspike:* A wooden bar used as a lever to move the ship's guns, or as a capstan bar.

107 *Chiloe:* An island off the Chilean coast.

108 *staple:* A metal loop used to secure a rope.

110 *Admiral Cochrane:* Thomas Cochrane (1775–1860), a British naval officer and hero then serving as an admiral in the Chilean navy.

113 *poop:* A deck above the quarterdeck, at the rear of the vessel.

116 *hove the log:* The log was a wooden apparatus used to help calculate the ship's speed. It was attached to the log line, a very long line with knots in it. When the log was thrown overboard, the speed with which the line ran out was timed with a half-minute sandglass, so the vessel's speed could be figured in "knots" per hour.

CHAPTER 8—*The Schooner* Zephyr

119 *on change:* At Boston's trading center, or exchange.

119 *standing royal yards:* The horizontal lengths of timber (yards) supporting the fourth sails from the deck (royals) were fixed to the masts, rather than being movable.

122 *vessels are moored to dolphins:* Mooring posts or bollards.

122 *John Hodshon, & Co.:* Possibly the correct spelling of the name was "Hodgson."

125 *news room:* For shipping news at the port of Boston.

CHAPTER 9—*More Pirates and a Sudden Squall*

128   *the Siam Twins:* Chang and Eng Bunker (1811–1874).

129   *hoy:* A small coasting vessel.

130   *anchors, and other fasts:* Mooring cables.

133   *placed a board over the light:* Over the window.

138   *Colombian government:* At this time, Venezuela was part of the federal republic of Greater Colombia.

143   *alcalde:* An administrative and judicial officer.

145   *the colonel had sent in a bill:* Presumably for the expense of guarding Tyng's vessel.

146   *she . . . could lay two points nearer the wind than we could:* A sailing vessel heading directly into the wind cannot move forward by catching the wind in her sails; she must steer at an angle (measured in "points") to the wind. A fore-and-aft rigged vessel is able to sail at a narrower angle, nearer to the direction the wind is coming from, than a square-rigged one can.

146   *making leeway:* Being driven sideways (off course) by the wind.

147   *under our lee:* Downwind from Tyng's ship.

149   *Lonja:* Merchants' lounge or coffee house.

151   *Burnham & Co.:* The building still stands in Havana, and is now called Casa Simón Bolivar.

151   *Matanzas:* A town on the north coast of Cuba, west of Havana.

155   *the sails soon got aback:* Wind in the sails was pushing the ship backwards.

156   *stern way:* Sailing backwards.

156   *I . . . had . . . the foretopsail yard fished:* Temporarily repaired.

157   *The foremast was sprung:* Broken; split or cracked.

157   *I then was married:* On November 11, 1826.

160   *Marblehead Capt.:* From Marblehead, Massachusetts.

161   *Palau Pinang:* Also called Georgetown, Malaysia.

161   *Mr. Peabody:* Probably Joseph Peabody (1757–1844) of Salem.

162   *the breeching broke:* A leather strap around the horse's hindquarters, intended to keep the sleigh from bumping against him.

CHAPTER 10—*A Belated Honeymoon*

164   *scaled our cannon:* Scraped out the cannon barrels.

166   *recherché style:* Exquisite.

167   *St. Domingo church:* St. Paulus Kerk, of the Dominican order.

167   *ignis fatuus:* St. Elmo's Fire; a glowing discharge of atmospheric electricity.

168   *more than fifteen years:* It was actually closer to thirteen.

CHAPTER 11—*A Man Overboard!*

171   *change hours:* Hours of business.

172   *a picture for a Hogarth:* William Hogarth (1697–1764), English painter, satirist, and engraver, was widely known for his popular engravings in series such as *The Rake's Progress* and *Marriage à la Mode.*

175   *we had to go by the lead:* Measure water depth using a long rope (the lead line) with a lead weight on the end.

175   *wore ship:* Came around on the other tack by turning away from the wind rather than tacking into it.

175   *sucked under the counter:* Pulled under the part of the stern that overhangs the rudder.

176   *louis d'ors:* French gold coins.

179   *not cleaned:* Entrails not removed.

180   *six reals per fanega:* A *real* is Spanish currency; a *fanega* is a 55.5-liter Spanish measure.

CHAPTER 12—*The Brig* Creole

184   *we rode there in volants:* The Cuban *volante* was a light, two-wheeled carriage, like a gig, chaise, or sulky.

184   *Lord Timothy Dexter:* A famously eccentric merchant (1747–1806) and author of *A Pickle for the Knowing Ones* (1802), a book whose punctuation was supplied on a page at the back, for readers to apply as "seasoning."

186   *met on the mole:* A mole is a harbor pier or breakwater.

187   *Western Islands:* The Azores.

193   *Bright's disease:* Nephritis, a degenerative disease of the kidneys.

CHAPTER 13—*The Wreck of the* Munroe

195   *the pintles of the rudder were broken:* Pintles are pins forming part of the hinge of a rudder.

201   *started the cut water and stem from the bow planks:* Tore loose the prow and upright bow timber.

202   *wrecks in Key West:* Salvaging and reselling goods from wrecks was Key West's major industry.

203   *stanchions:* Posts supporting the outside planks of the vessel's hull.

CHAPTER 14—*A Painful Loss*

210   *named after the English gentleman whose large estate and mansion house was on the banks of the river:* Harrison's Landing was the estate of the Harrison family, whose better-known members included Benjamin Harrison (1726–1791), a signer of the U.S. Declaration of Independence, and his son and great-grandson, the ninth and twenty-third presidents of the United States. The mansion house, Berkeley, built about 1726, is still standing.

211   *assassinated . . . the year previous:* Charles Ferdinand, duc de Berry, was assassinated in 1820.

212   *table d'hôte:* A communal dining table at the hotel.

CHAPTER 15—*Rough Passages*

215   *frame . . . was working badly:* Was loosened by the battering of the waves.

215   *chambers:* Chamber pots.

217   *Joshua Bates:* Bates (1788–1864) was an astute, highly successful financier, and the first great benefactor of the Boston Public Library, whose splendid reading room, Bates Hall, is named for him.

218   *hock:* Rhine wine.

218 *Mr. Martin Van Buren:* U.S. president, 1837–1841.

219 *purchase tackle:* Ropes and pulley blocks.

219 *Dungeness Point:* Between Dover and Hastings.

220 *Cardinal Wolsey:* Since Cardinal Thomas Wolsey (c. 1475–1530) is buried in Leicester Abbey rather than Canterbury Cathedral, Tyng is describing someone else's monument. He may have been thinking of St. Thomas à Becket (c. 1118–1170), whose shrine was the traditional goal of Canterbury pilgrimages, but the saint's present-day memorials do not fit the description given by Tyng.

221 *imposthume:* Abscess.

CHAPTER 16—*Dining Out in London and Paris*

230 *Havre:* Le Havre, the French port at the mouth of the Seine.

231 *Cannep:* Possibly Fécamp or Caen.

232 *four in hand:* A team of four horses.

233 *cabriolet:* A light two-wheeled one-horse carriage with a folding leather hood.

234 *smoking my cuba:* Cuban cigar.

234 *Abelard & Louise:* The legendary lovers Pierre Abelard and Héloïse, of the twelfth century.

234–35 *Some of the pictures are truly grand:* Tyng is describing *Scene of a Deluge*, by Girodet-Trioson (1767–1824). *The Wreck of the Medusa* is the work of Théodore Géricault (1792–1824).

235 *mostly built by him:* The Louvre was constructed between 1546 and 1670, with nineteenth-century additions by Napoleon III.

236 *He placed his hat in the beckets:* Brackets, storage hooks.

238 *Mr. Hutchinson:* William Huskisson (1770–1830), statesman and free-trade advocate.

239 *hauled up the courses:* Courses are sails hanging from the lower yards of a square-rigged ship.

239 *weather glass:* Barometer.

239 *got the tack down:* Completed the change of course.

239 *nearly threw her on her beam ends:* Almost blew the ship over on her side.

239 *A bark which was 3 to 4 miles astern:* A bark (or barque) is a three-masted vessel with foremast and mainmast square-rigged, and the mizzenmast fore-and-aft rigged.

239 *It is called a sympiesometer:* A barometer in which there is a gas above the column of liquid in the tube.

CHAPTER 17—*Out of the Frying Pan and into the Fire*

241 *The most violent speeches were made, one of the most violent by Governor Pinckney:* James Hamilton Jr., not Pinckney, was the governor at that time (1830–32).

242 *General Scott:* Winfield Scott (1786–1866).

247 *considered the crack resort:* Superior place to stay.

INDEX

Ackers, William, 134. *See also* William
    Ackers & Co.
Adams, John (schoolmaster), 12
Amsterdam (Netherlands), 119–25,
    152–54, 228, 237
Anderson, Richard, 209
Anderson (merchant), 137–40, 142–44
Antwerp (Belgium), 165–67, 170–71,
    173–74, 179, 235–37
Arieta, Joaquin, 180
Atkins, Dudley. *See* Tyng, Dudley
    Atkins
Atkins, Rebecka ("Aunt Becka"), 3,
    86, 206
Atkins, Sarah Kent (grandmother),
    xiii, 3

Bahia (Brazil), 79–82, 86
Baltimore (Md.), 55, 144, 194, 198,
    209, 243, 247–48
Barcelona (Spain), 188–93
Baretta family, 103
Baring Bros. & Co., 11, 154, 171, 174,
    213, 230, 237

Barnett, John, 186
Bartlett (secretary), 218–20, 230
Batavia (Indonesia), 89, 92–99, 103,
    105, 174
Bates, Joshua, 11, 217–18, 221, 230
Baxter (mate), 45, 47–48
Beal (retired merchant), 73–74
Belgium, 237. *See also* Antwerp;
    Brussels; Mons
Bennit (supercargo), 105, 106–10, 113
Bixby & Valentine, 119, 126
Bixley (mate), 132, 151–52, 155,
    135–37, 139, 143–44, 147
Black, Braddock, 46, 49
Blake, S. Parkman, 11
Blanchard (mate), 170
Bonaparte, Napoleon, 37–38, 40, 90,
    166, 235
Borroughs (captain), 114, 116, 117
Boston (Mass.), 5, 9–15, 42–45,
    51–53, 62–63, 105–6, 114,
    118–20, 125–26, 154, 157, 163,
    168–70, 179, 183, 205–6
Bowers, William, 88–89, 92, 105

Bray & Boit, 14
Brazil, 79–82, 116
Bremen (Germany), 39, 129–33, 237
Bridge, Nathan, 122, 124, 126,
    127–28, 154, 157, 163, 168–70
Bridgewater Academy, 4–6, 196
Brown (captain), 61–62
Brussels (Belgium), 166, 235, 236
Bryant & Sturgis, 207–8, 252
Byron, sixth baron (George Gordon
    Byron), xv, 85, 255

Cabot, Edward, 102
Cabot, John Higginson, 79, 85
Cabot, Samuel, 86–87, 102, 120
Cádiz (Spain), 180, 182, 188, 226–27
Cambridge (Mass.), 13, 15, 53
Campbell, Jack ("Neptune"), 19
Canterbury (England), 220
Canton (China), 11, 16, 28, 31–36, 70,
    73–74, 96, 99, 104
Cape Cod (Mass.), 42, 45, 47–48, 51,
    120
Caracas (Venezuela), 134, 137, 139–44
Carnes, Nat, 65, 66, 70, 77
Casilda (Cuba), 180–81
Chambord, Henri, comte de, 211–12
Champlain (captain), 218–20
Charles Drake & Co., 228, 243
Charleston (S.C.), 240–42, 247
Charles X (king of France), 188–89,
    211
Chesapeake Bay, 129, 194–97, 209
Chile. *See* Coquimbo; Valparaiso
Chiloe (Chile), 107, 108
China, xiv, 27–37, 118, 120, 256. *See
    also* Canton; Lintin Island;
    Macao; Whampoa
City Point (Va.), 129, 130, 209–10
Clark, W. (captain), 224, 236, 243, 248
Clarkson (captain), 129, 193, 228
Cleveland, Richard J., 183, 243–44, 254
Cochrane, Thomas, 110, 116, 255
Coffin, Abel, 128
Cohasset (Mass.), xiv, 6–7, 9–10
Conant (captain), 64, 67, 70, 72, 77

Coquimbo (Chile), 21, 23–24
Cowan (landlady), 184, 248–49
Cowes (England), 38–39, 68, 69, 75,
    222–24, 226, 238
Cramer & Wilkins, 211, 240, 242
Cuba, 57–60, 146, 165, 180, 184–85,
    227, 243. *See also* Havana;
    Matanzas; Trinidad
Cunningham (pilot), 209, 210
Curson, Margaret Searle ("cousin
    Peggy"), 3, 58–59
Cushing, Caleb, xvii
Cushing, John Perkins, 32, 47, 88, 96,
    101, 102, 104, 207, 252
Cushing, Nathaniel, 67, 75

Dacres, James R., 9
Delisle (merchants), 166, 167, 70–71,
    235, 237
Delius, Everhard, 130–32, 134
Delius, George, 129
Destout (merchant), 229–33
Deveraux (mate), 78
Dexter, Timothy, 184
Dimpsey (ship's boy), 106–7, 113
Donnett, Jean Baptist, 171–74, 176.
    See also Widow Donnett & Co.
Dover (England), 219–20
Dow, Henry, 17, 43, 44
Drake & Mitchell & Co., 148, 151,
    158, 170, 178, 180, 198, 202. *See
    also* Charles Drake & Co.
Ducatel (mate), 195, 197
Dumeresque, Philip, 96, 119
Duxbury (Mass.), shipbuilding, 127
Dwight, Edmund, 45

Eades (captain), 44, 94
East India Company, British, 100
Elliot, Catherine Atkins (aunt), 77, 86
Emerson, Ralph Waldo, 10
England. *See* Canterbury; Cowes;
    Dover; Greenwich; Liverpool;
    London; Manchester;
    Portsmouth; Yarmouth
Equator, crossing ceremony, 19

Farris (captain), 52
Farwell (captain), 193
FitzGerald family, xvi, 231–32
Flint, Jacob, and family, 6, 9
Forbes, John Murray, 252
Forbes, Robert Bennet ("R.B."), 102, 252, 254
Forbes, Thomas, 102
Forcade & Co., 172
France, 230–36

Gardiner family, 102
Gavecoot & Delius, 129, 130
George Wildes & Co., 237–38
Gibraltar, 187–88, 192–93
Gittings, Lambert, 198–99
Goldsborough, Louis M., 10, 114
Gomez, Stephen, 178, 206
Good Hope, Cape of, 37, 49, 51, 65, 69, 75, 91
Gosler, John B., 40
Graves (captain), 129
Gray, Horace, 11
Green (captain), 204
Greenwich (England), 71
Griswold, Alexander V., 78
Gulf Stream, 51, 57, 180, 196

Hall (captain), 186
Hamburg (Germany), 39–41, 52, 212, 237
Hampton Roads (Va.), 129, 197, 209–10
Hanover (Germany), 39; commissioners, 214–18
Harrison's Bar (Va.), 210
Harvard College, xiv, 13, 78, 128
Havana (Cuba), xvi, 31, 53, 55–61, 77, 148–51, 157–60, 165, 170, 171, 178, 183, 202, 206, 228, 243–49
Havre (France), 230–32
Hawaii, 24–27
Hebbert (captain), 229
Hellevoetsluis (Netherlands), 174–75, 211, 213
Hendricks, John, 44

Henry (2nd mate), 64, 68–71
Henshaw, David, 126
Hickling, Sarah, xv, 44
Hickling, William, 17, 20, 22, 43, 44
Higginson, Henry (uncle), 45
Higginson, James P. (uncle), 203
Higginson, John (uncle), 14–15, 17, 19, 24–27, 34, 41, 79, 252
Higginson, Stephen, Jr. (uncle), 119
Higginson, Stephen, Sr. (grandfather), xiii, 9, 114, 118, 119
Hingham (Mass.), 9
Hodshon, John, 122–24
Hogan, Peter, 244
Holland, 120–24, 211, 237. *See also* Amsterdam; Hellevoetsluis; Rotterdam
Horn, Cape, 21, 42, 114, 116, 117
Horseman (sailor), 107–8, 112
Houqua (merchant), 32, 67
Howe (schoolmaster), 10
Howland (merchant), 151, 153
Hubbard, Henry, 4
Hubbell, George, 104–7, 113
Hubbell (clerk), 105, 107–8, 113
Hull, Isaac, 12, 113
Hull, William, 11–12
Hunt (captain), 212
Hunter (consul), 222, 224
Hunter (lieutenant), 114

Iceberg, 124–25
"Irish pennant," 22
Italy, 82–85

Jackson, Andrew, 241–42
James (river), 129, 209–10
Janosin & Co., 166
Japan, 94–95
Jarvis, Samuel Farmar, xvi, 78
Java, 37, 92, 97. *See also* Batavia
Jones, Warrick, 5, 52

Kamehameha I, 26–27
Key West (Fla.), 77, 202–5
Kin, Tom, 30, 48

King, John, 14, 17, 31, 41, 43–44
Knight (merchant), 59, 244

La Guaira (Venezuela), 131–45
Langdon, Woodbury, 206
Lawrence, James, 8
Lee, Thomas (cousin), 14–15
Leghorn (Italy), 81–85, 256
Leopold I (king of the Belgians), 236
Libbey (mate), 129, 132–33, 135–36
Lincoln, Joshua, 90
Lintin Island (China), 100, 252
Liverpool (England), 237, 238, 241,
    242, 248
London (England), 71–73, 213,
    217–22, 229–31, 237–38
Louis Philippe (king of France), 189,
    236, 237
Louvre museum (Paris), 234–35, 255
Lowell, Frank, 4
Luce (captain), 183
Lunt, Micajah, 129

McAlpine family, xvi, xvii
Macao, 47, 73–74, 101
McFales (schoolmaster), 3
Mackay (ship chandler), 110, 112
McLoud (doctor), 73
Magee, Charles, 17–18, 20, 22–23, 29,
    41–42, 44, 87–100, 104–5, 252–53
Malays, 68–69, 96–98, 102–3
Manchester (England), 238
Manila (Philippines), 101, 102–4, 108
"Marblehead" (captain), 160–62
Marseilles (France), 186, 188–89
Martha's Vineyard (Mass.), 160–62
Matanzas (Cuba), 151–53, 206, 248
Medford (Mass.), shipbuilding, 118, 207
Mermaid, 94–96, 99, 101, 105–6, 255
Mitchell (merchant), 148–49, 244
Molasses, storage and sale, 172–73
Mons (Belgium), 236
Morales (count), 150–51
Moreland, John, 193

Nantucket (Mass.), 51, 82, 160
Nash, Joshua, 64–66, 70, 72, 74–77

Neef, Henry ("Harry"), 64–65,
    68–70, 77
Netherlands. *See* Holland
Newburyport (Mass.), xiii, xvi, 3, 76,
    81, 86, 117, 128, 129, 169, 188,
    206–7
New York (N.Y.), 117, 154, 157,
    196–97, 199–201, 206, 228, 233,
    240, 247, 252
Nickols (undertaker), 158
Norfolk (Va.), 197–98, 209–10
Nullification controversy, 240–42

Opium: smuggling, 100–101, 104,
    255–56; use in China, 35
Ostend (Belgium), 176, 237

Paine (merchant), 93–94, 255
Paris (France), 232–35
Parsons, Clement, 2, 163–64, 170,
    175, 178, 182, 188
Patterson (merchant), 172, 198
Peabody, Joseph, 161
Peabody Essex Museum (Salem,
    Mass.), xviii
Peck (sailing master), 114, 116–17
Pedro I ("Dom Pedro"), 79–80
Pelham (captain), 53–55, 57, 59, 61
Penguins, 21
Perkins, Barbara Higginson (aunt),
    44, 252
Perkins, James, xiv, 14, 43–44, 252
Perkins, Samuel G. (uncle), 13, 14,
    252
Perkins, Thomas, Jr., 86, 96, 119
Perkins, Thomas Handasyd ("the
    Colonel"), xiv, 14, 43, 64, 72,
    77, 86–88, 102, 118, 252, 254
Perkins & Co. (Boston), 40, 64, 78, 86,
    102, 118, 119–20, 207, 252, 256
Perkins (merchant in Batavia), 93–94
Perry, Matthew C., 95
Petersburg (Va.), 129, 209
Philadelphia (Pa.), 78–79, 194,
    198–99, 229, 243
Phillips Academy (Andover),
    12–13, 46

Philippines. *See* Manila

Physick, Philip S., 78

Pickersgill family, 237–38

Pirates: Atlantic seaboard, 56–57; Caribbean, 146–48, 164–65, 254–55; Malays, 68–69, 97–98, 254

Pisa (Italy), 84–85

Polignac family, 211–12

Portsmouth (England), 213, 221–24, 230

Potter (captain), 168

Quincy, Josiah (3rd), 12

Rand, Edward, 129

Reynolds & Bros., 198–99

Rich, Benjamin, 11, 89

Richards (mate), 105, 107–8

Richmond (Va.), 129, 209–10

Rio de Janeiro (Brazil), 116

Ripley (mate), 105, 107–8

Roberts, John, 198, 209, 210

Rotterdam (Netherlands), 69–70, 168, 209, 211–14, 221, 237, 242

Rouen (France), 232, 235

St. Helena (island), 37, 69, 91

St. Marys (Azores), 56, 187

St. Salvador. *See* Bahia

Sampson (shipbuilder), 127

Sands (mate), 213, 222, 224–25

Sandwich Islands, 24–27

Sanger (schoolmaster), 4–5, 9

Sargent (pilot), 88–89

Savage family, 167

Savannah (Ga.), 237, 246

Scheldt (river), 69–71, 174, 237

Scott, Winfield, 242

Searle, Thomas (cousin), 237

Selfridge (captain), 128, 133

Shaler, William, 183, 243–44, 248

Sharks, 80–81, 254

Shaw, Zebulon, 13

Siam Twins, 128

Smith, Charles, 78, 85, 86

Smith (mate), 163

Southampton (England), 218, 229

Spain, 23, 243. *See also* Barcelona; Cádiz; Catalonia

Stewart, Charles, 110, 113–17

Stoney, John, 240, 242

Sturgis, Russell, 10–11

Sturgis, William, 207–8, 252

Sugar, production, 184–85

Sumatra, 37, 68, 96–97

Tacón, Miguel, 149–50

Tay (mate), 226

Tennant (merchant), 198–99

Thames (river), 71, 217, 219

Thompson family, xvii

Ticknor, George, 85

Tilden, George, 90, 105

Tod, Francis, 129

Trinidad (Cuba), 180–81, 185–86

Tucker, Nathaniel, 123–24

Tudor, William, 114

Tyng, Anita E. (daughter), xvi–xvii

Tyng, Anna McAlpine (wife), xvi

Tyng, Anna Arnold (wife), xv–xvi, 157, 164–67, 178, 179, 186, 188, 194, 206–7, 255

Tyng, Charles: boyhood, xiii–xiv, 3–15; career summary, xv, xvi, 252–56; death, xv–xvi; first voyage, 14–44, 252–53; marriage, xv–xvi, 157; memoir, xiv, 251–56; photo, *ii;* ships' encounter, xiv, *2,* 188. *See also* Vessels

Tyng, Charles (great-grandson), xiv

Tyng, Charles (son), xvii

Tyng, Dudley Atkins (father), xiii, 3–6, 9–10, 12–14, 16, 53–54, 76–77, 114, 128, 193, 253

Tyng, Dudley (brother), xiii–xiv, 13, 50, 76, 78

Tyng, Elizabeth Higginson (stepmother), xiii, 9, 15, 53–54, 76

Tyng, Francis C. (grandson), xvii

Tyng, George (brother), xiii–xiv, 78, 102

Tyng, George (son), xvii

Tyng, James (brother), xiii, 9, 76, 78

Tyng, Mary (sister), xiii, 9, 43, 63, 167

Tyng, Sarah Higginson (mother), xiii, 3, 22

Tyng, Sarah (sister), xiii, 217

Tyng, Stephen Higginson (brother), xiii–xiv, 12, 13, 78

Tyng, Susan (sister), xiii, 63

Uran, Richard, 45, 46–48, 169

Valparaiso (Chile), 23, 105, 106, 108, 109–14

Van Buren, Martin, 218

Venezuela, 131–45

Vessels (Tyng passage★; voyage★★; charter†; ownership††): *Allioth,* 129; *Arnold Wells,* 224; *Augusta*★★, 53–61, 63; *Barbara,* 64; *Bashaw*††, 124, 207–11, 213, 218, 221, 223–28, 235–38, 243, 248; *Bolivia,* 55; *Bulwark,* HMS, 7; *Cadet*★★, 87–113, 252, 256; *Caledonia,* 69; *Calhoun*★, 247; *Carabobo,* 147–48; *Caracas,* 145–46, 151; *Chesapeake,* USS, xiv, 7–9; *Constitution,* USS, 12; *Cordelia*★★, xiv, 14, 16–46, 49, 64, 88, 252–53, 256; *Cortez,* 56; *Creole*††, xiv, 2, 186–93, 207, 228; *Dollar,* 161; *Dolphin,* USS, 112–13; *Douro,* HMS, 147; *Eight Sons*††, xiv, 2, 77, 123, 127–48, 151–60, 163–65, 167–82, 188, 207, 210, 222; *Elizabeth,* 108; *Eurotus*†, 240, 242; *Franklin,* USS★, 113–17; *General Stark*★★, 52; *Globe,* 112; *Golconda,* 129; *Greyhound,* 118–20; *Guerrière,* HMS, 118–20; *Halcyon,* 77; *Harbinger,* 167; *Henry Clay,* 161; *Heroine*★★, 78–86, 256;

Houqua★★, 64–78; *Jaliff*★, 214–18; *Las Adamantis,* 146–48; *London Packet,* 72; *Majestic*★, 206; *Margaret Forbes,* 207; *Munroe*†, 194–98, 203, 210, 256–57; *Newton*★, 183; *O'Higgins,* 109–10, 112; *Roscoe*★, 109–10, 112; *Sally*★, 245–47; *Savannah,* 52; *Shannon,* HMS, xiv, 8–9; *Suffolk*★★, 45–52, 64; *Volant*★★, 61–63; *Woodstock*★, 240; *Zephyr*†, xv, 119–27, 152, 154.

Victoria (queen of England), 238

Vives, Francisco D., 149

Walcheren island (Belgium), 176–78

Waterloo, Battle of, 37, 167

Webb (judge), 204

Wendall (mate), 73–75

Whales and whaling, 82–83, 91–92

Whampoa (China), 28–30, 33, 47–49, 67, 74, 100

White (drydock owner), 222–24

Widow Donnett & Co., 173–74, 255

Wilde, Samuel S., 157

Wildes (merchant), 237. *See also* George Wildes & Co.

William Ackers & Co., 134–36, 138–39, 142–45

William I (king of the Netherlands), 166

William Marsilly & Co., 174

Williams, Abraham, 207

Williams, Caleb, 44

Willoughby (merchant), 76, 78

Winslow (captain), 173

Winthrop, Robert C., 10

Yarmouth (England), 216–17

York (captain), 238–39

Young, John, 180

Young Tom, Jemmy (shopkeeper), 34, 48, 67